EDEN'S EXILES: *ONE SOLDIER'S FIGHT FOR PARADISE*

Also published by Protea

Forged in Battle (2014)

Eden's Exiles

One Soldier's Fight for Paradise

Jan Breytenbach

PROTEA BOOK HOUSE
PRETORIA
2015

Eden's Exiles: One Soldier's Fight for Paradise – Jan Breytenbach

First edition, first impression in 1997 by Queillerie Publishers
Second edition, first impression in 2015 by Protea Book House

PO Box 35110, Menlopark, 0102
1067 Burnett Street, Hatfield, Pretoria
8 Minni Street, Clydesdale, Pretoria
protea@intekom.co.za
www.proteaboekhuis.com

Editor: Danél Hanekom
Proofreader: Carmen Hansen-Kruger
Cover design by Hanli Deysel
Set in 10.35 on 13.15 pt ZapfCalligr BT by Ada Radford
Printed and bound by Interpak Books

© 1997, 2015 Jan Breytenbach

ISBN: 978-1-4853-0259-9 (printed book)
ISBN: 978-1-4853-0260-5 (e-book)
ISBN: 978-1-4853-0261-2 (ePub)

Contents

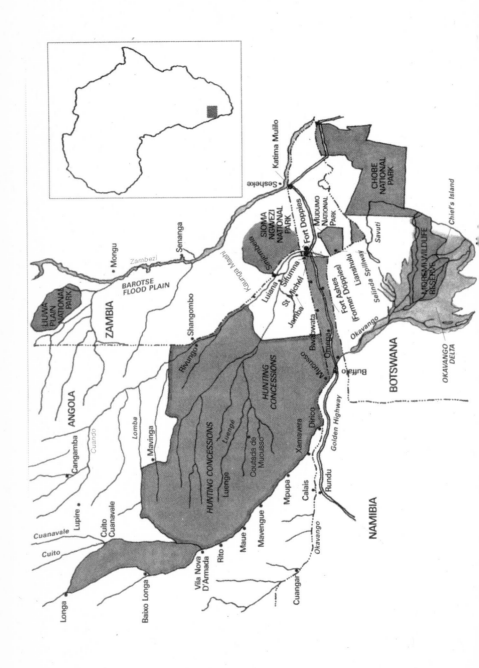

Preface

This is a story about two irreconcilable concepts: warfare and conservation.

Nevertheless, these diametrically opposed elements had to be brought face to face with each other in what was probably Africa's last pristine wilderness area. Warfare claimed both priority and complete freedom of action.

The result? Dire consequences for the game population in remote savannah areas, formerly visited only rarely by modern man.

When the god of war gate-crashed paradise, he spread destruction and violence, annihilating peace in one of its few African strongholds.

This story describes a peaceful wilderness area as it was first encountered by a vanguard of awestruck soldiers, rather tentatively deployed in the Cuando-Cubango region of Angola as the opening shots were fired in a war that lasted from 1966 to 1988.

It progresses through various situations which persuaded the same military men to opt for conservation rather than mindless destruction of the wildlife around them.

This, in turn, led to running skirmishes between poachers and warriors, and frequent clashes with uncaring, often corrupt, authorities. For the soldiers it was a losing battle, but for this last outpost of the African wilderness, it was a disaster. Yet there were compensations. Bonds of friendship were forged between men at arms and some of the more savage denizens of the savannah forest – three lions, Terry, Rufus and Dayan, and one leopard, Taunu, who moved disdainfully within a close circle of human friends until the time came for them to bid their military companions farewell.

These unusual relationships gave rise to many unexpected situations, mostly humorous, and to the tying of an unbreakable knot of love and respect between soldier/conservator and the untamed savannah.

When the poachers descended in overwhelming force on this treasure chest rich with ivory and abundant in rhino horn, the soldiers fought the onslaught with all their might.

But the forces they could muster against the devastating plundering were feeble. They could not know that this attack on the wildlife was not only well orchestrated, but planned and led from the highest levels in the South African Defence Force and launched in cooperation with its erstwhile allies, Jonas Savimbi and his Unita guerrillas.

The outcome is there for all to see. The massive campaign succeeded and the puny, resisting soldier/conservators were steamrollered and pushed out of the way.

The Cuando-Cubango and much of the western Caprivi became a sterile, green but lifeless wasteland, littered with the detritus of war, criss-crossed by innumerable deep-rutted vehicle tracks, polluted by modern waste and liberally sown with anti-personnel and anti-vehicle land mines.

We should, however, not surrender. The war is over, but small groups of renegades continue to plunder the countryside. Unita must be forced to quit the Cuando-Cubango and the entire area must be given enough breathing space to reclaim the virgin and savage African savannah. Modern man's meddling and oppressive hand must be removed so that nature can heal itself and once again find its own equilibrium to restore the most productive environmental system on the continent of Africa.

A plea is made for this wilderness area to be rehabilitated as a matter of urgency. It should include most of the Cuando-Cubango, northern Botswana (including the Okavango swamps) and parts of Zambia, Zimbabwe and the eastern Caprivi. Ideally, this would be an international effort, motivated by the desperate need for protein to sustain the people of this subcontinent.

Such an area could become the red-meat larder of all southern Africa, in perpetuity.

I want to thank my wife for the hours and days she spent

typing the manuscript and for correcting my spelling and grammar mistakes. In particular I want to thank an old friend of mine, Dewald de Beer, for the material on Terry the lion and information relating to poaching incidents in the western Caprivi.

Finally, I want to dedicate this book to the overworked, underpaid and unsupported nature conservators and game rangers of Namibia, especially those based in Katima Mulilo and Rundu. They have had to contend with their own spectre, the avaricious intrusion of ambitious politicians who, like the god of war, recklessly trample everything underfoot in their selfish rush to the top of the dung heap.

Jan Breytenbach

Introduction

During a century or more of intensive exploration by persistent adventurers of awesome stature, Africa – known as the dark continent because of its hidden secrets and treasures – slowly became exposed.

Livingstone, Stanley, Selous, Speke and others opened up the continent for missionaries, hunters, traders and European farmers. Only a few uncharted corners remained where the white man's foot had hardly trod because the cost of exploitation would be prohibitive both in money and in human life.

These areas became the last sanctuaries for the remnants of a profusion of wildlife that once roamed the African plains, forests and swamps. A harsh climate, remoteness and the tsetse fly formed a formidable defensive barrier which could not be breached by greedy man bent on wielding his nonselective rifle and wilfully destroying the last vestiges of a treasure which he, impoverished in spirit, failed to acknowledge as vital to his own continued existence on planet Earth.

The Cuando-Cubango, the western Caprivi and Botswana north of the Selinda spillway are, perhaps, the last areas open to Africa's free-ranging wildlife outside proclaimed game reserves. The pathetic remains of the vast antelope herds, the hundreds of thousands of roaming elephants, majestic prides of lions and the widely scattered cheetahs and leopards were clinging desperately to an inhospitable territory ignored by man.

It was my fortune – and at the same time my misfortune – to be propelled into the forbidding harshness of this wilderness by the circumstances of war. On the one hand, I experienced with an intensity not granted to the less blessed among my comrades, the infinite variety of primeval Africa, each facet incredibly rich and intricate in its composition. On the other hand, I witnessed the final wave of destruction gathering momentum and beginning to overwhelm this last stronghold with a relentless and unstoppable greed which has made me fume in impotent rage.

Until the early seventies, no one but the Bushmen and a few scattered bands of miserable black Angolans tried to scratch a living on this harsh and forbidding land, the Bushmen doing so with far greater success than the Angolans.

From time to time intrepid trophy hunters ventured into the tsetse-fly-infested interior to shoot the Big Five – lion, leopard, elephant, buffalo and rhino. On the whole, however, the region was given a wide berth by the comfort-loving whites and blacks living on its fringes.

It is a huge area, bordered to the west by the Okavango River, to the east by the Cuando River, the Okavango swamps, the Linyanti swamps and the Selinda spillway in the south. The northern limits are marked by a line through Menongue and Cuito Cuanavale to a point due east on the Cuando River.

Within these boundaries are found a myriad of crystal-clear rivers with the sweetest water, dense riverine forests, vast swamps forming the sponges from which most of the rivers are fed and thousands of square kilometres of hot, tinder-dry bush. In the summer months the onset of the rainy season sees a magical transformation to a verdant, overpowering, green jungle steaming with humidity.

Through this vast territory, elephants roamed at will in their hundreds of thousands. They fed from the bountiful shrubs and trees, ploughed up reed beds in the swamps in winter and pushed over trees by the million to gain access to the succulent topmost leaves, at the same time clearing the bush for the benefit of the seemingly endless herds of grazers.

In the thickets, black rhino dozed stupidly in the heat of the day, oblivious to the fact that they were the last of the Chobiense subspecies – almost certainly extinct at the time of writing.

Huge herds of buffalo, sometimes several thousand strong, made their way through the long grass of the flood plains to their water holes like Zulu impis on the march, the sun flashing off their glistening, black horns.

In the late afternoons, strings of majestic sable antelope moved out of the shade of the fringing forests to graze in the *omurambas* or flood plains, their curved sabres borne proudly to indicate their noble disdain for lesser creatures.

Here and there, the curled horns of magnificent kudu bulls could be spotted through the thick shrubbery as they nibbled at the tips of twigs and shoots.

Herds of red lechwe moved like flocks of sheep across the islands of the swamps and rivers while hippos grunted and chuckled from every pool.

Zebras and blue wildebeest trotted along the dusty *omuramba* valleys when disturbed or wheeled around to watch one's passage with intense curiosity from a safe distance.

The fleet-footed tsessebes, fastest antelopes in the world, flitted through the dappled shade of the forests to get out of one's way and into the welcoming arms of the undergrowth where they could disappear in a nondescript pattern of shapes and colours.

Small family groups of ring-tailed waterbuck watched alertly as one passed within a stone's throw along one of the abominable tracks bordering some of the region's rivers.

Towering over all of this, the heads of giraffes swivelled ludicrously at the ends of their long necks, often topping the tree canopies from which they were feeding, investigating the unexpected intrusion before loping off in sedate, slow-motion strides, their tails curved up against their haunches, their necks undulating to the tempo of their long, thin legs.

At night, one heard the "whoop!" of hyenas, the irascible trumpeting of elephants duelling over a particularly tasty shrub, the snorting and splashing of hippos leaving the rivers to feed along the banks. Towards morning, the distant roar of the king of beasts boasted of his skills as a hunter after a good kill.

And when the sun poked its head above the eastern horizon it was always greeted by the piercing call of the fish eagle – the most dramatic way to awaken to a new day in paradise. All of

Africa's forgotten history, creatures, rivers and plains are encapsulated in that call as it pierces the stillness of the morning air.

In early 1970 I was introduced to this remote world of wonders, of savage beauty, and wildness, harshness and searing heat. Enveloped in a cloak of primeval perfection, pristine in the purity that permeated all its component parts – animals, bush, swamps and rivers – to make up a pulsating, inextricably interlocked life system, it begged not to be disturbed by anything dangerous and foreign to its delicate equilibrium.

Then the war brought a serpent to paradise and I was part of it. The war was the reason I went there. The purpose of my journey was not to do some sightseeing and photograph wild animals, but to fight against Swapo guerrillas and their Fapla supporters.

ONE

Getting Acquainted with Paradise

Because I had passed a Special Air Service selection course, I was given the task of getting the South African Special Forces off the ground towards the middle of 1970. Four of us had just returned from an exasperating and futile African war a long way from home, in Biafra, and our experiences had convinced us there was a definite need for Special Forces in the Defence Force.

Therefore, we four formed the nucleus around which I had to start building a completely new and extremely unorthodox unit. For the next few weeks, I travelled around South West Africa and South Africa to round up men I knew well or who had been recommended to me.

Within a fairly short time, I had gathered twelve men, inevitably to be called the "Dirty Dozen", to form a core from which the unit will be expanded. Later, it became officially known as I Reconnaissance Commando. Others in the army soon abbreviated this and gave us the nickname of the "Recces".

For some of us, an attack-diving course followed, our skills later being suitably honed and updated at the French attack-diving school in Ajaccio, Corsica. We also completed a short course in clandestine air-infiltration techniques, courtesy of the French paratroopers.

By August 1970 we were all back in South Africa and looking forward to conducting our first selection course to identify prospective recruits for the unit.

However, Lieutenant General Pop Fraser, then General Officer commanding Joint Combat Forces, had other ideas.

I was called to Pretoria and dramatically handed a sealed envelope to be opened only once we got to Rundu.

We departed for the "operational area" with high expectations of taking on Swapo externally in Angola and Zambia. The war was still at a simmering stage and concentrated mostly in the eastern Caprivi and Ovamboland.

I was therefore surprised and disappointed to discover that our "secret" mission was to plot all the water holes in the southeastern corner of the Cuando-Cubango, an area just inside Angola. We also had to plot water holes in the western Caprivi nature reserve.

We were to operate in a region reported to be the infiltration routes of both MPLA and Swapo insurgents. The possibility of picking up a good scrap with either one of the two movements was quite high according to sector headquarters in Rundu. This prospect cheered us enormously.

The Portuguese military leadership was very sensitive about maintaining the image that they had Angola under firm control, possibly because they knew that most of their troops were languishing in their bases, abandoning the African bush to the wild animals and the small bands of insurgents roaming through it without constraint. The Portuguese did not want us to clash with insurgents in areas which they had publicly declared completely pacified.

Our arrival in Rundu therefore heralded an unprecedented round of patrols by Portuguese forces from their bases in Luiana and Coutada de Mucusso into the areas we would be covering.

We found ourselves six so-called Sabres, long-wheelbase Land Rovers with machine guns mounted behind the driver's compartment. I divided the "Dirty Dozen" into three teams of two Sabres each and assigned each to a sector of the south-eastern region of the Cuando-Cubango. Each patrol team picked up an additional six Portuguese troops who were supposed to act as our armed escorts in the dangerous interior.

In high spirits, having completed our preparations and fitted out the Sabres to our complete satisfaction, we set off for our bases.

I was to lead my patrol into the extreme south-east quadrant of the Cuando-Cubango, checking out the whole area eastwards from a line between Mucusso on the Okavango River, and Coutada de Mucusso, a hunting camp to the north, as far as Luiana in the east and down the Cuando River to Sifumna on the South West Africa border. I selected the police base at Sifumna as my patrol base.

We left Rundu early one afternoon for the police base beyond the Bagani ferry, 180 kilometres inside the wild and mysterious western Caprivi.

We slept that night at Bagani police base, crossed the wide Okavango River by ferry early the next morning and drove into the belt of tall trees fringing the river on a barely discernible, narrow track en route to our first scheduled stop, Bwabwata.

August is not the best time of the year to be in the Caprivi. The bush is tinder dry and often burnt down by the Bushmen. The days are extremely hot.

The sand tracks had deteriorated into long stretches of finely powdered dust. As black soot from the burnt grass mixed with the dust kicked up by the Sabres, we soon looked like the Second World War Long Range Desert Group on an extended mission into the Sahara desert to get behind the German lines. Our dust goggles completed the picture. With .30 Brownings mounted on the back of our Sabres, from which all unnecessary items such as doors, windscreens and canopies had been removed, we looked quite dramatic as we ploughed along, trailing long rooster tails of dust behind us.

The going was tough. It took us the whole of the forenoon to cover less than 100 kilometres to the police base at Bwabwata.

We saw no game. The few loin-clothed Bushmen ambling along with long forked sticks on their shoulders and small packs of scrawny dogs at their heels, paid scant attention to us as we passed.

Obviously they were not westernised, still hunter-gatherers in the true sense of the word.

We reached Bwabwata by lunch time, to be greeted by a somewhat inebriated police captain. He welcomed us with cold beer and a substantial, but tasteless, meal during which he cheerfully informed us that we would never return from the Cuando-Cubango. Our bones would be picked clean by vultures and hyenas. We would simply get lost, stuck in the sand forever and die of thirst, never to be seen again.

According to him, no one had ever ventured into Angola from any of his police-patrol bases.

Well, we had a job to do and I decided to ignore the captain's gloomy predictions.

In the two Sabres making up my patrol, we set off for Sifumna the next morning. The other two patrols decided to use Bwabwata as their base of operations.

Progress, once again, was exceedingly slow and it was quite dark by the time we reached the Cuando River which marks the eastern boundary of the western Caprivi.

We switched on the headlights, but my Sabre's lights were neither too bright nor properly adjusted. They illuminated only a smallish patch of Caprivi sand about 20 metres ahead of my vehicle.

It therefore came as no surprise when Trevor Floyd, my driver and team buddy, suddenly slammed on the brakes. The Land Rover skidded to a halt with its nose right under the rear end of an elephant and we found ourselves looking almost straight into its somewhat larger-than-normal rear orifice. I did have time to note that the elephant was definitely a cow.

Unperturbed, the animal ambled along, one among a small group of dark shapes we could just make out beyond the extreme limits of the Sabre's headlights.

Their bellies rumbled, they broke branches alongside the track and generally went about their business in a leisurely fashion, paying no attention to us whatsoever.

Finally, they disappeared into the night. We resumed our journey and arrived at Sifumna in time for a cold supper of burnt maize porridge and a tough hunk of tasteless, over-cooked meat. There were no beers for the thirsty travellers.

There were no beers in the base, period. The police commander at Sifumna, a lieutenant, was the complete antithesis

18

of his colleague at Bwabwata and we had to attend a lengthy prayer meeting before we could turn in for the night.

The next morning we arose and attended a parade, again featuring a lengthy scripture reading, sermon and prayer, before we were judged ready to face the day and, possibly, the enemy.

At that time, the Sifumna police used to patrol the cutline demarcating the border between Angola and South West Africa up to a point where the so-called Delta *omuramba* crossed the cutline, down this *omuramba* to the Golden Highway, the main road from Grootfontein to Katima Mulilo, east to the ferry at Kongola and from there up the Cuando back to their base. An additional patrol often went all the way down the river to the Botswana cutline, west for about 30 kilometres and then north and back along the Golden Highway to the base at Sifumna.

All these patrols were carried out in Ford pick-up trucks and the Sifumna police were more fortunate than their colleagues at Katima, who as regular as clockwork ran over anti-vehicle mines on the cutline between Zambia and the eastern Caprivi, often with fatal consequences.

Quite a few policemen were killed before the Council for Scientific and Industrial Research in Pretoria developed an extremely effective anti-mine vehicle, a cumbersome-looking contraption that was promptly christened "the Hippo" because it looked rather like one of these animals.

Mines were sometimes found on the western Caprivi cutline and also on the sandy track leading to the Portuguese platoon base at Luiana, 30 kilometres to the north of Sifumna.

We had to collect our Portuguese "escort" from this particular base and it was with some trepidation that we took the sandy track marking the western limits of the expansive Cuando flood plain.

Reluctantly, the police allocated to us the services of July, a Bushman tracker and guide. He was the chief of the nearby Bushman village, peopled exclusively by his somewhat extended family.

July was a typical little Vaskela, brown skinned, straight as a ramrod, brown eyes always staring into the distance, with peppercorn hair, a wrinkled face, filed teeth and tattoo marks on the bridge of his flattened nose. He had sinewy arms and legs with steel cords for muscles that unquestionably indicated a physical stamina far beyond the capability of any average man.

July wore a pair of shorts far too big for him, old police boots, inside which his small calloused feet slid around from side to side, and a threadbare jacket which reached down to his knees.

Around his waist he carried the standard Bushman knife, a crudely sharpened double-edged steel blade with an elaborately carved wooden handle. The knife fitted snugly into an equally elaborately carved wooden sheath.

I was struck by the fact that when July clambered on board my Sabre at the start of our extended patrol, he had nothing else except a single blanket. He had no luggage to encumber him on his anticipated laborious travels through the African bush of the Cuando-Cubango.

Our Sabre, in contrast, was piled high with our bulging rucksacks containing at least two pairs of everything – shirts, socks, underpants, trousers, jackets and handkerchiefs, plus our personal camping equipment such as groundsheets, sleeping bags, spare water bags, one-man gas cookers and spare gas bottles and even strong spices and condiments, according to taste, with which to make palatable the "delicacies" commonly found in army ration packs.

In addition, we carried water bottles, knives, compasses, some rations and spare magazines for our rifles on our belts, and some of us even strapped on a pistol or a revolver to enhance our ferocious appearance.

I marvelled at July and his simple lifestyle, and looked ruefully at all the paraphernalia we, as Westerners, had to take along to ensure reasonable comfort in the remnants of an environment that had become somewhat hostile to us while we diligently reshaped most of it into something more acceptable and materialistic and in tune with our Western outlook.

July looked at all our gear and, no doubt, came to the conclusion that we were mad.

With the dire predictions of our police friends still uppermost in our minds, namely that we would certainly get lost in the trackless Cuando-Cubango wilderness, we crossed the deep-rutted sandy tracks of the cutline into Angola. It was the first time most of my men had set foot outside South Africa or South West Africa.

The crossing was unremarkable. There was no customs post, no fence to cross and no sign of welcome or farewell on either side of the border. We just trundled in low gear, four-wheel drive, at a slow and gentle pace across the cutline. Our wheels were firmly caught in the deep ruts of the Portuguese army vehicles which had been there before us and which led to Luiana, our destination for the night.

Of course we were conscious of the danger of land mines almost every second of the journey northwards. I questioned July about mines on the track but he was noncommittal. I asked him to keep his eyes peeled for the slightest surface disturbance on the track ahead. He smiled widely with a mouth full of shark's teeth and nodded his head while scanning the bush on either side of the track for any sign of wildlife. His lack of interest in the enemy's "mining" activity was total.

So we travelled on with a peculiar, pinchy feeling around our southernmost orifices as a constant reminder that we could become violently airborne at any moment.

Trevor drove somewhat gingerly at first until familiarity took the edge off our continuous anxiety and we pushed up the speed.

To our right, the wide, swampy flood plain stretched to a barely discernible thin blue line on the eastern horizon. That line was the far bank of the Cuando swamp and river system and also the western boundary of Zambia. According to the map, the whole of the Cuando river system is located inside Angola.

The plain was covered with vast stretches of reeds and papyrus. Horseshoe lakes, long narrow lagoons, thin threads of secondary water channels and sheets of shallow water glinted in the early morning sun.

Dotted all over the plain were isolated islands, lushly covered with huge African ebony trees, knobthorns, sycamore and swamp-fig trees, mangosteens, sausage trees and palm trees. These islands were usually embedded in the middle of acres of blue-grey reed beds, the reeds hiding vast stretches of dark water and mud under their leaves and feathery flower heads.

Their unapproachability made these islands mysterious little paradises on which it was virtually impossible to set foot because of the swamps all around them.

The main stream of the Cuando River was nowhere in sight.

Immediately to our left, the tree-clad sand dunes often rose for several hundred feet, forming soft cliffs, recessed bays and prominent peninsulas butting proudly into the swampy, level plains at their feet.

The dunes were covered in camelthorns, Rhodesian teaks, red syringas, a solitary African ebony and shrubs that we used to call the Jewish peach. The leaves of most of the trees and shrubs on the dunes had fallen, so that the brownness of the dunes stood out starkly against the lush green of the swamps and islands.

The rutted, sandy twin tracks clung to the base of the dunes, the camber to the right threatening to slide us into the still pools of the swamps.

Suddenly, we came across a huge impi of buffalo, their black horns glinting in the sun as they turned in a solid-black phalanx to face the two Sabres laboriously ploughing towards them along the sandy track.

July, on the back of my Sabre, laughed excitedly as he started pointing out particularly juicy beasts for the attention of our rifles.

The herd was well over 1000 strong, standing knee-deep in the brown grass of a dry, flat plain.

They stared at us for a while and then, as one, they turned to their right to thunder off in a cloud of dust to get beyond the head of the nearest promontory.

However, our track turned away and led us across the neck of this feature, so that we parted company with the buffaloes. We started to inch our way upwards in the now thickening sand, hoping we would not get stuck. On reaching the top, we drove for a while on level ground, then started to descend, through the thick trees, to the flood plain below us.

We had just emerged from the trees on to level ground and were picking up speed when July started to jabber excitedly.

I turned around and saw the advancing buffalo impi right behind us, and closing fast. They showed no sign of veering left or right, and were headed straight for us.

After stampeding around the head of the promontory, the herd had cut back towards the track, by which time we had crossed the neck and were now ahead of them.

It looked like a classic bison or cattle stampede from a Hollywood Western and for those of us on the ground, just as dangerous as it appeared on the screen.

If we had stopped in our tracks, nothing would have happened to our fragile bodies or our equipment. The herd would have split and streamed past us as far as their stamina could carry them.

Being relative newcomers to the African bush, however, we did not know this.

A desperate race began between the vast herd of buffalo and the two tiny and vulnerable Sabres. Those who could, had their eyes turned firmly backwards, looking in awe at the thundering hooves and a most magnificent array of horns stretching in an almost unbroken line of black shields for at least 100 metres on both sides of the track.

The horns bobbed up and down as the buffaloes thundered along, a thick cloud of dust rising above the mass of black bodies.

It was a magnificent sight, albeit a rather frightening one, as they started catching up with the Sabres.

I had visions of us being trampled underfoot in our vehicles by the charging herd.

Of course, we had plenty of firepower in the shape of machine guns and rifles, but not one of us even considered resorting to such extreme measures.

It was their country after all and we were the intruders. We just had to get out of their way.

The Sabres hit firmer ground and soon pulled away from the herd still charging in hot pursuit. We drove up the side of the next promontory while the buffaloes decided to follow the contour line along the foot of the dune.

We stopped and got out to take a last look at the disappearing herd, each of us silently impressed by this marvellous introduction to the Cuando-Cubango. July was the odd man out. He was somewhat disconcerted by the fact that we had passed up a splendid opportunity to bag a juicy buffalo for the pot.

However, there was still a long way to go to Luiana and to be stationary for longer than a minute was to invite thousands of tsetse flies to settle on bare necks, faces and arms.

So we got back into our Sabres, resigned to the fact that all driving in the Cuando-Cubango was a tedious slog. The tsetse-fly cloud faithfully followed the Sabres in a bid to catch up and suck some more "boer" blood out of us – perhaps a new experience for them, since they usually dined off Portuguese and Bushman blood.

As the sun rose higher, the heat began to mount. Towards midday the sun hovered over the landscape with a leaden, blast-furnace ferocity. We sweated like leaky water bags, but the moisture brought no respite from the heat. Our eyes stopped straying to the plains and forests in search of game. The animals had moved back into the deeper shade of thicket and forest, seeking shelter from the searing heat, their flanks heaving, ears flapping or breath panting in an effort to drop body temperatures by a degree or two.

The landscape had become lifeless, an eerie, still hiatus on the fringes of the heat of hell.

The Cuando-Cubango would not treat us kindly in the weeks to come. Ours would be an ongoing struggle against an unforgiving, harsh environment in which we were the intruders, to be dealt with mercilessly when we stepped out of line, or grudgingly accepted if we learnt to live with it by accepting it unconditionally in all its moods.

Not fully appreciating the importance of complying with this one-sided code of conduct, we drove on listlessly towards Luiana and, hopefully, a rendezvous with some ice-cold Cuca beers.

We crossed the Luiana River, a narrow but very deep and barely moving stream, by means of a rickety and rotting wooden bridge, hoping that it would not collapse under our weight and deposit us, Sabres and all, in the black water below.

We skirted some brown and dusty agricultural plots where a few peasants were vainly trying to coax some life from the sullen soil with listless stabs of their ancient hoes.

Very dirty and very thin, dust-coloured children, attired in barely adequate rags, stared at us without much interest as we drove past, across the landing strip and into the sprawling *aldeamento*, a protective village squatting, almost obscenely, on the western approach to the fortress-like Portuguese military base on the edge of the Cuando flood plain.

A red and green Portuguese flag hung limply from a home-made flagpole at one end of a hard, compacted parade ground. Adobe huts sprawled along the eastern, southern and northern edges of the parade ground, the thick mud walls pierced with tiny paneless windows like vacant eye sockets. We stopped in front of the most important-looking building and were met by a neatly dressed Portuguese lieutenant, his olive drab uniform fitting like a glove, with knife-edge creases in his trousers and highly polished black boots.

He was flanked by a weird apparition enveloped in a huge black cloak, a pair of shorts and sandals and topped by a cowboy hat. He also carried a blue wildebeest tail switch to keep the swarms of flies at bay. He turned out to be the doctor, seemingly masquerading as Batman!

We were soon ensconced in the lieutenant's headquarters, each with a Cuca beer in hand, while we stated the purpose of our visit and our plans for the immediate future.

The lieutenant listened with great interest. When his turn came, he kicked off with a diatribe against the Portuguese metropolitan government and all Portuguese in general.

We discovered that he was, in fact, an Angolan and the son of the only Angolan to have reached general's rank in the Portuguese army.

He was more than willing to assist us.

We were allocated one of the dark and airless little huts and made ourselves at home as best we could.

July made his way to the *aldeamento* to look up some family. The sprawling, unhygienic-looking mass of hovels turned out to be mostly occupied by Vaskela Bushmen who had been forcibly removed from their widely scattered, small family settlements, known as *kimbos*, deep inside the bush, and resettled in order to "drain away" the life-sustaining river of humanity in which the guerrilla fish was likely to swim.

Not that the Bushmen had any sympathy with the MPLA or Unita cause; certainly not.

Almost without exception, the Bushmen hated the black Angolans bitterly, having been their chattels and slaves for hundreds of years, their women sexually exploited at leisure, the men forced to tend the black man's livestock or till his meagre lands.

But the Portuguese were only marginally better in their treatment of the Bushmen. While at Luiana, I saw black and white Portuguese troops wandering around the Bushman huts, disappearing into the dark interiors with young Bushman damsels and reappearing half an hour or an hour later, adjusting their clothing. Satisfied, the soldier would stroll back to camp casually, without as much as a smile or a wave at the browbeaten families who had been squatting miserably outside in the dust, waiting for the intruder to finish his business with their daughters or sisters.

July, understandably, was livid with anger when he reported to me the next morning.

I therefore piled our small Portuguese escort into the second Sabre to keep some distance between July and our allies. I never saw him address a single word to any of them. Neither did he go near them. He just stared at them from a distance with naked hatred burning in his dark eyes.

This was our first encounter with the rampant animosity between the different races in Angola.

The white and mulatto Angolans hated the metropolitan Portuguese because they were ruthlessly exploiting the country and exporting all their riches to Portugal. They also despised the black Angolans and Bushmen below them.

The black Angolans, in turn, hated the white and mulatto Angolans and the imported Portuguese from "metropole". They felt they were being scandalously used by all those above them, but at the same time, they despised the Bushmen. Where possible, they kept them as property, at a common level with their domesticated animals.

The Bushmen hated everybody above them, but had no one below them to despise. By nature, and because of their culture – based on survival – the Bushmen had a far closer affinity with the wild animals, to which they were often compared, than with their fellow human beings.

Whenever we, as South Africans, appeared on the scene, the Bushmen clung to us as if we were their only life raft in a stormy sea of conflict and racial tension.

In time, some sections of the black Angolan population were to adopt the same attitude to the South Africans who, because of the war, had to work closely with them.

I was beginning to see a faint glimmer of the profound significance of inherent African racial differences although, I must admit, I was too dense at the time to appreciate how these differences related to the African environment.

For the next few weeks we ploughed laboriously through the thick sands of the dunes or bounced painfully over endless bumps and potholes, caused by elephants digging for roots in the extensive *omurambas*.

A large part of northern Botswana, all of the western Caprivi and most of the Cuando-Cubango must have been a huge desert many thousands of years ago. The hot winds of the desert piled up the sand in long dunes running roughly from east of south-east to west of north-west. Between them formed lower lying depressions, many miles long, with a harder surface composed of fine, black soil particles probably leached from the adjacent sand dunes.

As the rainfall increased, so the black soil on the low-lying strips of land built up into layers of turf resting, like the sand dunes, on layers of calcrete that underlie the whole area. The long, low-lying strips are called *omurambas*. Depressions formed into round, low-lying pans instead of narrow valleys, are known as *chanas*.

The vegetation found on the dunes and in the *omurambas* and *chanas* differs markedly.

The dunes are extensively covered in red syringas interspersed by stands of kiaat, or mukwa, a highly-prized hard wood, occasional large stretches of mopani along the edges of the *omurambas*, manketti groves (producing huge nutritious nuts, almost indistinguishable from walnuts) solitary false mopanies with wide-spreading and evergreen crowns, here and there a few pod mahoganies, also sought after for their timber, and in some areas, thick baobabs. The sandy surface among the trees is covered with a dense carpet of shrubs, some of them delectable to all browsers and to elephants. Camelsfoot, or bauhinia, grow in abundance. The sickle bush, loved by kudu and impala, is found in great profusion. However, the grasses on the dunes are mostly annuals. In a good rainy season they can grow very thick and very tall, almost to the height of a man, only to disappear completely during winter.

Except in one place that I know of, water holes are never found in the dunes.

Between the dunes the *omurambas* lie like long narrow plains extensively covered in perennial grasses, including the highly nutritious "red grass" so valuable to cattle farmers in South Africa. The trees and shrubs are mostly from the acacia and combretum families. Therefore, one finds an abundance of camelthorns with their nutritious seed pods, knobthorns with bark which is stripped off by elephants during the dry season, umbrella thorns, sickle bush and others. The combretum family is well represented by a wide variety of shrubs and trees, among them the well-known leadwood tree with beautiful black wood that can keep a fire going for weeks but which is too hard to be turned into furniture or other objects.

Where the underground water is within three or four metres of the surface, one can expect concentrations of the most magnificent tree of them all, the jakkalsbessie or African ebony. Sausage trees also dot the long narrow plains, usually in the vicinity of water holes.

The biggest attraction of *omurambas* for all game species are the extensive water pans found in all of them. In the rainy season, they are filled to the brim with sweet water.

These pans habitually form along only one edge of the *omurambas,* like strings of pearls strung together by well-trodden elephant footpaths. They are rarely more than a few hundred metres apart and vary in size from small pans, hardly ten metres across, to very large expanses which can be several hundred metres in diameter.

When the rains come, the turf soil becomes a sponge, soaking up and retaining the water. In a good year, these sponges become oversaturated and the *omurambas* turn into vast, sticky traps for any vehicle, no matter how well designed for cross-country work it may be.

The pans then become covered in water plants, including the showy water lilies, which in turn attract water birds, insects and frogs in large numbers. The knobnosed goose is much in evidence as are the spur-wings. Coots, jacanas, gallinules and ducks swim around on the surface, run along lilies and water grasses or dig around the muddy fringes.

Red and yellow bishop birds build nests or flit around among the tall water grasses. Plovers kick up a fuss when one gets too close to their ground nests. Finches, flycatchers, shrikes, both the swamp and red-breasted species, waxbills and even parrots fly around or chatter among the branches of trees and shrubs.

Francolins, bustards, guinea fowl, quails and other ground birds scuttle singly or in pairs through the grass or feed in flocks from the myriad of insects and grass seeds.

Over it all sound the calls of the mourning dove, the hornbills and the penetrating cry of the fish eagle.

Bateleurs, brown and martial eagles soar in wide arcs over the plains below, their sharp eyes riveted to the ground to detect the slightest movement among the grasses and shrubs.

Initially, we moved through this thirsty land with our eyes closed to the teeming life around us. It was only much later, once our senses became properly attuned to the African bush, that most of us could begin to appreciate the virility of the tropical African savannah. For a few, however, the bush remained a closed book forever.

Quite naturally, we were looking for the big game, the lions, elephants, rhinos, buffaloes and such and we were not to be disappointed in our quest. But it is all too easy for the uninitiated to gain a lopsided impression of what the African savannah is all about, if the lesser animals are ignored.

Over the weeks that followed, we saw and heard literally thousands of elephants and buffaloes, especially along the Luiana River.

We also saw herds of the most majestic of all antelopes, the proud sables with their sickle-shaped horns sweeping back in grand arcs. We saw plenty of the bellicose roans, always staring at us morosely from a safe distance.

Zebras galloped along parallel to our Sabres for hundreds of metres before swerving away into the cover of trees or shrubs.

Blue wildebeest likewise dashed away in clouds of dust to stop and look, before trotting back towards the Sabres, then suddenly wheeling around and madly dashing for cover.

They usually followed us for quite long distances, their curiosity seeming to get the better of them despite the potential danger we posed.

In the dunes we often came across herds of giraffe, looking intently at us from their dizzy height, perfectly blending with the burnt and brown colours of the trees, only their swishing tails betraying their presence. They always stood dead still for a while, all heads facing the intruding Sabres, before sedately turning and galloping off with an undulating, slow-motion gait, their stilt-like legs, elongated necks and curled tails a flowing display of grace as if they were ballet dancers performing on an enormous stage.

At night, the roar of lions and whoops of hyenas were heard as we slept in a tight circle around our Sabres. Night was also the time for elephants to trumpet loudly or growl angrily at each other as they broke down branches, pushed over trees or stripped the bark from marulas or knobthorns.

We had a surfeit of large game species to look at as we travelled the length of the Biongue *omuramba*. Much wider than most, amply endowed with water holes and pans, it has extensive red-grass plains and is therefore a favourite concentration area for all the major game species, from elephants to warthogs, and eland to steenbok and duikers. All the species were represented on the plains, except for the bush-loving kudus who peered shyly from the forests and came down only to drink in the early evening.

It was here that we ran into our first pride of lions, about six or seven lying next to the track in the long grass. We pulled up next to these big cats in our open Sabres and man and beast stared at each other, to the discomfort of July, who did not believe in getting too close to the king of the bush.

The lions twitched their ears, looked at us from only a few metres away, got bored with the spectacle of two-legged humans ensconced in smelly, air-polluting vehicles, yawned and carried on daydreaming or grooming themselves.

We drove on, and some kilometres further along the Biongue, came across our first hunting safari.

The Cuando-Cubango was almost exclusively allocated to Simões Hunting Safari, operating out of Angola, and his safari business as a hunting concession. However, because of the size and harshness of the environment, he never had so many clients that the area could be overrun or the hunters have a noticeable impact on the game. In fact, the hunters were conspicuous by their absence during 1970.

We were therefore surprised to see a single file of Land Rovers and two big Mercedes trucks approaching us in what we had thought was the most desolate place on earth.

The convoy soon drew level and stopped. The safari leader was a tough, husky man with powerful arms and chest. His name was O'Flanagan, a local from Windhoek, and he was taking a party of Americans, with a burning ambition to bag the Big Five, into the blistering heat of the Cuando-Cubango.

The prime hunter in the group was a tall American armed with a steel longbow and some fierce-looking arrows. Evidently he had already shot grizzly bears, polar bears, brown bears, pumas and other assorted wild animals with his bow and was intent on adding the African Big Five to his collection of trophies. He had already shot a leopard, an elephant and a buffalo and wanted to complete his collection by adding a lion and a rhino.

We watched the hunters as their heavily laden, bush-scarred Land Rovers and trucks moved eastwards, one truck particularly smelly under a bulging load of skins and horns. They were obviously shooting other lesser animals as well.

The Portuguese were not too happy about venturing away from their isolated but culturally familiar camps at Luiana and Coutada de Mucusso.

Inside these bases, everything was Portuguese. Outside was primeval Africa. To venture into the unknown interior of the Cuando-Cubango was akin to deliberately setting off into the remote interior of the Sahara to die a horrible death from thirst and madness.

There were no landmarks, because the earth was indisputably flat here. Even the sun refused to cooperate, beyond rising in the east and setting in the west. For the rest of the day, it marked time almost overhead, so that direction-finding by looking at the broiling orb was not all that easy.

Our Portuguese friends, particularly from Coutada de Mucusso, were convinced that we were totally lost every time we ventured off the few known tracks. The lieutenant in charge of the Coutada escort used to approach me every time we stopped, insisting that we should return to his base, since nowhere was there water to be found and we were, in any case, driving around aimlessly in circles. We would all die of thirst, according to him, and our bones would be picked clean by the roaring, grunting and whooping predators we heard prowling around us every night.

Fortunately, once upon a time, I was a navigator by profession, and therefore not unduly concerned about our whereabouts. July, of course, always backed me up. He had a sense of direction that was simply uncanny.

The unusual sight of wild animals at close quarters tended to unnerve the Portuguese even further. When July got hold of the biggest python I had ever seen and put it, along with the Portuguese, in the rear Sabre, their cup of discontent ran over.

Mind you, it took some doing on July's part to get hold of the snake. He spotted it sliding along through the grass as we were on our way to Luiana, promptly jumped off the Sabre and grabbed the snake by its tail.

The python was slithering into a hole. July's desperate effort to pull it back into the open by its tail only increased the snake's determination to reach safety and shake off the persistent little fellow.

It was rather disconcerting to see him being pulled along by the python as if he were a little trailer being towed by a strong truck. The snake began to disappear into the hole, with July hanging on grimly like an anchor man in a tug-of-war contest.

"He is pulling me in! He is pulling me in!" shouted July desperately.

Trevor jumped out of the Sabre and rushed to assist July in capturing his snake. Between the two of them, they slowly tipped the scales. More and more of the snake emerged from the hole in reverse, until its head finally reappeared.

Like whiplash, the snake turned around and lunged at Trevor and July. Hastily they released their hold, whereupon the snake made another determined bid to escape into its hole as fast as it could.

But July wanted that snake badly. He once again latched on to its tail like a leech, followed by Trevor, who was beginning to enjoy this unusual sport.

The performance was repeated several times before the snake was finally beaten into submission with a very substantial stick, and finally came to rest among a bunch of rather alarmed Portuguese.

Not long afterwards, July suddenly shouted for me to stop. I looked around and saw Portuguese troops scattering in all directions from the Sabre behind me. In the back the snake had reared up, and was glaring ferociously at the back of the head of Kernaas Conradie, the driver. Before the Sabre even came to a stop, Kernaas was also on his way. He was never very fond of snakes.

Once again, July belaboured the python with a stick until it finally collapsed in a crumpled heap.

But an hour later we had an encore. Once more Portuguese troops, accompanied by Kernaas, scattered in all directions. July had no intention of cutting off the python's head, or even having it shot. It was meant for his father, who evidently relished the meat of the python, and had to have it prepared in a certain traditional way. I was told that the python had rejuvenating powers but only if the head remained intact and attached to the body.

We stopped for a brew-up towards noon and July walked back to check on his snake. It had absconded. Complaining bitterly about the useless Portuguese, he searched the Sabre high and low for his snake, even checking under the loose spare wheel, and finally, he cast around for the snake's spoor.

He found the trail and caught up with the battered python some 50 metres from the vehicles. It was desperately trying to put distance between itself and the persistent attention of the little Bushman.

Once more the snake was "killed", this time for good. We measured it back at Luiana and found it was more than five metres long.

One animal we came across fairly regularly was, believe it or not, the black rhino. On one occasion, Kernaas Conradie and Koos Moorcroft were chased by one in the thick sand of the

Angolan cutline. Because of the deep ruts left by the police Ford pick-up trucks, Kernaas could not get out off the track and out of the way of the charging rhino. The sand slowed the vehicle down as Kernaas ploughed along laboriously, anxiously trying to coax more speed from the Sabre.

The rhino was within a few paces of the fragile rear end of the vehicle when Kernaas got out of the thick sand of the dune and on to the firmer surface of the *omuramba*. He picked up speed and left the rhino several hundred metres behind, but inevitably, there was another dune with heavy going ahead. Once again Kernaas slowed down to a crawl with the black, steaming locomotive rapidly gaining, following the same rutted track as the Sabre.

Koos was moving in behind the machine gun when the Sabre hit another hard patch. This time, Kernaas changed direction, and the runaway juggernaut rolled eastwards and past them, having never wavered in its deadly determination to flatten the Sabre if it ever should catch up with it and its human occupants.

The rhinos were also fairly plentiful along the Luiana River. It was here that I saw a strange encounter between a rhino and a lone elephant bull.

I had left our temporary overnight base early one morning to perform my ablutions down-wind from the camp. As I came out of the thick forest I heard an angry trumpeting almost in front of me.

Twenty paces away was an irate elephant bull in the middle of a clearing, his trunk wrapped around the head of a rhino bull. He was shaking the rhino around like a rag doll while the latter screamed in fear. This went on for perhaps 15 to 20 seconds while the two wheeled around in a cloud of dust, the elephant's trumpeting almost drowning out the rhino's screams.

Finally, the rhino broke loose and rushed into the thick scrub surrounding the clearing. The elephant shook its head for a moment, flapped its ears, snorted loudly through its trunk, then placidly ambled off towards the nearby water hole.

Apparently, the elephant had become annoyed when he met the rhino insolently making its way back on *his* footpath after having had a drink at *his* water hole. To add insult to injury, the rhino had not respectfully stepped aside, giving the lord of the African bush the right of way as he should have done. The rhino, therefore, had to be taught a lesson in jungle manners in no uncertain fashion.

Much to the amazement of the Portuguese lieutenant, we did get back to Coutada de Mucusso. While still apparently deep inside the trackless forest with not a sign of civilisation, I deliberately told the lieutenant that the base was only a kilometre or so ahead.

When we broke the embrace of the thick forest shortly afterwards and drove straight on to the landing strip, it flattered my considerable ego to see the lieutenant's mouth drop open in astonishment. With exaggerated nonchalance, I folded my map and put away my compass.

In spite of my proven ability as a navigator, the lieutenant refused to accompany us on any of the remaining patrols. He had had enough of Africa.

Unlike the Luiana garrison, made up of roughneck Angolan infantry, the Coutada de Mucusso garrison housed a refined company from one of the elite metropolitan regiments. They all wore yellow scarves to indicate that they were cavalry, and therefore several notches higher in status than mere infantrymen. Fittingly, the captain's surname was Carvalho.

He came from a wealthy and perhaps influential family, judging by his tailor-made fatigues and always impeccable turnout, including gold wristwatch, gold-rimmed sunglasses and handmade boots.

The first time I saw Coutada de Mucusso was after a long, hot and dusty week in the unforgiving harshness of the sweltering savannah, trying to accurately plot the few perennial water holes that we had found.

We were filthy as we drove into the Portuguese base, covered in soot and ash from the burnt bush and with parched throats yearning for ice-cold Cuca beers.

The Portuguese welcomed us with unstinted hospitality. We showered, changed into reasonably clean clothes and settled down on the verandah with cold beers. The African sun went down in a blaze of colour. The sky was painted a deep red and orange as the sun sank through the haze caused by the extensive bushfires always burning at that time of the year.

Across the Luenge flood plain we watched herds of buffalo coming down to drink. Here and there we spotted small herds of lechwes on the islands in the middle of the swamps getting in a quick evening feed before nightfall.

It came as no surprise when we were offered plates of splendidly prepared tender buffalo steaks and chips.

Only the Portuguese know how to turn a tough buffalo steak into a delicacy that would not be out of place in the best restaurants of Europe. The steaks were, of course, accompanied by Portuguese red and white wines, all of this in the heart of the African bush.

We turned in tired but well fed, and I was more than a little put out at being woken up from a deep sleep at midnight by my travelling companion, the Portuguese lieutenant. The captain required our presence at his birthday party, which was about to begin.

We were guests and therefore had no choice. Reluctantly, I kicked the rest of my crew awake and, in due course, we set off for the mess where a party was already beginning to get up to flying speed.

Sleepily we stumbled into a simply unbelievable scene, bearing in mind that the nearest decent-sized Angolan town was something like 300 kilometres away.

Tables were laden with all the exotic delicacies one could think of, including crayfish tails, shrimps, tasty bits of mutton and steak, chicken drumsticks and even caviar, which most of us had never come across before.

"What are these things?"

"Fish eggs!"

"Ugh!"

There were little pies, tarts, cakes aplenty and all sorts of other sweet things.

Bottles of Napoleon brandy, Chivas Regal whisky, Antigua brandy, the best white and red Portuguese wines and, of course, the best ports in the world, already opened, were arrayed on the tables, waiting for thirsty throats to drain them.

We were welcomed as honoured guests by the captain who had all the refreshments flown in from Luanda by Dakota – at his own expense – shortly before our arrival. The party must have cost him thousands of rands.

So we sat down and started eating and drinking on already full stomachs. Speeches were made, of which we understood nothing, but nevertheless cheered and clapped every time.

I made a speech which neither our hosts nor, probably, my own men understood, but they all thumped the tables in appreciation.

Then the *fado* singers appeared and we all joined in, or tried, as this perhaps greatest of Portuguese cultural happenings was performed.

As the night wore on, our Portuguese improved concurrently with our companion's fluency in English. It wasn't long before we rendered our own version of South African *fado* by singing paratrooper songs, some of them rather bawdy.

This, among a musically educated audience, went down like a lead balloon. We received no encores which was rather disappointing.

We staggered to bed as the sun came up and had a couple of hours sleep before setting off again into the searing heat of the dry African bush – excellent medicine for hangovers.

Our constant search for water holes brought us into contact with some of the more bizarre aspects of the war, as well as manifestations of colonialism.

The biggest natural threat was, of course, the tsetse fly. They made it impossible for even the indigenous people to penetrate deep into the remoter parts of the Cuando-Cubango and the western Caprivi. Around the fringes, black Angolan cattle farmers were waiting hungrily to push their scrawny beasts into what they perceived to be the luscious grass pastures of the inviolate savannah. They also wanted to get their hands on the thousands and thousands of wild animals on the hoof to feed themselves and their protein-starved families.

Traditionally, Africa's indigenous people regard vast herds of moth-eaten cattle as a visible sign of wealth. They therefore refuse to kill them for food and eat only those that keel over from disease or old age.

In spite of the tsetse fly's burning and irritating bite, I have learned to regard it with great affection and consider it the best game ranger in the world. I was to cross swords with the Department of Veterinary Services on several occasions on the tsetse fly's behalf.

The Portuguese were making half-hearted attempts to eradicate the tsetse fly in the Cuando-Cubango by cutting down trees and clearing strips of bush over long distances in an attempt to contain the insects in demarcated blocks. For some reason, the tsetse fly does not like to fly across open spaces in sunlight. The blocks were then tackled successively and dark-barked trees were sprayed up to about three metres off the ground. The fly rests on the shadowy side of dark-barked trees and does not fly higher than three metres above the ground. The reason for this habit is not known. Maybe the tsetse fly has a fear of heights.

We found these cutlines in the most unexpected places in the Cuando-Cubango, but never saw a sign of the tsetse-fly control teams, until one day when we crossed a particularly wide *omuramba*, at least ten kilometres south of the Luiana River.

There, in the middle of this remote *omuramba*, close to a clump of ilala palms, we came across the filthiest camp I have ever come across.

Some scruffy tents were pitched in the hot sun, their sides rolled up. Inside lolled the filth-encrusted, bearded members of a tsetse-fly control team. Outside the camp there was a huge pile of animal skins, bones and rotting meat, crawling with maggots and flies. The stench was overwhelming, but evidently the Portuguese were used to it. Maribou storks covered the heap and the plain around it in their hundreds stalking along on stilted legs, their bellies swollen with muck and offal. Nearby, on the edge of an island of trees, there was a sizeable *kimbo*, populated by a band of Bushmen, whose women, as usual, were at the beck and call of the smelly soldiers.

July was nearly beside himself with anger and disgust and laid into the Bushmen with angry clicks and clacks which no doubt drove his message home in no uncertain fashion.

The control team had long since abandoned the fight against the tsetse fly. It was far more profitable for them to engage in large-scale poaching. Judging by the number of tusks and rhino horns they had in their possession, they were not doing too badly.

On our next call at Luiana, I reported the matter to the Angolan lieutenant who made it his business to get the police in from Sá da Bandeira to arrest the poachers.

In due course, and with the greatest satisfaction, the lieutenant informed me that all the members of the team had been jailed. The team leader was evidently sentenced to several years, which was no less than he deserved.

We never saw another tsetse-fly control team in the area, though others soon donned the poaching mantle discarded by the renegade band when the police moved in.

To avoid the bureaucratic bog of two separate armies, the Portuguese and the South African, we usually replenished our supplies at either Sifumna or Bwabwata, just inside the western Caprivi. On clocking in at Bwabwata with our Luiana escort, we met up with our two other teams, both escorted by the metropolitan Portuguese from Coutada de Mucusso. We established ourselves outside the base in two separate groups. The Portuguese elected to form their own little colony while my men from all the Sabre patrols clustered in.another circle around our vehicles.

I indicated to my Angolan escort that it would be in order for them to join their friends from Coutada de Mucusso. However, they refused to budge, and sat fingering their rifles while glaring at their compatriots. The sergeant informed me that they would rather stay with us than with the colonialists from "metropole", and we all settled down ... until the police captain called for me.

I had entered his base when we arrived earlier to say hello, but he had not been available. I was told that he was resting in his tent.

I found the captain, clearly "rested", sitting in the mess tent with a bottle of Antigua brandy in front of him. He staggered to his feet and indicated a chair.

"Who gave you permishion ... permission to be in my bashe ... base?" he asked angrily.

Tact was called for and I proceeded to inform him that without his help we would never be able to do the job we were there to do.

With the help of his genuinely concerned warrant officer, the captain was eventually placated and soon I had to drink a tot of brandy with him, neat from the bottle, despite the terrific heat of a tropical afternoon.

I broke away as soon as I could, accompanied by the warrant officer who informed me that the only patrols they undertook were to the Portuguese border town of Mucusso to replenish the Captain's supply of Antigua from time to time.

The next day the captain was up and about quite early, and evidently, sober for the first time in weeks.

I soon discovered that the reason for his sobriety was a visit by high-ranking police officers, including one I knew well from Operation Wildebeest, during which we cornered the first Swapo guerrilla patrol to infiltrate into South West Africa at a place called Ongulumbashe.

I was duly invited, with my other officers, to attend a special lunch with the captain's men and his important visitors. A Cessna brought the police officers to the base, and after the usual briefing, we adjourned to the mess tent for drinks and a splendid meal.

All we had on the table, in the way of alcohol, were cans of Castle or Lion beer, but the lunch was very good. We sat back, replete on the rations the police garrison had acquired specially for the occasion.

The police captain did not touch a single beer during lunch, and was stone-cold sober as he rose to his feet and started to make a speech.

"Welcome to general so and so, brigadier so and so, colonel so and so and our friends from the army. The food you saw today, general, is not the usual fare ..."

I "rogered" that in my own mind, because usually their food was just maize porridge and dry chunks of venison, virtually inedible.

"We do not have time for the usual comforts. We are constantly on patrol ..."

I looked at the stony-faced policemen around me and thought about the regular booze patrol to Mucusso.

"The beer you see on the table is the first we have had during our service here on the border. General, I want to assure you that I, as commander, have refrained from drinking a single beer up till now. That is why I did not drink a can of beer today either. I believe in setting the example ..."

"You hypocritical bastard," I thought. My eyes met those of the warrant officer and we smiled. Of course, the captain wasn't really lying. He never deigned to touch a beer, but he was into the hard stuff with a vengeance.

I was called out by one of my men soon after lunch. O'Flanagan's party was shouting desperately for assistance. He took me to a decrepit-looking Land Rover, parked outside the base, with a hard-looking individual standing next to it.

The man addressed me in rather old-fashioned Afrikaans. He was O'Flanagan's assistant, by the name of Prinsloo and a descendant of the Afrikaner pioneers from the Thirstland Trek into Angola towards the end of the last century.

O'Flanagan was in a bad way. He had been attacked by a lion two weeks before, the wounds had turned septic and he was virtually on his last legs. Could we please help?

It was a fortunate coincidence that the police general and his party had arrived in an air force Cessna. I explained the situation to the general and he quite happily made the Cessna available.

However, the pilot, a young second lieutenant, was not so happy at the prospect of landing his frail little aircraft in the middle of an *omuramba*. There was no suitable airstrip within miles of O'Flanagan's party.

We talked the pilot round, explaining that *omurambas* were as smooth and level as billiard tables, especially in the vicinity of O'Flanagan's camp.

We said nothing about the havoc wreaked by elephants over large parts of *omuramba* surfaces, and Mr Prinsloo's optimistic assurance that landing a Cessna near their camp would be a "piece of cake" eased our consciences. Prinsloo also volunteered to show the pilot the way, thus convincing him that it could not be so bad a trip after all.

Soon the reluctant pilot was airborne, bound for the Biongue *omuramba*. About 40 minutes later, he was back at Bwabwata with O'Flanagan, Mrs O'Flanagan and Mr Prinsloo on board.

As the pilot stepped out of the Cessna, he swore that if he had known what was in store, he would never have made the trip. He looked at us accusingly while he checked his Cessna minutely for the slightest damage after what must have been a very hairy landing.

Yogi Potgieter, our own home-grown *medico*, took a look at O'Flanagan and declared that he had to be transported to a hospital as soon as possible. The man was in great pain and, quite obviously, destined for the critical list. In fact, I was of the opinion that he could die at any moment.

The police general once again stood aside, and while the Cessna flew O'Flanagan and his very pregnant wife to Rundu, the police party proceeded by Ford pick-up truck.

By this time we were all feverish with curiosity about what had happened to safari leader O'Flanagan. It was the first time any of us had encountered a man who had been mauled by a lion and, from what we had seen of O'Flanagan's injuries, we could almost visualise the ferocious battle between this giant of a man and the king of the beasts.

Prinsloo soon enlightened us.

It appeared that while the chief source of the problem was the American with his longbow, O'Flanagan was not entirely blameless and, in wanting to satisfy his client, he had done some very stupid things.

The American, whom I called Robin Hood, was hell-bent on bagging the fourth specimen of the Big Five species. The safari had spotted the same pride of lions we had encountered the day before their arrival in the Biongue *omuramba*. There and then, Robin Hood decided that a male lion had to be impaled on the end of one of his steel-tipped arrows.

The whole exercise was to be filmed by a fellow American, who bore some resemblance to Friar Tuck. Robin Hood wanted a record of his bravery on film, no doubt to be shown to captive audiences back in the USA.

So he convinced O'Flanagan to go after the peaceful little pride of lions.

The lions, of course, had no indication of what fate had in store and they viewed the approach of the open Land Rover with barely concealed boredom and equanimity. In front sat Mrs O'Flanagan, swollen bellied in an advanced stage of pregnancy, with the burly O'Flanagan at the wheel. On the back stood Robin Hood with his longbow, an arrow notched, bravely eyeing the strangely complacent lions as they approached the safari leader's terrifying rendezvous with destiny. Friar Tuck was at Robin Hood's elbow, film loaded in his camera, all the settings just right, finger on the trigger, taking preliminary background shots from time to time.

Also in the back was a wrinkled black outrider of O'Flanagan's, a loyal servant for many years to both master and madam. He was armed with a flimsy, home-made bush axe, the kind used by Bushmen and bush-oriented Angolan men to chop wood and reduce carcasses into suitably sized chunks for the pot.

There was not a single firearm among them. The Land Rover stopped ten paces or less from the sprawling lions, who looked up at the intruders and yawned.

O'Flanagan wanted Robin Hood to sink his arrow into the male where he lay, but Robin wanted none of that. It would be a singularly unimpressive movie if he was seen taking on a bored-looking animal at ten paces from the back of a Land Rover. Robin wanted to provoke the animal into a full-blooded charge. So, stupidly, O'Flanagan edged his Land Rover forward towards the male and started to nudge him with the bumper.

The lionesses and cubs angrily moved off into the bush and the male rose reluctantly to follow them rather more sedately, but he was slowly getting his dander up: It was annoying to be unceremoniously pushed around by a smelly, exhaust-fume spewing, tin monster without due regard for one's status.

So he strode off majestically in the wake of his pride.

Robin Hood, in his ignorance, was scornful of the oft-repeated fireside stories about the African lion's irascible temper and that he was the most dangerous animal in the African bush, after the African buffalo. Robin looked disdainfully at the retreating bulk of the king, then prevailed upon O'Flanagan to repeat his provocative performance.

Well, the client had to be satisfied, so O'Flanagan duly, albeit gingerly, followed the lion, nudging it with the bumper of the Land Rover. His bush instinct must have taken leave of him at that moment.

By now the lion's temper was being fuelled to an almost uncontrollable explosion by the undignified way in which he was being shunted around by mere human beings. He acknowledged one or two more bumps from the Land Rover with warning snarls, and then his patience snapped.

Suddenly, 200 kilograms of hard-muscled fury, armed with awesome claws and fangs, spun around like lightning with a blood-curling snarl and jumped on top of the open Land Rover's bonnet, his yellow eyes aflame with a desire to kill the man behind the wheel. In a split second, the docile king had turned into a furious, killing monster gone berserk.

He took a mighty swipe at O'Flanagan with his right paw, fearful claws fully extended, knocking him clean out of the Land Rover. From the front of the vehicle the lion launched himself on top of the safari leader, lying bleeding on the ground, and started to maul him with fang and claw.

Robin Hood took one frightened look at the lion, flung his longbow and arrows aside, jumped out of the Land Rover and logged it for the distant camp, hotly followed by a portly Friar Tuck, minus his expensive cameras.

Mrs O'Flanagan screamed at the top of her voice, slid out of her seat and wriggled under the Land Rover, swollen belly and all.

O'Flanagan's wrinkled old outrider was the only one left on the scene. Undeterred, he also bailed out, but instead of following the Americans, he jumped at the lion, his little axe raised in a gesture of defiance. He started to belabour the king around his head and face with his ludicrous-looking little weapon.

The lion's fury abated, and he left off shredding O'Flanagan's bulky body. With a few angry snorts he made off into the bush in the wake of his wives and children, his naive trust in the human species shattered forever.

O'Flanagan was lying on the sand, bleeding profusely from numerous bites and claw marks in his head, arms, shoulders and upper torso.

That was how Prinsloo found him. For two weeks, he tried to nurse him back to health, but eventually the wounds turned septic. Prinsloo had no choice but to seek help, leaving the American hunting party to their own devices and O'Flanagan in the hands of his hysterical wife.

We found the safari group the day after O'Flanagan had been rescued, encamped at a stinking, slime-covered water hole within easy reach of the cool, clear waters of the Luiana River. They, of course, did not know that the river was so close, literally within ten kilometres of their position.

We felt like the US cavalry coming to the rescue. Dirty, smelly Americans clustered around our Sabres and drank all our water within minutes.

They swore, all of them, that they wanted to shake the dust of Africa off their feet as soon as possible and forever.

They rapidly packed all their gear and, as we watched, the fetid caravan pulled out of what must have been a hellhole for them setting off towards the west and the nearest civilisation at Serpa Pinto, about 300 kilometres away. We had no regrets at seeing Robin Hood and his party return to whence they came.

Unfortunately for O'Flanagan, Robin Hood was making merry with his wife while he was ensconced between white sheets in the Windhoek general hospital. The safari leader was scarcely out of hospital when Mrs O'Flanagan and Robin Hood flitted off to the United States.

O'Flanagan never returned to Angola and died a very lonely man some years later, still troubled by the wounds inflicted by the king of the beasts.

Our survey of water holes in the Cuando-Cubango was duly completed and the maps suitably corrected and annotated were despatched to General Pop Fraser's headquarters in Pretoria.

We still had to survey the western Caprivi.

Again we split up into smaller patrols to cover the ground more quickly. I selected the more interesting-looking area adjacent to the Cuando River. After all, rank has its privileges.

Backwards and forwards we tracked along every one of the *omurambas*. Apart from wells dug by Bushmen and one or two water holes, there were no other sources of water away from the rivers.

The game was also less plentiful than it was north of the border. Elephants were conspicuous by their almost total absence.

However, there were quite large herds of buffalo along the river and, in areas adjacent to it, many small herds of zebra, giraffe, wildebeest, roan and sable antelope and quite large numbers of tsessebe.

For the first time, we found Bushman settlements some distance from the Golden Highway. Some larger settlements were found along the road where the Bushmen were already placing one tentative foot inside Western civilisation. They had begun to adopt discarded Western-style rags as clothing, and battered kitchen utensils such as old enamel buckets and bowls replaced the traditional clay pots and ostrich shells. Even the odd donkey was used to carry their meagre possessions or freshly slaughtered venison.

Deep inside the remoter parts of the bush, we came into contact with Bushman family settlements where the adults still wore skin loincloths, and the little ones wore nothing at all, except beads if they were girls. The Bushman bow and poisoned arrows remained much in evidence, however. These Bushmen smelled rank, but they looked a lot more lively and content than those squatting along the Golden Highway who were becoming dependent on hand-outs from passing military and police convoys.

The western Caprivi was, and is still supposed to be, a nature reserve although there was no visible sign indicating its status. The nearest nature conservator lived in Katima Mulilo, some 130 kilometres away, but he was not allowed to enter the reserve "because of the war situation".

The result was that the police had a free hand to shoot for the pot as much and as often as they liked.

The area also became the happy hunting ground of certain civil servants from Katima, as well as senior officials and politicians from as far afield as Pretoria.

The Cuando River and its western flood plains, the focal point of game concentrations in the dry season, were not encompassed by the reserve ostensibly to place the few Bushman communities on the river's western bank under the jurisdiction of the Katima Mulilo magistrate. This situation was the result of arbitrary action by the Commissioner General for Bantu Affairs in South West Africa.

It made a farce of the effectiveness of the western Caprivi as a game reserve. Most of the huntable game migrated from the protected areas, deep inside the reserve, to within shooting range of the expensive hunting rifles of the many hunters from Katima and the commissioner general's select group of hunting companions, who were more often than not drawn from South African government circles.

There are quite a few former cabinet ministers who can boast today that they have shot a buffalo or two, even an elephant or a lion, in Central Africa. The trophies are there for all to admire, mounted on the walls of various studies to prove their undoubted expertise as intrepid shots and big-game hunters. Others of less lofty stature, and rather more humble accomplishments, readily followed in the footsteps of their leaders.

We were settling down in our hide one night, a few hundred

metres off the Golden Highway, when a heavy truck pulled off the road opposite us. By the sounds emanating from the stopping place, I gathered that whoever was in the truck was going to stay there for the night. No one, except members of the security forces, was allowed to overnight in the western Caprivi because of its status as a combat zone.

Therefore, four of us set off as a small armed patrol to investigate. It was not too far-fetched that Swapo could use trucks passing through to plant mines on the only road between Rundu and Katima Mulilo, a tenuous supply line from the distant railhead at Grootfontein for both the police and the Defence Force in the eastern Caprivi.

We were armed with AK-47s, wore camouflage and our faces were blackened: normal battle attire for the Recces. We got close to the cosy little campfire and observed two men scoffing bully beef straight from tins, while taking copious swigs from a whisky bottle. One fellow, a fat hulk of a man, was celebrating the fact that he had got off, scot free, in the Katimo court that morning on a charge of poaching. He openly boasted that he had spun the magistrate an unlikely yarn and that the magistrate had swallowed it, hook, line and sinker.

Quite by chance, I knew that a man had been charged for shooting a hippo on the western side of the Kongola ferry. We were close enough to listen attentively from just beyond the circle of firelight to the poacher's tale of perjury. He was a man who unabashedly revelled in his lack of integrity.

He had told the magistrate that he had unexpectedly met up with a hippo on the road and that he unavoidably drove straight into it. The animal was badly injured. He therefore followed it into the bush and reluctantly put it out of its misery with his heavy-calibre hunting rifle, which just happened to be in the cab of his truck. Of course neither the police, nor the flora and fauna man (or conservator) produced any evidence during the trial that the animal was hale and hearty when the truck driver felled it with his ever-ready hunting rifle.

In the stillness of the Caprivi night, with four pairs of ears listening intently to every word, he admitted that he saw the hippo standing in the road in good time, stopped, took out his hunting rifle and deliberately shot the animal. Proud of his spectacular achievement in chalking up another big-game species to his credit, he left the animal thrashing around in its own blood, and drove on with not a twinge of conscience to bother him. What was one hippo more or less, anyway? There were plenty more where that one came from.

It was time to take action. We rose quietly and, with the expertise of true Recces, sneaked up behind the pair, still deep in conversation with one another and in close communion with the whisky bottle. I got within one pace of the standing poacher, my rifle pointed at his bulky back. He was shovelling globs of cold bully beef down his throat with a fork.

"Good evening," I said.

The huge body whipped around. He nearly swallowed his fork when he saw four ferocious-looking figures, AKs clasped in their hands, staring at him with white eyes set in pitch-black faces, no more than an arm's length away.

"Who... who are you? How... how did you get here?" he stuttered in panic.

His mate's mouth just hung open. Our sudden appearance at close quarters, without a sound, clearly frightened the hell out of them.

"Pack your things and get out. You are not allowed to camp here," was all I answered.

They quickly threw their few belongings on board the truck and were about to drive off without extinguishing the fire.

"Put out your fire," I ordered.

"Yes ... we will," they answered submissively. They shovelled sand over the still burning fire until I was satisfied that not the smallest glowing coal was left.

The truck, which turned out to be a tipper, raced off at speed, its taillights disappearing fast into the blackness of the night.

They must have flattened the bottle of whisky on the way, probably to steady their nerves, because by the time they reached the Bagani ferry, they were as drunk as skunks.

In their haste to get out of the sinister western Caprivi and into the safety of the Kavango, they started blowing their hooter a long way off as a signal to the Bagani river ferry that they were on their way and that the crew had to stand by to take them on board.

There was only one problem. The ferry had been put to bed for the night on the far bank of the Okavango River.

The truck made an impressive splash as it drove straight into the river, without stopping, at a point where the bank suddenly dropped away vertically to a depth of seven metres or more. Truck, driver and passenger disappeared in a cloud of bubbles into the cold, dark depths of the Okavango River.

Fortunately, the two sobered up immediately when the cold water gripped them in its clutches. They struggled to the surface and swam frantically for the nearest bank to escape the hungry crocodiles cruising around in the dark. They escaped the watery grave of their truck and pulled themselves up the bank wet, bedraggled and freezing, to spend a miserable night shivering with fear and cold until the ferry trundled leisurely across to fetch them the next morning.

Other better known poachers from Katima also joined the unequal fray from time to time. One of them was a well-known medical doctor who developed a particular weakness for elephants. He was never caught, although this wasn't for lack of trying on the part of the nature conservator.

Unfortunately, the poor conservator was viewed with a certain amount of derision by the white population of Katima. He was more or less treated as an outcast, excluded from community life because he interfered with their favourite pastime. This clearly demonstrated the general disregard for wildlife by the white public servants who made up the majority of the town's population. Everyone who could pull a trigger had a rifle and it was used as often as possible to ensure what was wrongfully perceived to be an inexhaustible supply of biltong (jerky) and ivory.

The black inhabitants – members of the Mafwe and Basubya tribes – also took a heavy toll of whatever animals strayed in front of their shotguns, rifles and antiquated blunderbusses.

The Caprivi was a mecca for the unlicensed hunter. Only a very few asked questions. Most law enforcement officers turned a blind eye and many partook in the slaughter.

A white pharmacist once drove to Kongola from his dispensary at the general hospital in Katima and on the way he came across a lioness with four young cubs next to the road.

In an incredible display of macho bravery, this fellow got out of his Land Rover and shot the mother and four cubs at point-blank range. He had shot five lions! He had made his mark as a big white hunter in Central Africa! The fact that the four cubs were too small to run away, let alone gnaw weakly at his custom-made hunting boots, was neither here nor there. He was a hero! He left the carcasses right there and drove back, pleased with his day's achievements and more than ready to boast over a sundowner at the club about his bravery in overcoming five lions all by himself.

But these were not the only people who shot wild animals inside or outside a proclaimed game reserve.

We could not pay July for the job he was doing as a tracker and guide. We were not provided with the necessary cash to do so. To set the army's administrative machinery into gear and acquire money would require a small tactical nuclear warhead to be placed under the buttocks of the chief paymaster, not to mention the civil service commission and other dried-out sticks reclining limply in their green office chairs while gazing languidly over the heaps of dusty, mouldering files in their pending trays.

Taking into account the Bushmen's social structure, way of life and the vast difference between their family-based hunter-gatherer culture and our materialistic, modern one, giving money to them seemed not the obvious choice in any case.

So I agreed to shoot a buck on a weekly basis for July and his family.

We could not shoot inside the game reserve, so the animals were shot in either Angola or Botswana. At the time, we were completely ignorant of the law that prohibited the import of game products across an international boundary without a permit.

The tsessebes were the most plentiful animals around, and I therefore resolved to shoot one per week rather than any of the other buck.

So, after our first week in Angola, we dropped off July and his newly shot tsessebe, at his kraal.

Soon the drums started to throb and the fires began burning high in July's kraal. As darkness descended, the Bushmen started singing in their peculiar monotonous manner. The drums beat louder and the singing grew noisier as the night wore on.

We lay in our sleeping bags, still unaccustomed to the ways of the Bushmen, listening to the mounting, discordant racket. A pack of howling dogs would have done better. In the early morning hours, quiet fell at last over the Bushman kraal.

As we pulled out on the Monday morning for our next patrol I asked July how they had enjoyed the tsessebe.

"It was good, but we are still very hungry," old July replied.

Several weeks passed and then we moved back to Sifumna. I decided to shoot two tsessebes, because the previous one was evidently not quite enough to feed all the mouths in July's family.

Once again we went through the painful experience of listening to the cacophony of a Bushman choir, accompanied by madly beating drums. This time, the party went on right through the night until late the next morning.

When Monday morning came around, I once again asked July, this time with a confident smile, how they fared with their two tsessebes. Was the meat to their taste and were they happy with our generous contribution to the family larder?

"Oh Major, it was quite good, but we are still very hungry."

The tsessebe is not exactly a small animal. In fact, it is quite big, comparable in size to a fully grown wildebeest. I said nothing while I tried to figure out how 35 people, of whom at least a third were tiny toddlers, could do adequate justice to two large animals in just one short night and less than half a morning.

I decided to shoot the biggest buffalo I could find.

By then we were surveying the Caprivi water holes, and towards the end of the week, we found ourselves on the Botswana cutline.

A buffalo bull would be found inside Botswana, without Botswana's knowledge, of course.

This, hopefully, would keep the Bushmen in meat for at least a week.

We walked into Botswana and finally found a small herd of buffalo moving away from us. The rear of the herd was covered by an old and very large bull, commonly called by us a "cement bull" since its back and sides showed grey, bare patches where the hair was becoming somewhat grizzled and thin, creating the impression that it had been sculpted out of concrete.

Kernaas begged for the opportunity to make his name as a big-game hunter. The old bull had stopped and was gazing back at us, no doubt wondering what it was that brought us there in the first place.

Kernaas took careful aim at the head of the bull with his R1 rifle and squeezed the trigger. The bull went down like a log in the long grass. The rest of the herd cantered off.

Carefully, very, very carefully indeed, we approached the place where we had seen the bull go down.

We had read and often heard of a buffalo bull suddenly coming to life, jumping to its feet with astonishing alacrity and goring its would-be killer before a second shot could be fired.

So we were thoroughly nonplussed, to say nothing of alarmed, that not a sign of the bull could be found. There was not even the smallest droplet of blood.

"You missed!" we all observed.

Kernaas, his claim to be a big-game hunter seriously jeopardised, could only keep his mouth shut.

July took the spoor and we followed. He made a few caustic comments about marksmanship which did not go down well with Kernaas.

After several kilometres, deep inside Botswana, we caught up with the herd again and, lo and behold, there was the cement bull in its customary rearguard position, quite unconcerned about its previous narrow escape.

Kernaas asked for another chance, but I decided a section attack on our quarry was warranted.

So at the command "fire!", four R1 rifles opened up on the doomed bull. Riddled with bullets, it sank to its knees and rolled over.

July did not mind that the meat was already tenderised with lead slugs before he got down to slaughtering it. The Bushmen are less fussy about the appearance and state of meat than we spoiled and fastidious Westerners.

Closer inspection revealed that Kernaas's bullet had lodged as a lump of metal on the thick boss of the bull's huge spread of horns. A 7.62 hard-nosed bullet just could not penetrate such thick armour at a range of a 100 metres, but the shock of impact had momentarily stunned the bull and brought it down.

We summoned a police pick-up truck and by using an overhanging branch and a thick rope as a block and tackle we got the buffalo into the truck. The Ford was sagging right down on its rear axle and the back legs of the huge animal were dangling over the rear edge. Its tail dragged on the sand as we set off for Sifumna.

July was all smiles and sparkling eyes as we drove into the centre of his kraal with his meat ration for the week.

We dropped the buffalo in the middle of the kraal while women and children danced around and clapped their hands in a show of undiluted joy.

Then our purgatory began. The drums started up and soon the women joined in with their rendering of a mixed jackal and hyena choir praising the bounty of Africa.

The sun went down, the stars came out and the tempo and decibels of the drums and singing rose to a crescendo.

I slept fitfully, waking every hour or so to the same discordant chorus, if one could call it that, and the same off-tempo throbbing of the drums. When the grey of dawn appeared in the east, the Bushmen were still at it, more enthusiastically than ever.

The sun rose and the party sounds showed no sign of abating.

We got up, serviced our vehicles and weapons, went for a swim in the river and came back. July and family were still at it.

Only towards midday did they slow down before stopping for an hour or two.

We were just getting used to the unusual quiet when a drum started throbbing again, soon to be joined by the others.

It wasn't long before the girls' chorus broke into the same aria from whatever bush opera July had chosen to inflict on our long-suffering ears.

The sun went down and the noise level concurrently went up. They probably had girls singing in relays and drummers pounding in shifts, because the crescendo was maintained throughout the night.

It was only at midday that the racket came to a halt, but only for a while. Towards evening, there was a final but half-hearted spurt, and then, at last, blissful silence descended on Sifumna and its surroundings.

The next morning, I asked a somewhat jaded July whether he and his people were happy with their buffalo bull.

"It was very good, Major but oh, the Bushmen are still very hungry," he replied.

They had scoffed the entire buffalo in virtually one continuous sitting. All that remained was the skin.

I just gave up and went back to shooting one tsessebe a week, much to July's disgust.

Finally, our mission came to an end. We had seen a raw and unspoilt part of Africa, probably the only corner still left that could claim to be in the same state as when it was created.

We were sad at having to return to Rundu, and from there, to Oudtshoorn, our home base in the RSA.

Little did we know that in just a few months, we would be back on a permanent basis.

TWO

Fort Doppies

We were soon given another mission, one that was more of a "fighting" job than the previous one – at least it had the potential to develop into a small-scale war with enough action to satisfy the more adventurous among us.

We had to train a hundred guerrillas as a nucleus around which a bigger irregular force could be built. Everything was to be done in utmost secrecy.

The problem was to find a place completely out of sight of inquisitive snoopers. The western Caprivi nature reserve was finally selected as the ideal location for clandestine training of this nature. It was, in fact, the only terrain in all of southern Africa where we could get away from the prying eyes of others, both friendly and hostile.

I arranged to meet a friend from Ongulumbashe, the first Swapo base in Ovamboland which we had attacked in 1966, who had been posted to Katima in charge of the security police, and he identified a suitable spot for our training camp. Knowing the Caprivi like the back of his hand, he suggested a position some 10 kilometres south of the Golden Highway and about 30 kilometres west of the Cuando River.

We flew there by helicopter and I found it to be ideally suited to our purposes.

Swanie, my security police friend, arranged for boreholes to be sunk, a water pump to be installed and a rough track to be scraped from the Golden Highway to our new base.

Tents were supplied, vehicles obtained, a 100-man field kitchen was installed and all the rest of the equipment sent to the Caprivi from army logistical depots.

Naturally, the equipment included rifles, ammunition, rocket launchers, bombs, mortars and their shells and at least a ton of explosives.

We were ready to start and some of my men were already there waiting for our 100 recruits to arrive.

After a spell of frustrating inactivity the would-be guerrillas finally made their appearance and I flew to the Caprivi from Oudtshoorn to be on the spot when training kicked off.

The base had been named Elephant Camp by Swanie, possibly because he assumed it to be located in an area frequented by herds of elephant.

Nothing could have been further from the truth. There was not an elephant in sight and it was almost a year before we spotted the first one clumsily limping past the base. It was virtually dead on its feet.

Another base through which our guerrillas were first routed for security checks was known as Rhino Base. Later, when it was taken over by so-called Unita refugees, this base was renamed Delta.

Rhino Base was, initially at least, not a misnomer. There used to be plenty of rhino in the area but most were subsequently shot by poachers.

Another area prepared for possible future expansion was further to the west. It was called Zebra Base again because of the presence of a small herd of zebra.

When I arrived at Elephant Base I was introduced to another newcomer to the unit by the name of Doppies.

Doppies had taken over the running of the base as quickly as he could. However, he was not very efficient and tended to create chaos and sometimes havoc among instructors and students alike.

Doppies was a vervet monkey and I never did find out where he came from. He had no particular master, and belonged to all of us, although he did seem rather partial to FC van Zyl, one of the original four Recces. But he certainly made his presence felt.

A monkey can be one of the most destructive little animals

one could ever encounter and Doppies was no exception. In fact, he was the bane of Alphonso's life.

Alphonso was our cook, an exceptionally good one, who was worth his bulky weight in gold.

Doppies had the knack of making his appearance in the kitchen just as Alphonso was starting to dish up lunch or dinner. He then proceeded to help himself to whatever was to be had, screeching shrilly when he inadvertently plunged his little black hands into a steaming hot concoction.

Alphonso's Afrikaans was decidedly earthy. He had learned the language mostly from crude soldiers and policemen who deliberately taught him all the wrong words and phrases. He was an Angolan from Luanda who could speak only his native language and Portuguese when he arrived at our camp.

One day, I was not surprised to hear a string of curses emanating from the kitchen. From the hut that served as my office I saw Alphonso, armed with a huge ladle, chasing Doppies who was scampering all around the kitchen.

"Doppies, you bugger! You crapped in the soup! I will kill you when I get my hands on you!" shouted Alphonso at the fleeing little figure. Doppies spotted me and made for his usual sanctuary on my shoulder, a normal drill to escape the wrath of the victims of his naughty pranks.

Full of bravado Doppies turned around and faced Alphonso from the safety of my shoulder uttering a long series of stuttering threats while baring his teeth in a show of aggression.

Alphonso walked away muttering to himself about the unfair protection granted to an animal which should really be done away with, threw away the contaminated soup and started a new batch.

Doppies sat back on my shoulder enormously pleased with himself for having once again the upper hand in the continuous contest between himself and Alphonso.

Others also suffered from the monkey's unwelcome attention. Dewald de Beer had his paycheck snatched from his hand when he opened a letter from home in the presence of Doppies. The monkey scuttled up a tree where he carefully examined both sides of his prize, while Dewald stood under the tree, threatening imminent destruction if Doppies did not come down and hand back his money.

Doppies took no notice and after a while decided that it was a worthless piece of paper, so he tore it up.

Uncle Spook, our mess caterer, showered every afternoon and Doppies soon learned his routine for future reference. Unfortunately, he also discovered that Uncle Spook was easily excitable and therefore an ideal target for the attention of a mischievous monkey.

One afternoon, Doppies surreptitiously followed Uncle Spook to the outside shower and watched him undress, turn the shower on and move under the spray where he started to soap himself.

Previously, Doppies would steal the soap and disappear with it into the tree so Uncle Spook made sure that he had a firm grip on his soap at all times while busy with his ablutions.

This day, however, Doppies spotted Uncle Spook's wristwatch and, quick as a flash, he came down from his perch to snatch the watch. Then he scampered back to his branch and proceeded to examine the expensive wristwatch like a connoisseur.

The heartbroken wails emanating from the shower were heard all over the camp, followed by a string of oaths and curses not normally associated with Uncle Spook.

Finally, Uncle Spook tried to reason with the monkey. "Please Doppies, you can't do anything with that watch. Please give it back to me."

Doppies sat in his tree, watch in hand, looking rather disdainfully at Uncle Spook below. Suddenly he flung the watch down from a dizzy height. Spook was not quick enough and a very expensive watch smashed to pieces on the concrete floor of the shower cubicle. Doppies nonchalantly swung off through the branches without a care in the world, leaving Uncle Spook speechless with rage and almost in tears at his costly loss.

While training our recruits, we also carried out operations from time to time, especially in south-western Zambia, where small groups from our base would harass Swapo bases and Zambian army garrisons which gave them support.

We killed quite a number of Swapo guerrillas and also a large number of Zambian army troops who persisted in ferrying Swapo to drop-off points just north of the border in Zambian army trucks.

In one incident we blew up a lorry load of 20 Swapo guerrillas killing all of them and utterly destroying the truck.

As a result both Swapo and the Zambian army withdrew completely from the south-western tip of Zambia, attacks on the South African police base at Singalamwe ceased and no more mines were planted along the entire border from the Okavango in the west to the Zambezi in the east. We had made life exceedingly dangerous and unbearable for both Swapo and the Zambian forces.

All our information about the enemy, our patrol activities, concentrations of local inhabitants inside south-western Zambia, infiltration routes and other data were carefully plotted with coloured pins on a map in our makeshift operations room. FC van Zyl was responsible for keeping our operations maps up to date.

Doppies thought he could assist FC in this task, and on several occasions he decided he should do his bit for the war effort by removing the coloured pins. FC was furious, but could never catch Doppies in the act. Then, one day, there was a tremendous din in the operations tent and judging by the sounds and the hysterical screeching Doppies was getting a terrific hiding.

I rushed into the tent to see Doppies sitting under the table crying his heart out and rubbing his little buttocks with both hands. FC was bent over double, head under the table, and wagging his long index finger giving Doppies a severe dressing down.

Painstakingly, FC replaced all the pins while Doppies watched dejectedly from under the table. Finally, FC walked out. Without a second thought, Doppies was back at the map, where, with rapt attention, he started pulling out the coloured pins and stuffing them into his cheek pockets.

On his first birthday we gave Doppies a dog, a nondescript puppy found by FC somewhere to the east of the Cuando. Doppies was duly presented with his dog named Dingo at a proper birthday party where, as usual, he consumed too much beer and staggered around knocking over beer and whisky glasses. We sent him to bed early, disgusted with his behaviour.

Doppies immediately took to his dog.

He played with him, rode on his back and groomed him from time to time. In fact, Doppies got quite attached to his pet.

Dingo, however, was always underfoot in the mess or in the pub and when a party of policemen came to visit us one of them made the mistake of giving Dingo a kick. He was attacked immediately by a furious grey ball of fur screeching dementedly with anger. Doppies bit the astonished policeman in his ankle and jumped back to protect the cowering Dingo. From there he threatened the policeman with worse consequences if he should dare to accept the challenge.

The policeman stared at his bloody ankle ruefully, then hurriedly retreated behind the protective screen of some of my men who, of course, treated the episode as a huge joke and sympathised with poor Dingo.

For all the time the policeman stayed in the pub he had to be protected from sneak attacks by a still furious little monkey.

The policeman left soon afterwards with his buddies and never returned. That monkey was too much for him.

We did not like the name Elephant Base since there were no elephants in sight and decided to find a new name for our camp. Suggestions were made, but none seemed appropriate and eventually I expressed my own preference.

I did not want the base to be named after some general, politician or anyone else who might seek to lay some claim to fame in the war we were fighting or who was above us in the command structure. So I suggested that the base be named after Doppies. His fame had already spread to all police, army and air force bases throughout the Caprivi. Everyone agreed whole-heartedly.

The base was officially named Fort Doppies at another party where Doppies once again misbehaved. As usual, he went to sleep in my sleeping bag where I found him later. He did not even wake up when I crawled in.

We took him with us as much as we could during training sessions. On route marches he would bum a lift from any of us or scamper from tree to tree along the route.

He even accompanied us in our kayaks on the river while we were preparing for a particular operation. For the first time in his life Doppies came face to face with hippos at close quarters and, to our alarm, decided to adopt a threatening posture. Fortunately, the hippos took no notice.

But we left Doppies in the camp with Uncle Spook and Alphonso when we went on operations, sometimes for weeks at a time. His presence on a patrol was unthinkable as he had no concept of the vital importance of silence and stealth when in close proximity to the enemy.

Though Doppies was never lonely – after all, he had Dingo, his dog, to play with as well as Sheila, the cat, her three kittens and both Spook and Alphonso to terrorise – he always missed us and we were greeted with unbridled delight when we returned to base. For hours after our arrival, Doppies would jump from one shoulder to another, nuzzling up to his pals and being affectionately stroked and cuddled by otherwise exceedingly hard-bitten Special Forces operators.

So it was a terrible blow to all the men when Doppies disappeared.

He used to go with us on our early-morning runs, cadging a lift on somebody's bouncing shoulder.

One morning, he joined the runners as usual, went halfway and decided to wait in a convenient tree by the roadside for our return.

But when we got back there was no sign of Doppies and he was nowhere to be found on the base. For the rest of that day and for the next several days we went around the area calling, searching, looking for spoor and scrutinising every troop of monkeys we came across, but to no avail.

He simply left without leaving a single clue to the manner of his departure.

Perhaps he had reached the right age to break away on his own or maybe he joined a passing troop of monkeys. Dewald thought that strange monkeys would have chased him away.

I don't know enough about the habits of monkeys to make an intelligent guess, but the fact is there was no sign of him whatsoever, dead or alive, and this seemed to point to his breaking away from his human companions and returning to the wild as he was free to do.

But he could at least have said goodbye.

Doppies was still with us when we were given the task of tracking down and intercepting a band of Swapo insurgents who had infiltrated the Cuando-Cubango across the Cuando River from a place called Kaunga Mashi inside Zambia.

The security police loaned us two Bushman trackers and guides, both Vaskelas and armed with antiquated .303 rifles. They were brothers. One, Antonio, could speak a smattering of Afrikaans, but the other, Kamaia, could speak only Portuguese and, of course, his own language.

We set off in our trusty Sabres to be briefed at Bwabwata by the military commander of the sector. By this time the army had assumed control of all the former police bases.

After a vague and unsatisfactory briefing we crossed the border into Angola with the two Vaskela Bushmen, instead of old July. They knew exactly where Swapo tracks were likely to be found, having lived in the area for most of their lives.

We headed straight for the Biongue *omuramba* to cast around for spoor and when we got there Antonio pointed out an old and well-used Unita base. He informed us that he was once a member of Unita which had a symbiotic relationship with the Portuguese troops at Luiana: Unita did not bother the Portuguese and the Portuguese did not bother Unita.

They also gave succour to Swapo gangs on their way through

to Ovamboland, Unita and Swapo having been on good terms with each other for a number of years.

It therefore came as no surprise when Antonio and Kamaia found Swapo spoor, perhaps a week old, in their old Unita base. The spoor led westwards.

We were soon on their trail with Dewald de Beer, the best white tracker I had ever come across, keeping a check on the Bushmen's capability.

He was expected to verify all their interpretations, but as the day progressed we soon brushed aside any doubt we might have had about their reliability.

We came across several temporary bases that Swapo had occupied and, significantly, found a large stock of dried elephant meat hanging in the trees in smelly, fly-infested strips, no doubt to replenish other Swapo gangs soon to follow along the same trail.

At one point I decided to break away from the spoor and leapfrog well ahead of our quarry with the intention of laying ambushes at the only two water holes in the area.

We pushed on northwards, past Bambangando to a point roughly in line with the Luiana River's junction with the Luenge River. Here we turned south until we reached the first of the two water holes.

I dropped half the patrol at this location and pushed on further south to set up an ambush at the second water hole.

We were no sooner in position than we made violent contact with the Swapo gang's reconnaissance party. We shot three of the five and seriously wounded a fourth who managed to get away. The fifth fled into the bush, only to run into a paratrooper patrol further to the east where he too was shot.

The remains of the guerrilla we wounded was found under a tree two weeks later by one of my patrols. His bones were picked clean and pulled apart by hyenas and vultures. His AK-47 was lying conspicuously in the open proving that he was indeed the sole survivor of the contact at the water hole.

However, we did not have it all our own way. On the spur of the moment, I decided to backtrack on the Swapo reconnaissance team's spoor all the way to their temporary base where I hoped to find the rest of the gang.

With Dewald sitting on the left front mudguard of my Sabre as tracker, we made good time on the spoor which generally followed an elephant footpath.

Suddenly Dewald signalled me to stop and urgently beckoned me to come and take a look.

He pointed at a fresh footprint, obviously made by someone getting out of our way in a hurry. "This spoor is not more than ten seconds old," he said.

As the significance of his information sank in, he calmly continued. "This means that we have unexpectedly stumbled into their temporary base ... they are probably looking at us right now through the sights of their weapons."

We had the knack of driving our Sabres silently down to a fine art. It was quite possible to get within 20 or 30 paces before the sound of the engines could be picked up.

We all got out of the vehicles and moved in an extended line on both sides of the fresh spoor. It doubled back in a semi-circle to cross our Sabre tracks, about 50 metres to the rear. Doggedly we moved on, fingers on triggers, every nerve tautly strung.

Suddenly we came upon their cache of equipment and rucksacks and at that moment a violent firefight exploded on our left flank.

I had to swing the extended line through 90 degrees to the left to form an assault line, while the machine guns on our stationary Sabres supported us from the left with automatic fire.

Unfortunately, one of my men, Lieutenant Zeelie, who was on the far left was cut down as he charged into the midst of the guerrillas, becoming the first South African soldier killed in the operational area.

Kamaia was with me, armed with an SKS Russian carbine. He had been complaining that his .303 rifle was too slow-firing to be of any use in a contact and pestered me until I gave him one of the weapons we had retrieved from the dead Swapo guerrillas at the water hole.

The bullets were flying thick and fast, especially every time

I shouted an order to the rest of the assault line, the guerrillas concentrating their fire on the source of the patrol commander's voice. Unperturbed by it all, Kamaia stood upright in this hail of bullets, calmly pumping away at the unseen attackers to the fore.

Then his rifle jammed and he immediately lost his composure, and strode over to me sounding off at the useless SKS I had palmed off on him.

Evidently, he expected me to produce another weapon from nowhere and at a somewhat inopportune moment.

I curtly ordered Kamaia to go and get his own .303 from the Sabres.

He walked off in a huff oblivious to the lead flying all around him and I thought that would be the end of the little man.

Within seconds, however, I heard the unmistakable bangs of an old .303 being fired to my immediate right.

I glanced in that direction and saw Kamaia, upright in the open, firing his Second World War rifle at the enemy as if he was having a go at some harmless guinea fowl.

"Are you alright Kamaia?" I asked.

"Yes, Major," grinned Kamaia. "This is a good rifle, not like the s**t Swapo rifles that don't work!"

We proceeded to the final assault charging through the Swapo base with Kamaia right beside me.

Swapo took off in a hurry, leaving everything behind, but dragging a badly wounded comrade with them. He died before they could get him to medical assistance.

We found Zeelie's crumpled body in the middle of the base and his death put a damper on the success of the operation.

But at least Kamaia and Antonio were smiling broadly. They had got their own back against the hated "long feet".

We headed south, away from the contact area and spent a rather restless night in a temporary base. The next morning a helicopter flew in to resupply us and to evacuate Zeelie's body.

We again followed the Swapo gang's spoor heading in the direction of Zambia with the object of overtaking them and wiping them out before they could safely reach their sanctuary.

The spoor led to a crossing site northwards across the Luiana, but we could not get our Sabres across because of the extensive swamps on both sides of the river.

I therefore requested a helicopter airlift to the known Swapo crossing sites opposite Kaunga Mashi in order to cut off the Swapo gang's retreat.

My request was refused and I was ordered to go to a somewhat mystical point in the bush where we were assured we would make contact with about 200 Swapos.

According to my own security police sources, there were no more than 80 to 90 Swapos in the whole of south-western Zambia so I refused to be sent on a wild-goose chase and decided to backtrack on the original infiltration route south of the Luiana River in the hope that our opponents would link up with their old trail again somewhere to our east.

The final straw was when I was peremptorily ordered to investigate fires burning to our south which the sector commander assured me appeared to be the cooking fires of vast Swapo hordes.

I knew for a fact that the fires were the smouldering stumps and trunks of leadwood trees after a bush fire had passed through the area. We had covered that particular stretch of bush about a week before and leadwood can smoulder for months on end after a bush fire has burnt itself out.

Nothing doing. My explanations fell on deaf ears. I was ordered south while the Swapo gang was heading away from us, east to their crossing sites opposite Kaunga Mashi.

Angry and frustrated I moved south with all four of our Sabres. We spent the night in a temporary base overrun by elephants and even a couple of crashing rhinos. Nobody slept much, the Bushmen not at all, until a few bursts into the air from one of our machine guns initiated a stampede of crashing, trumpeting and squealing elephants and rhinos that surprised and overawed the most bush-wise among us. There must have been hundreds of elephants spread all around us, peaceably but noisily feeding from trees and shrubs by tearing down the branches with explosive cracks like a huge gang of destructive vandals intent on eradicating the last vestiges of any vegetation from the face of Africa.

The next morning, under the direction of Antonio, we were taken south across the western end of the Biongue *omuramba* and into the dune areas beyond.

The trees changed from red syringas to large stands of false mopani and mankettis, both of them majestic trees. The false mopani's evergreen, widely spread canopy gives a pleasing parklike atmosphere to the otherwise brown and burnt garb of the African savannah in winter dress.

Game spoor became plentiful, particularly sables, zebras, kudus and roans.

We drove through the increasing lushness of this paradise until we were suddenly confronted by a sizeable pool of the clearest water right in the middle of a dune, a place where no water hole was supposed to be.

The pool, about 50 metres across and all but hidden under the huge spreading canopies of the false mopanies, was alive with fish, ducks, geese and other water birds.

The water was as sweet and clear as the best I had ever tasted from remote mountain streams.

The nearest *omuramba* was miles away, and there was no way rainwater could flow into this pool, and no sign of any streams feeding it. The water had to come from strong underground springs.

Antonio informed me that their parents used to have a *kimbo* there and we did, indeed, find the remains of a Bushman *kimbo*. His father had given him directions to this pool as he was very small when they left the area and therefore could not remember his former "home town".

Incredibly, Antonio led us over a distance of at least 20 kilometres straight to his birthplace, through trackless bush moving from tree to tree, ant hill to shrub, dried-up water pan to clearing as described by his father, who had long since departed this life.

From only a hundred metres away this idyllic pool of water was completely invisible.

A Bushman's navigational ability never ceased to amaze me.

Subsequently, many others, including Unita and South African liaison officers working with them, tried to wheedle the whereabouts of this pool from those of us who had been there. We all refused to betray the confidence Antonio placed in us. Someday, he and his family may want to go back there to escape enslavement by the black man and the white man's corrupt philosophy of life, clothed in the garish tinsel and synthetic sheen of so-called democracy.

I may even decide to join him there!

Antonio's birthplace is one of the few remaining spots in Africa where a man and his family can live off the bounty of the savannah.

At one's doorstep are the choicest freshwater fish in all of Africa, the well-known bream untainted by muddy water and therefore with a delicate flavour that would send any chef dashing for his frying pan.

The numerous ducks and geese would supply one with meat and eggs, judiciously collected to ensure a continued supply.

The guinea fowl, likewise, would offer meat and eggs, while the great variety of antelope, including the sought-after eland with its delicious steaks, would gladden the heart of the greatest epicures.

The nuts of the manketti tree taste just like walnuts and are in great abundance, offering a nutritious content rarely found in other kernels. Bring to the table the tubers, roots and edible shoots of certain plants, including water lilies, to provide the necessary vegetables and a meal would be as well balanced as anything the best restaurants in South Africa can serve.

Add to this the wild honey and marula beer and one can have a party into the bargain, with the grandfather of all hangovers to follow.

The place where Antonio's life began is a little paradise, flowing with milk and honey, that pool of clearest water forming the focal point, nestled in the most isolated part of the remote Cuando-Cubango and no one had even begun to search for it because they had no idea where to start. It must be the ultimate bolt hole for any "drop out".

We reached Bwabwata and sector tactical headquarters in a somewhat better frame of mind after our passage through paradise, only to be met by confusion and downright wishful thinking. The sector was going to drop two companies of paratroopers on the spot where the imaginary 200 Swapos were said to be.

When I heard that the operation was based on information already two years old, supplied by Chief of Staff Intelligence in Pretoria, I blew my top and refused to take part in any more operations with the sector.

We departed for Fort Doppies in a huff but relieved to be released from the farce into which the operation had deteriorated. But not for long.

We had hardly removed our "black-is-beautiful" make-up when we were asked to proceed by helicopter to the Kaunga Mashi crossing sites, post haste, to cut off the still retreating Swapo gang.

The elaborate airborne assault on an imaginary Swapo concentration had, as predicted, turned up nothing except peaceful, undisturbed bush with not even a very old Swapo spoor as compensation for all the wasted effort.

Somewhat disgruntled and convinced that the bird had flown, we set off for the crossing sites.

We were six hours late.

The Swapo guerrillas were probably disembarking from their *makorros* (dugout canoes) on the far side of the extensive Cuando swamps at the same time we were rapidly deploying from our helicopters on the near side to cut off their retreat.

If those hidebound staff officers at tactical headquarters had only possessed the wisdom to listen to the operators on the ground, we could have cornered all of them and avenged Zeelie's death.

On the other hand, we would not have had our side-trip through paradise.

Round about this time we saw our first elephant in the Fort Doppies area. It was a gaunt bull, still young in years, but almost paralysed on one side. He staggered past our base one afternoon, completely ignoring our presence, no doubt painfully looking for a place to die peacefully.

I sent Dewald out to go and shoot the animal and put it out of its misery.

He did, and on closer examination he found a bullet lodged in one side of the elephant's brain and a suppurating wound on the surface. Somebody had taken a shot at it with a .303 rifle.

Fortunately, the other game species were multiplying at a pleasing rate. I laid down strict ground rules in an attempt to conserve what game there was in the area and to attract animals from other areas which were under tremendous pressure from a barrage of poaching rifles throughout the rest of the western Caprivi.

I managed to get a large chunk of the western Caprivi declared a prohibited area by the Chief of the Defence Force, Admiral Hugo Biermann, for the sole use of 1 Reconnaissance Commando.

A distinguished sailor, he seemed to have an affinity for wildlife on land, a quality found rarely among the top brass in the army whom one might have expected to be closer to the bush than a man who spent much of his life on the seas and oceans of this planet.

We immediately set about protecting our fief against all comers and especially those officials who surreptitiously carried hunting rifles in their baggage when they came to visit the Caprivi.

At the time, a civilian road construction company was building a new highway to reduce travelling time between Katima Mulilo and Grootfontein to more manageable proportions. It sometimes took an army convoy two weeks to cover the distance between the two towns in the rainy season and, obviously, this was not good enough for army units at the end of a thin and fragile logistical string.

Some of the officials from the construction company came equipped with luxurious caravans, a goodly supply of liquor to while away their leisure hours, other commodities such as tinned vegetables, canned fruit, potatoes, even some bully beef, but, of course, no fresh meat.

Almost all of them had the foresight to secrete in some recess or another at least one or two hunting rifles to shoot for the pot. Sometimes they also shot for the pocket should an unwary elephant stray into their sights.

They were not allowed to go further than 400 metres from the road they were building. They were, after all, operating in a game reserve and the game had to be protected.

Unfortunately, that factor became less of a stumbling block as time wore on, and some of the construction workers began to roam further afield as their hunting fervour got the better of them.

Driving southwards from the Golden Highway and the roadside construction camp one day, I was angered by the realisation that, not long before, a heavy truck had travelled down the track marking the western edge of the Cuando flood plain towards the Botswana border.

I followed the spoor determined to find out what the occupants of the truck were doing inside our prohibited training area.

The truck had turned off into the flood plain and I soon came across it stuck in the deep, black mud of the swamp. It was submerged up to the axles and two white men, hunting rifles slung over their shoulders, were staring disconsolately at the trapped tipper. There was no way they could get the vehicle out of the sucking mess without outside assistance, so they were glad to see me.

"Can you please help us get our truck out of the mud?"

"What are you doing here in the first place? You are not supposed to come into this area at all."

"Well, we only wanted to catch some fish," volunteered one of them sheepishly.

"With rifles? Were you going to shoot the fish?" I asked.

"Well no … The rifles are for our own protection."

"Where are your fishing rods?"

"I don't know … We must have forgotten them," answered one lamely.

I started to turn my Land Rover around.

"Aren't you going to help us?"

"No."

"Well … Can you give us a lift back to the construction camp then?"

"You can walk back."

I drove off, leaving them there in their misery. Much later, on my way back from the Botswana cutline, I found their footprints in the rutted tracks, showing distinct drag marks as they neared the end of their long and hot slog through the bush. I drove to their caravan and found two very footsore, would-be poachers sipping cold beers on the porch.

Needless to say, they did not offer me a beer and sat glumly regarding this hard-assed army officer with distinct hostility, their bare, blistered feet propped up on chairs.

They told me that they needed the truck the next day to carry out their contract commitment, which was to transport gravel for the company involved in putting a new surface on the Golden Highway. With the truck stuck in the mud, they could not fulfil their obligations.

I replied that I sympathised with their dilemma, but reminded them that they were restricted to a 400-metre strip of bush on either side of the road and that access to the truck to recover it would, regrettably, not be possible.

"But our contract is at stake," they replied.

"Well you should have thought about that before, shouldn't you? Anyway, I cannot give you permission to recover your truck, as it is well inside a prohibited area. I suggest that you approach Windhoek to sort out the problem." I was at my bureaucratic best and, frankly, enjoying every minute of it.

I left them disconsolately contemplating the future. Back at Fort Doppies, I arranged for a small standing patrol to prevent them from recovering their vehicle.

About two days later I was approached by the police at Kongola Fort requesting permission for the two would-be poachers to recover their truck. My answer was "no".

A week went by, then another. The hapless pair lost the contract for their employer in Windhoek, who promptly fired them. I then graciously stepped down off my high horse and allowed the company concerned to recover the truck.

The incident served as a lesson for the remaining road construction crews, who until then had been waging relentless war against the game of the western Caprivi park. No one had been able to stop them, as neither the police nor we were involved in game conservation. From time to time we had come across the freshly shot carcasses of animals with only choice portions cut away for human consumption, and we had even found the carcass of a kudu hidden underneath a pick-up belonging to the company, but no one could tell us who the poachers were.

The situation had called for drastic action and the truck incident stopped the depredations by the construction workers, but other aspirant poachers continued to still penetrate our training area, almost at will.

So I decided that the access roads had to be mined. Kernaas Conradie, my intrepid engineer, was ordered to prepare small, four-ounce explosive charges which could be activated by the wheels of a trespassing vehicle.

To inform unwelcome visitors of the dangers facing them, we liberally displayed the standard triangular red mine warning signs at intervals along all the tracks. A clear notice at the entrance to the prohibited area announced to all and sundry that the tracks ahead were mined.

Many heeded the warnings and turned around hurriedly to return home to Katima Mulilo or wherever else they came from, but one adventurer decided that it was a huge bluff. He decided to drive southwards along the river road towards the Botswana cutline, merrily passing one triangular "Danger – Mines" sign after another.

His flippant mood did not last long. Suddenly there was an almighty explosion and his ten-seater Land Rover came to an abrupt halt in a cloud of dust and smoke.

Angrily, he climbed out to find his right front wheel completely blown away. His Land Rover was tilted on its front axle directly below yet another warning triangle nailed to the trunk of a tall tree.

That is where I found him several hours later raging almost incoherently and threatening dire consequences such as court cases, compensation and all sorts of other nasty acts of vengeance.

"Can you read?" I asked.

"Of course I can read. What the hell do you mean?"

"What does the sign say?" I asked pointing to the red triangle clearly visible on the trunk of the tree beside the road.

"I can read what it says!" he shouted. "You don't have to be sarcastic."

"Right, you had ample warning that the road was mined, so if you persist in being stupid then you must pay the price."

"I will take you to court!"

"Please do."

I drove off leaving him fuming and spitting in his fury.

The police were called to recover the Land Rover and Kernaas was available to guide them through the minefield.

Nothing came of the court case, although the police did come to take a statement but, with the exception of security police patrols, no one ever entered the area again unless accompanied by one of us. The security police were mates of ours who used to overnight at Fort Doppies and who knew that, in reality, the "minefield" was a hoax except for the few charges we had planted to catch particular poachers.

In time, Fort Doppies grew from a tented camp to quite a luxurious establishment with picturesque, thatched buildings clustered around the central bar and open-air braai area.

The man responsible for all this development was Nic Visser, my irrepressible second-in-command, known throughout the army for his sense of humour and practical jokes.

He was also well known for his extraordinary initiative as a scrounger, sometimes using rather unorthodox methods to obtain what he needed.

While most people would call it "stealing", Nic Visser called it "liberating" desirable equipment from people or organisations that really had no good use for it or whose need was not as great as ours.

For instance, we needed building materials such as corrugated-iron sheets to construct walls for our buildings, creosote poles to bear the roofs and cement to lay the floors of the huts and pave the entertainment area, including our bush pub. We also needed tools for the job.

Nic mustered all our ancient Bedford trucks and sallied forth to Katima Mulilo to collect the poles and whatever else he could find. The poles belonged to the Bantu Development Corporation, a government organisation against which a night raid was executed, the trucks returning in due course, heavily laden with more than enough poles for our needs.

Another trip was arranged to acquire some sheets of corrugated iron. Luck was on our side because as Nic entered Mpacha Air Force Base, a C130 transport aircraft had just landed bearing a cargo of corrugated iron, steel girders and cement for construction of a goods hangar in Mpacha's freight control area.

Nic coolly drove up to the C130 with his Bedfords and informed the loadmaster that he was there to collect the building material.

Assisted by willing hands from the SAAF ground crew, his trucks were soon loaded and Nic disappeared westwards into the unknown depths of the western Caprivi with a hangar that had been "liberated" from the air force.

When I left the Caprivi in 1988, the air force still had an open docket on a hangar stolen in 1973 ...

As the need arose, we liberated additional cement from the Bantu Development Corporation – Kernaas plastering away at the Fort Doppies end and shouting for more, and Nic, at the Katima end, scouting out unattended stocks of cement.

Finally Nic decided that saws, hammers, pliers and other tools were needed, so he took a truck back to Mpacha, this time with Wannies Wannenburgh as his accomplice in an after-dark raid on the air force's toolshed.

With Wannies outside the shed, Nic was passing tools to him through a gap between the roof and wall. This went on for quite a while and Nic was about to wrap up the exercise when an air force sentry suddenly entered the shed to investigate the unusual and suspicious noises emanating from its dark interior.

"What are you doing here?" asked the sentry rather nervously as he saw the looming hulk of a Free State rugby loose forward. Rugby was a sport Nic was uncommonly good at.

"Where the hell have you been, you little nitwit?" shouted Nic, bristling with anger.

"I have been in here for at least an hour, making as much noise as I could and nobody came to investigate. I could have stolen all the tools in this shed!"

The sentry gulped and stammered, "I am sorry, sir. I only came past the shed now. I have a big area to cover."

"That is not good enough," replied Nic relentlessly. "Come on, let's go and see the orderly officer. I must report to him that his base security is nonexistent. I have my men infiltrated all over the place and not one has yet been picked up."

Nic left the shed with the sentry, taking care to stay in the shadow. For a while he stood outside the shed, contemplating the situation, then he turned to the despondent sentry.

"I tell you what," he said in a kinder tone. "See if you can track down the other infiltrators and perhaps I'll be able to produce a somewhat more sympathetic security report for counter-intelligence."

"Yes, sir," agreed the sentry, visibly relieved at his unexpected reprieve. He lost no time in making his way to some hangars in the distance and the vulnerable aircraft in them.

As soon as the sentry was out of earshot, Nic climbed back into the shed to complete his task and we were soon the proud owners of a comprehensive collection of tools, courtesy of the air force.

Our raids on air force installations notwithstanding, we found some eager accomplices among the helicopter crews. They often spent nights and weekends with us out in the sticks, away from the bureaucracy of an overlarge operational air force base and were therefore just as concerned about the comforts of Fort Doppies as we were ourselves.

The magnificent base Nic built included a kitchen, dining and sitting room complex and a charming little pub.

Apart from the most basic furniture, however, we had nothing with which to furnish our splendid recreational area. There were no armchairs, bar stools or coffee tables to give our bush camp a tinge of class and comfort.

However, in Katima Mulilo there was a grand recreational club, lavishly furnished with the items we so desperately needed.

The subsector commander, Minnaar Fourie, was an old friend of mine who had a rather soft spot for us, perhaps because he knew exactly what our top secret operations were really about.

I did not want to hurt his feelings by involving my men in the liberation of items from the splendid clubhouse, of which he was justifiably proud, so we did it through the chopper crews in dribs and drabs hoping that Minnaar would not catch on too quickly.

Every time a Puma helicopter came to Fort Doppies for a weekend stay, it had to bring a couple of armchairs or some other items to pay for the crew's "board and lodging".

Gradually, Minnaar's club furniture was being transferred to Fort Doppies and as his club's amenities became sparser, the living areas at Fort Doppies became more luxurious.

Minnaar had the habit of visiting Fort Doppies unexpectedly from time to time, but he always had to fly in by helicopter. We had arranged with the chopper pilots to give us a "beat up" over the camp if Minnaar was on board and then to make a long and leisurely approach to the landing zone in the *omuramba* about a hundred metres from the base.

This gave us enough time to grab armchairs, coffee tables and bar stools and rush into the bush where these items were hidden until Minnaar had departed.

One day, Minnaar stood in our unfurnished lounge, gravely taking in the bare cement floor (there were no carpets as these were hidden with the furniture), the few lonely and uncomfortable plastic chairs and forlorn dartboard against a wooden pillar.

"I see you also have a problem getting furniture out of the quartermaster general. You have been like this for months now. Is there any particular reason for them not supplying you?"

"Probably not budgeted for," I replied lamely.

"Yes, if you don't budget in time for furniture you won't get any. I also have a problem with furniture at my club. For some reason the place seems to be getting barer every time I go in there for a drink," said Minnaar.

"That's strange," I replied. "Somebody is probably pinching your stuff."

"I am sure somebody is. For a while I thought it was you and your people, but I see now that you don't have much either."

I decided to spread the word that the quartermaster general had relented, and that we would be getting furniture in the not too distant future.

Meanwhile, the furnishing of Fort Doppies at the expense of the sector's club went on apace until we felt that we were nice and comfortable.

Then tragedy struck.

Most of us were back in Oudtshoorn, our home base, when I was called to the radio urgently. Jack Dippenaar was calling from Fort Doppies with the news that the whole base had burnt down, Minnaar Fourie's furniture and all.

A gas bottle had exploded in the kitchen, a strong wind was blowing and the flames swept through Fort Doppies within a matter of minutes. There was no way they could fight the fire and virtually everything in the base was destroyed except weapons and ammunition stored in bunkers or tents well beyond the range of the fire.

Nic Visser was virtually inconsolable.

I flew up to Doppies a few days later and found Jack Dippenaar and his "students", a group of former Portuguese servicemen desirous of joining the Recces, miserably ensconced under a tarpaulin on the edge of the burnt-out and blackened camp.

There was soot everywhere, even on Jack and his students. They looked like refugees from Cambodia who had barely escaped the murderous clutches of Pol Pot and his Khmer Rouge.

The situation was very depressing. I decided to move Fort Doppies completely to the vicinity of the so-called horseshoe lagoon on the Cuando River. It would be pointless to build a new base on the ruins of the old one. Besides, our water supply from two boreholes had some rather unpleasant purging qualities. It tasted as if it had been liberally dosed with Epsom salts.

The water from the river was sweet, clear and plentiful.

With Jack in charge, the base was gradually shifted to the thick riverine forest fringing the beautiful horseshoe lake.

It was wonderful, although we had to go back into tents. A few huts were built from local materials and soon we were comfortably in situ with all our equipment and our bevy of cats.

We even acquired two large white pigs, promptly christened with the first name and surname of a particularly odious Bureau of State Security spymaster who was based in Katima Mulilo and who continuously tried to poke his nose into our affairs.

Meanwhile, Dewald de Beer went in search of an alternative site for our permanent base.

This was found closer to the Golden Highway and in due course the South African engineers began construction. I made sure that each building was sited exactly where Dewald and I wanted it and that not a single tree or large shrub had to make way for any building or installation.

Consequently, the new base was constructed around and under the trees of the dense riverine forest. The result was a camp completely tucked away under the shady foliage of towering knobthorns, camelthorns, fig trees and jakkalsbessies, with all the buildings nicely moulded and blending into the natural African bush.

Below us flowed a sidestream from the most beautiful of Africa's rivers, the Cuando. Across the stream was a large island dotted with dozens of lechwes peacefully grazing among the swamps.

A little further downstream was a large herd of hippos, snorting and splashing in a dark pool among the reeds.

Within a hundred metres of our selected swimming place, a huge crocodile used to bask on a clean, white sand spit, seemingly uninterested in the splashing bodies of homo sapiens within striking range.

Old concrete slabs were brought from the original Fort Doppies, henceforth known as Fort Ashes, to the new Fort Doppies to pave a central area which was then officially named Freedom Square.

If a junior had a grudge against a senior he could take his senior to Freedom Square and tell him exactly what he thought of him without fear of a disciplinary comeback or any other retribution.

Away from the square, of course, the military disciplinary system had to be strictly enforced.

Much to my disgust, I had to leave 1 Reconnaissance Commando before the new base was completed. I had neither asked for nor anticipated a transfer. I was happy in the bush; the many operations we were conducting were both successful and extremely hurtful to the enemy and my hopes and plans for the future of the Recces had still to be fulfilled.

As far as I was concerned, outside the army, life could pass me by, as long as I was left in command of the Recces and allowed to carry out the tasks assigned to me to the best of my ability.

But there is always some grey little man tucked away in an obscure office somewhere who considers himself to be the master of one's destiny. All he has to do is write a two-lined signal, after the year-end flurry of personnel committee meetings to move the pawns around, get the man above to approve it, and the process of personal and emotional upheaval, endemic in all transfers, gets underway.

Somewhere in the stratosphere of the top military command structure, somebody had decided that for the benefit of his own career, Jan Breytenbach had to be brought out of the dark, savage interior of the African bush and deposited in the enlightened and civilised atmosphere of the corridors of power at army headquarters.

They dragged me there kicking and screaming all the way, and I grimly resolved to get back to the bush as soon as possible.

THREE

Poaching – An Endemic Disease

Dewald de Beer became synonymous with the Fort Doppies training area in particular and the eastern half of the western Caprivi in general. No other man knew more about this part of Africa than Dewald, except maybe one or two of the older Bushmen.

There was also no one in the entire South African Defence Force who surpassed him in bush knowledge. Some tried, but they always came off second best.

Even highly qualified botanists and zoologists who pitted their academic learning against the practical experience and skills of a man with modest educational achievements eventually had to throw in the towel.

It was therefore inevitable that Dewald would be posted to Fort Doppies on a permanent basis, initially to run survival and minor tactical courses, later to take charge of the base and the whole training area.

Dewald grew up on a firm in the north-western Transvaal. From a very young age he had an affinity for the bush and all its creatures, even acquiring a rather alarming habit of collecting all kinds of live snakes.

He was a slightly built young man, with blue eyes and curly blond hair, forever looking for the chance to pull a trick on some unsuspecting victim.

He had learned to live in and accept the harsh environment of the African savannah because, as a poacher, he was forced to do so. He poached in Botswana, where the authorities are not known for their compassion towards those who break the laws of the country.

He came to the Recces endowed with an uncanny ability to track over the most difficult terrain, shoot extremely well and live comfortably using only that which he could find in the environment around him.

To my mind, Dewald was streets ahead of all the other so-called survival experts I have ever met and usually a short head in front of most of the Bushmen.

During his youthful spell as a small-scale poacher he had hunted strictly for the pot and he was imbued with an all-consuming love of the African bush, especially the western Caprivi. This made him somewhat biased when it came to allowing others to encroach on his domain.

Consequently, Dewald was the ideal man in the right place when illegal, albeit "official", hunting expeditions were put together by certain individuals in high places.

I was still bemoaning my fate at army headquarters in Pretoria when I got a frantic message from Dewald that a certain brigadier was about to visit the area with some highly placed guests to shoot an elephant or two, a handful of buffaloes, a couple of lions and perhaps even a rhino if it was unfortunate enough to wander into their line of fire.

In my capacity as a staff officer at army headquarters, I despatched a signal to the brigadier, then stationed in Rundu, forbidding him and his party to enter the Fort Doppies area. I unashamedly sent the signal in the name of the Chief of the Army.

Of course the brigadier realised that the signal was from me, and in angry retaliation, restricted all the Recces to a radius of 1000 metres from the base. This effectively brought all training to a grinding halt.

Although not under his operational command, the Recces fell into his military sector and according to him it was his right to take away our training area if he felt so inclined.

I decided to write a letter directly to Admiral Biermann, placing on record all my complaints about the brigadier's interference in Special Forces training and that he wanted to take some of his drinking pals on a hunting spree in the western Caprivi.

Among his friends he counted a fellow who shifted the western Caprivi border so that he could get at the game concentrated on the Cuando flood plains in winter where the animals became easy prey for his high-powered hunting rifles.

The admiral soon put a stop to this nonsense, but I made another enemy for life.

The man who fiddled with the eastern boundary of the game park was well known throughout South West Africa as a greedy poacher who had absolutely no concern for the environment.

His culpability in getting the Kaokoveld desert elephants and rhinos placed on the endangered wildlife list, was great. His voracious appetite for hunting led to one or two scandals which were never satisfactorily explained, the whole sorry business having been swept under the carpet because of the potential threat to the "integrity" of individuals and the South African government.

There is a well-documented case of official intrigue involving two conservation officers who stumbled on a trail of slaughter littered with desert elephant carcasses and the remains of specially protected black-faced impalas.

These impalas are found only in the Kaokoveld, the western extremities of the Etosha reserve and, perhaps, in isolated pockets in south-western Angola.

The uniqueness of this subspecies meant nothing to the man who shifted geographical borders on a whim or commandeered military helicopters from which he could shoot at his defenceless prey. He was the worst kind of bloodthirsty slaughterer of game.

A former helicopter pilot told me at a later stage that he was flying a Cessna from Opuwa, the administrative centre of Kaokoland, at the height of this man's poaching career. The drill was for the pilot to get airborne with the official in the passenger seat, plotting the location of desert elephant herds on a map. Back at Opuwa, the poacher then hastily commandeered a helicopter from which to bag his prey before they could move off to safety.

Neither the Cessna nor helicopter crews could refuse to ferry this ruthless character. He held a position in the top structure of the South West African civil service, his authority equal to that of the highest ranking military officers, and later became a well-known politician in an independent Namibia.

Back at Fort Doppies, Dewald soon began to get the measure of the local poachers.

Most of them came across the river from a kraal called Lazauli, situated near the southern extreme of the boundary between the eastern and western Caprivi; from induna Maplanka's kraal opposite the centre of the Fort Doppies training area, and from a kraal called Choi, not far from Kongola Fort.

They usually targeted the lechwes within easy reach on the islands or those hippos reckless enough to make themselves at home in the main stream of the Cuando or in pools on the eastern Caprivi side of the flood plain. Sometimes they came across the river to shoot elephants and rhinos for the dealers in Katima Mulilo.

Dewald built a special cell for these poachers and kept them there for days before nature conservation officials in Katima were informed of their capture. Dewald resorted to this harsh treatment because all acts of poaching were dealt with extremely leniently by the local magistrates. Before long, convicted poachers were back in business, laughing contemptuously at Dewald's puny efforts to stop them slaughtering the game.

A stay in Dewald's cell was anything but pleasant. It was small, constructed of corrugated iron and out in the open, fully exposed to the fierce sun of the western Caprivi. The dark interior soon became a stifling oven as the scorching heat baked down on the metal structure.

At night, the situation was reversed, especially in winter. The corrugated iron radiated the day's heat back into the black sky almost as rapidly as it absorbed the broiling heat by day, and the bitter cold penetrated the very bones of the unfortunate occupants.

To make things worse, hyenas and other nocturnal predators would sniff around the isolated little cell, scaring the wits out of those inside, who knew full well that help would not be forthcoming, even if the Recces at Fort Doppies base camp did hear frantic screams.

In later years, I dealt with poachers caught red-handed in more or less the same way, but I also made it a rule to surreptitiously bend the barrels of their captured rifles. Next time around, once the poacher had served his ludicrously light sentence and his rifle had been returned to him, he would, hopefully, miss his prey by a mile.

If he got trampled by an enraged elephant, gored by a furious buffalo or rhino or torn into strips by a vengeful lion in the process, that was just too bad.

It took a long time for magistrates to start handing down stiffer sentences and then only after numerous submissions by the conservation authorities. Too many law enforcers regarded the shooting of an elephant as no more serious than a parking offence.

Even suspended sentences were dished out to people who virtually regarded such "punishment" as a licence to carry on poaching.

Many magistrates did not realise that by merely warning culprits, or suspending their sentences, they were making a joke of the law which became something to be sneered at as being too weak to keep people within the boundaries set by that law. This leniency did nothing to encourage a law-abiding citizenry among both the white and black population.

Stoking this witch's brew of "justice" was a mainly white administration with a tendency to indulge in a fair amount of private poaching themselves.

Sometimes this was done fairly openly or at least with the knowledge of many in authority. At its worst, the practice took the shape of "official hunting expeditions", as already mentioned.

And since what is sauce for the goose is also sauce for the gander, it is little wonder that the black Caprivians took to poaching with such gusto.

All elephant and rhino poaching was conducted on an organised basis. The dealers were all white men who, in time, emerged as members of one of the biggest ivory and rhino horn-smuggling rackets that the African continent has ever seen.

It was difficult to pin down these sophisticated poachers because there was almost always somebody high up in the civil service with his own filthy finger in the pie to protect the criminals below.

In short, for its size, Katima Mulilo was the most corrupt place I had ever come across. On second thought, Rundu, in the Okavango, might have won by a short head.

Virtually everyone in town was involved with some racket or another, be it the illegal export of wood, smuggling of ivory and rhino horn, selling unlicensed and unroadworthy second-hand vehicles to the local inhabitants, diamond smuggling, dealing in dagga (marijuana), smuggling mandrax from Lusaka to Johannesburg or providing the black market in Sesheke, inside Zambia, with luxuries stolen from government stores and warehouses on the South West African side of the Zambezi River.

Development capital could be obtained only by greasing the right palms. Monopolies were concentrated in the hands of a few corrupt and powerful politicians. Brothels made vast amounts of money and spread venereal diseases like wildfire. In recent years, AIDS erupted in the Caprivi, and by the end of 1989, an estimated 16 per cent of the population tested HIV positive.

In the prevailing milieu of lawlessness we had to take drastic action to keep the poacher's rifles away from the dwindling game herds of the western Caprivi. We effectively had to take the law into our own hands to stem the swelling tide of poachers and the result was our home-spun system of justice.

Dewald did his bit extremely successfully, as did I when I returned to the Cuando after an absence of several years.

We sank the poacher's *makorros* whenever we found them on the western side of the flood plain. We fired shots over the heads of distant predators, safe on islands surrounded by swamps as they attacked the lechwes with volleys of rifle fire. We locked those we caught in solitary confinement before handing them over to the game rangers, derisively called "goat-keepers" by some of Katima's less law-abiding citizens.

Dewald showed no mercy when he ran into a group of poachers. He single-handedly caught dozens of them, and was so effective that poaching virtually ceased in the Fort Doppies training area.

One day he found the spoor of some poachers near the Botswana border. He was on his own but decided to follow the spoor as far as he could in an effort to capture them before they could cross into Botswana.

It wasn't long before he came across three poachers around the carcass of a freshly killed elephant. Dewald tried to arrest them, but two got away. Dewald apprehended the third, but he was determined to get his hands on the two who had escaped and were rapidly making tracks for Botswana.

Undaunted, Dewald hacked a chunk of meat from the ribcage of the dead elephant, laying bare a huge bone. He carefully stripped the meat off the massive rib, then snapped one end of the handcuffs which he always carried with him around the bone and the other to the poacher's wrist.

It was late afternoon when Dewald set off at a trot on the spoor of the other two, leaving behind a petrified poacher securely chained to the huge carcass of a very immobile elephant.

Dewald crossed the cutline into Botswana as the sun sank below the western horizon and soon had to give up on the spoor. He decided to bed down for the night, and resume his hunt in the morning.

Meanwhile, darkness descended on the unfortunate poacher as well, and soon the creatures of the night began to crawl out of their holes, emerge from their dens in the undergrowth, climb down from the trees or slither out of the nearby swamps to start scavenging and hunting for food as part of the 24-hour cycle that had ruled their lives for millions of years.

It wasn't long before the poacher heard the first "whooo-oop!" of an approaching hyena. He shivered in terror as he faced the inevitable, knowing that not only the hyenas would soon appear, but that lions could well come in the wake of the hyenas' whooping call.

It was a long night for the poacher. Dewald returned to the elephant carcass in the late forenoon the next day, the other two poachers having given him the slip when they crossed the Cuando back to the Lazauli area in a *makorro*.

He found the chained poacher almost incoherent with fear. During the night he had scraped a ditch in the soft sand as he tried to keep the hyenas at bay by throwing sand at their faces when they came too close.

The snapping of powerful jaws, their excited giggles and the slobbery gnawing of flesh on the other side of the carcass where the hyenas feasted out of reach of his sand missiles had kept the poacher terrified throughout the night, but that was the last time he crossed the river to shoot elephants or any other animal in the western Caprivi, even although he was never charged for the crime he had committed.

Another time, Dewald stumbled across a so-called lion gin trap. This is a monstrous thing, which needs the strength of at least two people to set, the springs that snap the serrated jaws shut being particularly powerful. As the name indicates, this trap is often used to capture lions, pound for pound probably the most powerful beasts on earth. Against them, the comparatively puny little traps used on other animals, even on the bigger antelopes or smaller carnivores such as leopards, are useless. To catch a lion in this barbaric way, the trap has to be the biggest on the market.

Dewald found the lion trap set up and concealed on a hippo footpath. The obvious intention was to catch a hippo while it was entering or leaving its watery sanctuary on its nightly foraging expeditions into the grassy pastures of the flood plain.

Dewald followed the spoor of the poacher until he found the exact spot where he had beached his *makorro* when he came across to set the trap. Then he carefully removed the trap, and reset it, at the exact spot where the poacher had landed. He camouflaged the trap carefully and erased all signs of his presence.

Just a day or so later, Dewald heard from one of his Bushmen that a great tragedy had befallen a hippo poacher from Maplanka's village.

Confident that his trap had been sprung, the poacher crossed the river by way of numerous byways such as pools, sidestreams and backwaters. It was a rather circuitous and lengthy trip and must have taken at least an hour, perhaps longer, because crossing the swampy Cuando in any kind of a boat is never a straightforward affair. Those who don't know the river, got lost among the reeds, swamps and numerous streams going in all directions of the compass. Visibility is rarely more than a few paces.

But, at long last, the bow of the poacher's *makorro* ran aground on the small muddy beach where the hippo footpath entered the water. The poacher stepped out of the *makorro*, around the bow and straight into his own trap.

The powerful jaws snapped shut around his lower leg with a resounding clang. The pain and shock must have been excruciating. No doubt the poacher screamed, but there was no one for miles to rush to his aid. He was utterly alone in the wilderness of the Cuando flood plain.

He probably tried desperately to wrench open the jaws of the trap, but the springs were far too strong for his single-handed efforts.

Finally, in unspeakable pain, the poacher manoeuvred himself into his *makorro*, the huge trap clumsily and heavily clamped to his leg. It must have been an inhumanly painful process.

A *makorro* is a narrow little vessel, and it takes all one's sense of balance to keep it upright while poling along or across a swiftly flowing stream. Free board can be measured in only a few inches, as the boat is always hollowed out from a particularly heavy log, usually African ebony.

A lion trap is an unwieldy and huge load in itself, without a poacher firmly stuck between its steel-toothed jaws. With this cumbersome, awkward contraption clamped to one leg, the poacher had to carefully arrange his stance in the *makorro* so that the trap would lie fore and aft, and not athwartships.

Once ensconced in the narrow boat, the poacher would have to stay in the same position for fear of capsizing and coming to a watery end with a heavy metal sinker around his leg.

It could not have been a pleasant journey back to Maplanka's kraal. It certainly took him hours to get there. The poacher could not sit down to rest, because the boat would overturn. Nor could he shift his stricken leg to lessen the pain, or pass out during his agonising voyage. He no doubt fervently hoped that no hippo would suddenly burst from the reed-smothered banks to upset his tender craft with a tremendous bow wave, or even attack him in its fury.

It would have been impossible to shove the *makorro* quickly into the reeds and jump out to escape a massive hippo thundering down upon him with its vengeful little eyes burning red with hatred.

At long last, the injured poacher reached the opposite side of the flood plain. Maplanka's people probably removed the trap before they took him to hospital, but whatever they tried to do, it was too late to save the poacher's leg, which had to be amputated in Katima.

Another poacher had been removed from the scenario, at least as far as Fort Doppies was concerned.

Elsewhere, however, the poaching curve was rapidly becoming exponential in its rise. In fact, after 1976, the tuskers were rapidly moving into focus as an exploitable resource from which huge piles of money could be made, turning struggling civil servants, poverty stricken refugees from Angola and near bankrupt businessmen into cigar smoking and champagne swilling, instant millionaires.

But before this would happen, a great many changes were to come in the western Caprivi.

The first of these was manifested in the Bushmen, slowly at first and then suddenly, with a bang, when the Portuguese colony of Angola collapsed without as much as the whisper of a warning.

FOUR

The Fate of the Bushmen

I once asked Tokoloshe, the chief of the Bwabwata clan of the Barakwena (or Barakwengo) tribe how many years his people had been living in the western Caprivi. He replied: "Colonel, the Bushmen have been living here ever since God made us."

Now that is an extremely long time to live in one locality, but it is generally accepted that the Barakwena were settled in the eastern and western Caprivi, northern Botswana, the eastern parts of Okavango and parts of south-eastern Angola long before the arrival of black tribes migrating southwards and eastwards from Central Africa.

The Hambukushu lived around Katima Mulilo at first, but when they were threatened by the conquering Balozi tribes coming from the north down the Zambezi River in the nineteenth century, they packed up their goods and chattels and migrated to the Cuando flood plain in Angola. When the Portuguese began to capture them as slaves, the Hambukushu moved further west, finally trekking across and along the Okavango River into the area of present-day Namibia known as the Okavango. They occupied the eastern part of it and are now commonly known as the Mucusso.

It wasn't long before the newcomers began to enslave the indigenous Barakwena, exploiting them mercilessly. They took their daughters, and sometimes wives, by force as concubines and captured the youngsters to be herd boys to their cattle.

The vacuum left by the Hambukushu in the eastern Caprivi was filled by the Lozis, particularly the Mafwe tribe, which settled in the western half of the area, and the Basubya, who settled in the eastern, swampy parts. The eastern Caprivi is wedged between the mighty Zambezi and the Cuando, Linyanti, and Chobe rivers and their associated swamp systems.

Once again, the Barakwena fell prey to the invaders. Those living east of the Cuando were quickly enslaved and exploited, while those west of the Cuando tried to stay out of the way of the raiding Mafwes by moving deeper into the dry bush of the western Caprivi.

I asked Langman, a Bushman of indeterminate age, to describe the lot of the Barakwenas living along the Cuando in the face of exploitation by the Mafwes settled opposite them on the east bank of the Cuando flood plain.

He spat into the sand and got quite excited as he explained to me how the "long feet", as the Bushmen call all black people, came across the river with *makorros* at night to raid the scattered Bushman villages on the west bank. They captured young girls and boys, the first to serve as the concubines of their black masters, the latter to become perpetual slaves.

This state of affairs continued well into the 1960s, when the first South African police contingents arrived to fight the Swapo incursion, and inadvertently formed a shield for the Bushmen against the depredations of both the Mafwes and the Hambukushu.

Primed by more than a century of bitter hatred for their black oppressors, the Bushmen rallied round the South African security force colours the moment they realised that they could revenge their past by becoming soldiers in a war against Swapo insurgents.

However, forced enslavement and subsequent miscegenation left an indelible physical mark on many of the Barakwena. In time, many of them grew blacker and taller, although many Bushmen characteristics are still unmistakeably evident in the present generation.

Many, of course, have retained the lighter, peach-coloured skins of the original Bushman tribes, and their shorter stature. They all still speak a typical Bushman language with its characteristic clicks.

To the north of the Barakwena, inside Angola, a purer strain of Bushman was found, probably because contact between them and the nearest blacks was of a more fleeting nature.

The south-eastern Cuando-Cubango was so remote and so infested with tsetse flies that this tribe, the Vaskela, was left more or less to its own devices. The country was, and still is, unfit for cattle farming or, indeed, any other kind of farming. For centuries, therefore, the Vaskelas lived on land away from the major rivers in their isolated family kraals, or *kimbos* as they are commonly known in Angola, and were relatively safe from exploitation by the black tribes.

However, Vaskelas living along the fringes were subject to raids and the practice of capturing slaves and concubines persisted. In 1977, the commanding officer of the Bushman Battalion, an old friend of mine, was dead set on tracking down and killing a particular black man who had abducted some Vaskelas as his slaves from an area inside the Cuando-Cubango.

Langman also told me that the Barakwena had to move away from the Cuando River to find refuge, far from open water, in the Bwabwata area.

The scoundrel Maplanka immediately occupied the west bank vacated by the Bushmen, until the tsetse flies drove him, his Mafwes and their cattle back across the river. However, to this day Maplanka lays claim to the eastern part of the western Caprivi.

Over in the west the Hambukushu, in turn, lay claim to the area just east of the Okavango River inside the western Caprivi. They openly state that the Barakwenas who escaped across the river to settle in the western Caprivi are their "property", just as cattle are their property.

These are Bushmen from the Bangani clan of the Barakwena tribe, and their chief, who goes by the strange name of Chipi, is an educated man who at one time studied to be a minister of religion, but decided to assume the mantle of clan leadership instead.

When we arrived in the Caprivi in the early 1970s, most of these were still living as typical hunter-gatherers. There could not have been more than 400 of them in the entire region.

Their little kraals, or *kimbos*, were ramshackle, temporary affairs, scattered all over the Caprivi, but concentrated mainly around Bwabwata and the area just east of Bagani on the Okavango River. Some of them were already settling near the recently established police posts, the men being used as trackers against Swapo gangs.

However, the majority still lived as Stone Age hunter-gatherers, clothed in skimpy, animal skin loincloths and "dresses", the children running around naked as the day they were born.

They used bows and poisoned arrows to hunt the bigger game and snares to trap the smaller animals. The women collected an ample and varied supply of berries, nuts, bulbs and tubers from the surrounding bush, and they dug shallow wells on the edges of *omurambas* to tide them over the dry months. The underground water was close to the surface, especially near Bwabwata, where it could be found three to five metres down. In the rainy season there was an ample supply of water from the numerous pans scattered along the length and breadth of all the *omurambas*.

Theirs was a hard but innocent and idyllic life. The family formed a close-knit unit and there was no strife within the clan. All their possessions were shared, except knives and bows and arrows.

All worked together to contribute to the daily challenge of constant survival, and they never raised their voices in anger. To give a child a hiding was something completely foreign to their culture and, in any case, unnecessary, because nature dished out its own punishment for those reckless or disrespectful enough to step over the line.

To their detriment, the war changed all of that.

War came to Angola first long before it spread into northern South West Africa. It was started by the FNLA, in Bakongo territory, and gradually spread southwards and eastwards when the MPLA decided to take up the cudgels against the Portuguese colonial power. The MPLA used western Zambia as a home base and inevitably the south-eastern corner of the

Cuando-Cubango became a favoured infiltration route. Soon, MPLA guerrilla gangs were marching through the wild, unoccupied bush of one of the last wilderness sanctuaries on earth to reach their more populous destinations in the west.

They even established bases in these remote areas from which they could harass Portuguese settlers and the colonial army scattered around the fringes.

Some bright young Portuguese officers quickly realised that the conventionally trained Portuguese from "metropole", were completely ineffective in the African bush and black Angolan soldiers were inducted into the army. Of profound significance for the future of the Vaskelas, large-scale recruiting was also undertaken among them, for the so-called Flecha units (the Portuguese for "arrow").

The moving force behind this scheme was a brilliant paratrooper named Oscar Cardosa, at one time also a member of the Portuguese DGS or security police.

He knew the Vaskela Bushmen better than most other Europeans.

The first problem was to weld a bunch of highly individualistic hunters into a body of men that could react and fight together when the right commands were given.

Cardosa resorted to a centuries-old instrument, the parade ground, to infuse discipline and teamwork into his Bushman warriors.

He then introduced them to the G3 or FN rifle and found, to his astonishment, that they were natural-born marksmen.

Apart from constant shooting practices and parade-ground work, no other training was given. The Bushmen were not taught to attack, withdraw, defend, ambush, raid or do anything else normally found under the heading of small-unit tactics. Neither were they taught how to survive in the bush or how to navigate.

Oscar merely devised a simple system of grid squares on a map, in accordance with which his Flechas had to report back to him by radio about the location of any MPLA movements or bases.

The Bushmen are intrepid ambushers and skilled stalkers by nature. They love to stalk an unwary enemy, to shoot the hell out of him and then disappear like a shadow into the bush before the victim can react.

To shake Bushmen out into an assault line to attack and overcome a well-defended enemy position is virtually impossible. It has been done by a few who know them well enough to motivate them adequately, but only with much sweat and many tears. Such formal military drill cuts right across their Bushman character and the habits of the hunter-gatherer.

So Oscar wisely left them alone to kill MPLA guerrillas in any way they saw fit.

In this they were so successful that soon the MPLA began to tremble in their Russian boots the moment they discovered that Flechas were on their spoor.

I know a Vaskela Bushman by the name of Kampembe who was one of Oscar's Flechas. This Bushman became an extremely successful operator, often working on his own with only his FN rifle and his bow and arrows as defence against the MPLA gangs. He used to track them down as regularly as clockwork and was eventually decorated with one of the highest Portuguese awards in recognition of his efforts. It's an impressive-looking award and hangs from a gold chain around the neck.

One particular incident will serve to illustrate the ability of this man.

A gang of about 20 MPLA guerrillas crossed the Cuando River from Zambia into Angola and set off on a course, presumably for Cuito Cuanavale or Serpa Pinto, now called Menongue.

Kampembe, clad only in his loincloth, was soon on their trail. Over the next week or two, he stalked them relentlessly, every time they paused for a rest or a longish stop. He took a toll almost every day, killing at least one guerrilla with either his rifle or his poisoned arrows.

Nothing the MPLA did could stop Kampembe from getting to his prey nor could counter-tracking on their part shake him off their spoor.

In sheer terror they eventually turned around and rushed back to the Cuando with Kampembe in hot pursuit.

Only three or four of them made it back across the river into Zambia.

Some of the Portuguese saw the potential in the Bushmen to contribute to their war effort in a most uncommon way and actually understood the Bushman and his culture far better than many so-called experts in the field of ethnology.

Others did not. To them the theories of guerrilla warfare, and suitable measures to counter it, were of more importance than the practicalities of war and tribal life in the sweltering Angolan bush. One theory in particular – that the population is the water in which the guerrilla fish has to swim, in accordance with Mao Tse Tung's little red book – made a strong impact on certain staff officers reclining in offices in far-off Lisbon and Luanda. For them, the correct counter-measure was to remove the water, so that the guerrilla fish would be left floundering on dry ground.

So a large-scale removal of the local population from their remote *kimbos* in rural areas was launched. The uprooted indigenous people were concentrated in *aldeamentos*, protected villages in close proximity to Portuguese garrisons scattered throughout the wilder parts of Angola.

The removals included the poor, confused Bushmen, who hated the MPLA bitterly, but who were nevertheless treated as supporters of the guerrillas. They were rounded up from scattered *kimbos* all over the Cuando-Cubango and deposited in the stinking slums fringing most Portuguese garrisons.

I shall never forget the filth and depredation of the Bushman *aldeamento* at Luiana. In one fell swoop, the Vaskelas had been uprooted, their umbilical cord with the African savannah brutally severed, and deposited in overcrowded, squalid settlements, where their souls were systematically destroyed.

To hasten their spiritual demise, the Portuguese soldiers wilfully exploited the Bushman women to satisfy their sexual appetites exactly as the "long feet" had been doing for centuries.

There was no escape. The *aldeamento* policy was based on the sinister premise that anyone found in a depopulated zone would be shot on sight.

They had no choice but to submit to the inevitable, which spelled nothing less than the annihilation of their culture, and their downfall as a people.

Their removal from the African savannah environment was not only a tragedy for the race, but a terrible loss to mankind. It was also a severe setback for the environment.

In the distant past, homo sapiens was entrusted with the mission of reigning over all the lesser species, whether plant or animal, and utilising them for man's benefit.

Over thousands of years, the ruler of nature's realm "evolved" into sophisticated modern man, to become estranged from the environment from which he had sprung. He began to abuse his former home by recklessly exploiting it, all the while driven by a perverse desire to "improve" on the creator's handiwork.

Only small splinter groups of the human species remained true to their original mission, among them the people derisively called "Bushmen" by the more civilised and technically advanced species.

In the prehistoric environment, the Bushman filled a particular niche. He was both a primary consumer (plant eater) and a secondary consumer (carnivore). But he consumed in such a way that the environment benefited from his hunting and gathering.

He took only what he needed, without destroying the rest, in this manner contributing to the rate and quality of reproduction. When a species is kept just below the optimum, sustainable capacity of the surrounding environment, the rate of reproduction will increase in an attempt to fill the continuous void.

Conversely, overexploitation can lead to a situation where the few surviving individuals are unable to sustain the species in an environment which has tragically become a threat to its survival. The species will then die out.

The Bushmen also contributed to the "fire regime" in the

Cuando-Cubango. In the dry season, usually in August and September, just before the onset of the summer rains, they burnt down large tracts of bush. This practice ensured the removal of the old, dead grasses, and the sprouting of young, fresh grasses, eager to soak up the first showers.

There is no doubt that a fire regime, whether caused by Bushmen, lightning or both, has a profound influence on the character and physical contours of the African savannah.

The trees are largely fire resistant, and recover quickly after the rains start to fall. Bush and tree encroachment can be kept in check because young seedlings are killed off during the bush fires. The savannah's grazers can therefore count on ample supplies of grass.

The Bushman's role in the fire regime, inherently part of the savannah's growth cycle, has never been adequately researched. What I have said about his contribution must therefore be regarded as pure speculation on my part. However, my personal observations left me with no doubt that the Bushmen following their traditional lifestyle caused no damage whatsoever to the savannah, including the animals, through overexploitation of its bountiful resources.

As far as modern society is concerned, we lost our last link with Mother Nature when we abruptly tore our Bushman cousins from her embrace.

Bushmen could have shown us the way back to living in harmony with nature. They could have taught us the secrets of the bush, such as tracking, survival, the habits and life cycles of animals and plants, their uncanny ability to find their way through virgin forest and untracked desert, and how to feel at one with the spirit of ancient Africa. They could have taught us to become part of Africa and to accept as normal its harsh realities including the heat, thirst, flies and mosquitoes, instead of angrily fighting these discomforts in an effort to tame and distort nature to meet our sophisticated but artificial standards.

We have lost, forever, a golden opportunity to increase our scientific knowledge of the savannah by using them as a guide to probe its mysteries.

I have a hefty book called *The Mammals of Southern Africa*, an excellent reference book written by Doctor Smithers, undeniably an outstanding expert on the subject. But even he admits that there are huge blank spaces in respect of virtually every species described in his book.

Just imagine the contribution the Bushmen could have made, especially in regard to those species found in the tropical African savannah and the deserts to the south. Over thousands of years they have learned all the intimate secrets that any human being can possibly learn about the species they have hunted for food, or those which posed a threat to their lives.

The same applies to the plant, bird and insect life of these regions.

But, because modern man deliberately and recklessly intruded, insinuating his destructive power into the life and culture of the Bushman tribes, that knowledge has been lost, probably forever.

The pace of estrangement between the Vaskelas and the bush accelerated dramatically when the Portuguese elected to hand over Angola, as quickly as they could, to the Marxist MPLA government in Luanda.

Overnight the Vaskelas were faced with the spectre of genocide from the guerrillas their Flecha battalions had brought to heel so successfully during the drawn out counter-insurgency campaign.

Some conscience-stricken Portuguese commanders negotiated with the South Africans to provide refuge for the Flechas and their families and a mass exodus of virtually all the Vaskelas occurred. They trekked from the Cuando-Cubango into the western Caprivi with all their pathetic earthly possessions. Thousands of them arrived under the control of a small staff of Portuguese instructors, and a new base, called Alpha, was set up for them. The intention was to continue using them as Flechas but this time against Swapo.

The arrival of the Vaskelas had an adverse influence on the precarious situation of the indigenous Barakwenas of the western Caprivi.

Although both groups were Bushmen, they were from two different tribes. To relocate the Vaskelas in a favoured situation inside Barakwena territory and pamper them with decent housing, hospitals and schools as well as regular rations and even salaries, did not impress the Barakwenas.

Once again the theorists ensconced in claustrophobic offices, this time in Pretoria, burnt the midnight oil to arrive at a solution to the problem.

They decided to be even-handed, and the Barakwenas were offered the same opportunity to espouse civilisation and become soldiers in the South African army. Their families were granted the same facilities and benefits as the refugee Vaskela families, inside a new, giant army base. Like a rampant cancerous tumour, the base was burgeoning, right in the middle of the western Caprivi game reserve.

But the "do-gooder" and all-knowing theorists took the project several steps further. The Bushmen would not be left to flounder without hope in the filth and squalor of a typical Portuguese *aldeamento*, but would be "uplifted" from their Stone Age existence with a gigantic heave into the computer age of the twentieth century.

To assist them in this task they released into the field of battle a clutch of ethnologists, none of whom had ever clapped eyes on a real Bushman but all of whom were instant experts on the subject of Bushman folklore and culture. One ethnologist in particular, who ruled the roost, became as persistent as a housefly around a dog's faeces.

This fellow actually tried to impose his expert opinions on my own unit – 32 Battalion – in an attempt to prescribe to seasoned soldiers how tribal blacks from Angola should be handled. I refused to have anything to do with him or his cronies. I could see only problems in relationships ahead if he was allowed a toehold inside the unit. I therefore peremptorily ordered him never to come near 32 Battalion, irrespective of what Pretoria had to say on the subject. It apparently never occurred to this idiot that we had just fought a bloody campaign with our black soldiers, and that we consequently knew them better than he ever would.

But a housefly is not easily deterred, and one day when I was not around, he gained access to the unit. He ended up in the pub, rubbing shoulders with my somewhat rough and ready company commanders and platoon leaders.

"Who are you?" asked one of the platoon leaders.

"I am Captain so and so," answered the ethnologist.

"I don't know you. Do you serve in this unit?"

"No."

"Well, what are you doing here?" asked the lieutenant belligerently.

"I have come to examine your tribal situation to determine how your troops should be handled."

The lieutenant stared at the captain, light slowly dawning in his infantry man's brain.

"What is your name again?"

"Captain so and so."

"Oh, so you must be that ethnologist the colonel warned us against."

"Well yes, but I have Pretoria's permission to be here."

"You don't have the colonel's permission."

"The colonel has no say in the matter."

"You had better leave, Captain, or else you will pick up a problem or two."

"Nobody can force me to leave. I am here with Pretoria's authority."

"Oh yeah? Boys! This guy refuses to leave the unit. Shall we dump him in the river?" shouted the lieutenant gleefully to his mates.

"Yes, let's go for it! Into the water with you, Captain, and there are plenty of crocodiles."

They grabbed the ethnologist and unceremoniously hurled him as far as they could into the fast-flowing Okavango River. The ethnologist swam for his life, frightened out of his wits by the possibility of a leviathan taking him for dinner. He made it to the bank, lined with laughing infantry officers. Wet and bedraggled, he was promptly deposited outside the unit gate and told never to return.

He never did.

The Bushmen, however, were not so fortunate and their "upliftment" proceeded apace.

For the first time, the majority of them were introduced to modern medicine, proper child care, hygiene, housing, running water, showers, water-borne sewage, Western-style furniture and other "blessings" of civilisation.

The population began to explode, as most babies survived infancy.

Other refinements soon followed, including the latest in Western-style clothing, bicycles, pick-up trucks, even the odd Mercedes Benz and a self-service store with shelves filled with tinned meat, jams, canned fruit, clothing, electrical equipment and other items Bushmen had never seen before.

At one stage, expensive hunting rifles, bridles and saddles were sold in this particular store, in spite of the fact that it was in the middle of a game reserve.

Of course the Bushmen drew salaries, and they were paid at standard army rates. To further syphon off excess cash, an enlisted men's club was opened and alcohol made available to these little Stone Age men. Drunkenness became widespread and Bushman troops and their wives staggered around the base in an alcoholic daze. They simply did not know how to handle liquor.

From widely scattered family communities throughout the tropical savannah, thousands of Bushmen were squeezed into a single compound. Neighbours were within spitting distance of one another, children squabbled and got up to all kinds of mischief. Mothers competed against one another with new dresses and useless baubles, displaying their personal wealth and garishly proclaiming their status in the community.

Men started to covet their neighbour's wives and prostitution reared its ugly head. For the first time, the Barakwenas made their acquaintance with sexually transmitted diseases and ultimately even AIDS put in an appearance, the final sign that the Bushmen had shed their traditional and age-old values in favour of Western morality.

The fur soon began to fly. Restricted to a relatively confined space, Bushmen took pot shots at each other with their army rifles. Several murders were committed and there were even some cases of suicide. Children became rebellious and undisciplined and began to despise their elders. Fights were common.

In place of the former filial affection that spread its blanket over the small, remote family *kimbo*, a dark cloak of resentment, jealousy, anger, lust, spite and envy descended over the new Bushman urban community.

Upliftment was complete. The out-of-touch theorists from Pretoria proudly showed parties of important visitors around the modern hospital, the church, the messes and modern *kimbos*, the home crafts shop and so on. The guests admired the neatly dressed but somehow remote little soldiers, and referred to them as South Africa's own Gurkha troops – the terror of Swapo which, sadly, they were not.

Visitors always spent a delightful evening and night in the bosom of the battalion with lots to eat and drink, romantic wooden huts in which to sleep and the beating drums from the Bushman *kimbo* to remind them that they were in deepest Africa.

They returned to the Republic with nothing but praise for the battalion and a wholly superficial impression of the Bushman soldiers and their families.

The tragedy is that in this process of being uplifted, the Bushmen lost all their empathy with the African bush and its creatures. They also lost respect for their traditional culture. Inadvertently perhaps, they were taught to view their former existence as hunter-gatherers with distaste, and even with a sense of shame.

The gulf between the older and younger generations became pronounced. The older ones tried desperately to cling to some vestige of their familiar lifestyle. The younger ones viewed anything connected with the African savannah with derision.

It eventually got so bad that there were no Bushmen worthy of the name among the younger soldiers to act as trackers. For them, the bush beyond the perimeter fence became as strange, and sometimes even as menacing, as it was to young white soldiers fresh from South Africa.

The command element decided to try and rescue the situation, and started bush schools where Bushman children were reintroduced to their traditional culture and bush lore. The experiment was not successful and the children viewed the re-education programme with a certain amount of contempt and barely concealed irritation.

Our ethnologist from Pretoria and his colleagues had done their job so well that in a few short years they totally destroyed an innocent, environment-oriented primaeval culture and offered in its place the cynical, greedy, selfish culture of Western man.

Today the Caprivi Bushmen find themselves in the same sorry state as many of the Australian aborigines. They lounge around drunk, listless, quarrelsome and utterly incapable of competing economically with the blacks or whites of southern Africa. They are helplessly caught in the web of a world they cannot understand, and which is sucking their ancient spirit out of them like an insatiable spider.

Inevitably, the soldiering ability of the Bushmen deteriorated in direct proportion to his "growth" in the materialistic world prescribed by Pretoria.

On the battlefield, the Bushmen became unreliable, especially when used in larger formations during conventional direct assaults. They lost much of their bush sense, including their once phenomenal ability to track down and take out small groups of Swapo insurgents. As a military fighting unit, they became more of a liability than an asset.

Here and there remnants of the old-style Khoisan were still to be found, but they were getting too old to keep on carrying the torch.

At Ndashwa Pan, Tokoloshe somewhat haphazardly and ineffectively held sway over those Barakwena families who opted to live in the bush rather than in the military base. They were, in fact, mostly the older generation – mothers, fathers, uncles, aunts, grandfathers and grandmothers of the young Bushman soldiers at Omega, formerly known as Alpha Base.

Among them old Bott still tried to be something of a witch doctor, but no one ever listened or heeded probably the ugliest and most evil-looking Bushman I have ever seen.

Tokoloshe still went out trapping or poaching giraffes and even elephants for the ivory smugglers in Katima Mulilo. Sometimes, he renewed his painful acquaintance with Dewald's sjambok after some or other poaching incident.

Shorty, the "political" man, could keep one busy for hours with his complaints about the seemingly inevitable takeover of the western Caprivi by Unita troops.

On the Okavango side, opposite Bagani, the Khoisan became helpless targets for exploitation by the Hambukushu. Racketeering became a way of life and ranged from large-scale poaching, especially elephants, to the keeping of brothels, cuca shops (shebeens or illegal bars), dealing in marijuana and other equally disreputable activities.

On the Cuando River, Dewald kept a tight rein on "his" Bushmen. He had a platoon of young soldiers who guarded the base and patrolled the Fort Doppies training area. They lived in a *kimbo* some distance from the main base and it was kept spotlessly clean under Dewald's close supervision.

They and their families still lived fairly close to the bush, but there was a little primary school for the Bushman children which at one time was also attended by white children from Fort St Michél.

Old Captain Jack was their chief and inevitably he resented Dewald's usurpation of what he perceived to be his mantle of authority.

The resentment smouldered for quite a while until Captain Jack decided to invite Dewald to his *kimbo* for formal discussions.

Dewald duly turned up, deliberately late so as to make an entry, and found Jack and the Bushman troops sitting around a large fire ready for the indaba.

Jack had seated himself grandly on a chair on one side of the fire and they were arranged in a circle around the flickering flames, squatting Bushman-style on their haunches in the sand. Jack indicated a place for Dewald to squat among the men.

Dewald immediately realised that this was to be a clash of wills between the two of them. He calmly strolled into Jack's hut, removed one of his better chairs, took it to the opposite side of the fire and sat down, staring at Jack through the flames and smoke from a slightly more elevated position, much to Jack's discomfort.

Dewald then proceeded to dominate the discussions, laying down the law as regards hunting, the possession of vehicles, schooling, distribution of rations and so on. The troops soon ignored Jack and fixed their eyes attentively on Dewald, who spoke with such authority, while their own chief had to look on meekly. The contest of wills had been decisively won by Dewald.

Jack accepted the outcome and from that time on supported Dewald in every way possible. He trusted Dewald to such an extent that he began to disclose some Bushman activities perhaps best kept secret and which were, no doubt, part of the mysticism of their way of life.

One day he insisted that Dewald had to take him to a remote spot in the featureless bush some distance from the river. They drove for a considerable time, weaving, under Jack's directions, through trees and across *omurambas* until they arrived at a spot that was quite inconspicuous and therefore hard for a non-Bushman to locate.

Jack got out and began to dig. Finally, he hauled three nicely cleaned human skulls from the hole, and proudly showed them to Dewald.

The skulls, he said, formerly rested on the shoulders of three "long feet" from the hated Mafwe tribe. They had been a source of grief to Jack and his clan for some years until Jack decided to do something about it. Somehow he lured them across the river, presumably one by one (his Afrikaans was not too good when he told the story) and terminated their lives by some means or another. For a reason best known to himself he buried their skulls at that particular spot and dug them up from time to time, either to make sure that no one had pinched them, or perhaps to give them a ceremonial cleaning!

Before the police set off post haste for this dark scene of violent crime, they should know that old Jack is no longer with us. He has moved off to the supreme hunting ground where all real Bushmen go when they depart this earthly life. And it is highly unlikely that anyone will ever be able to find the exact spot again. The three skulls are probably still there, carefully hidden and patiently waiting for old Jack to come along and have another word or two with them about their crimes against his people.

One of Jack's sons, Ben, was something of a slippery character. Jack, of course, had a whole harem of wives, and Ben was the offspring of one of the lighter skinned women. Jack himself was almost a pale creamy colour, thus still a purebred Barakwena with little, if any, Lozi blood in him.

Ben, however, unforgivably married an Ovambo "long foot" woman, in addition to the Bushman wife he already had, and was therefore closer to the "long feet" than his siblings, and tended to follow the Ovambo customs. Much to Dewald's annoyance, he started to keep goats, which inevitably disturbed the pure savannah environment. Ben soon started to complain that the "tigers" – that is either cheetahs or leopards – were killing his goats.

Unfortunately, Ben also replenished his larder from time to time with an illegally shot kudu, sable, impala or anything else that crossed his path.

His half-brother, Langman, was unquestionably one of the best trackers at Fort Doppies, if not the best. His mother, one of Jack's many wives, had quite a dose of Mafwe or Lozi blood, and Langman was deeply dark-skinned.

On the whole, he was a reticent sort of fellow, and quite tall for a Bushman, as his name indicates. But he, too, had his problems, preferring to live apart from the westernised Bushmen in the small clan. This led to others of similar ilk being attracted to Langman's *kimbo*.

The conflict between a western way of life and the former Bushman lifestyle was sharply evident in Langman. He hankered after the bush but the "new age" movement instituted by the theorists in their offices in Pretoria captured him in its grasp, irrespective of what people like Dewald had to say on the subject.

Then there was Kampembe, the Flecha hero from the Portuguese-Angolan war. He preferred the Fort Doppies situation to the Bushman base at Omega.

All the other Bushmen had a healthy respect for this little man from the north who was, without a doubt, the ace tracker among them all. He always carried his bow and poisoned arrows with him, along with his army-issue FN rifle.

Kampembe and Dewald became almost inseparable for a while, Dewald learning as much as he could from the little man's fantastic treasure of bushlore. Strong bonds of friendship developed between them.

Unfortunately, a blustering and – to say the least – moronic army captain one day ordered Kampembe, the one Bushman everybody looked up to with admiration and respect, to carry out some degrading, menial task. Had he obeyed the captain's orders, Kampembe would have lost face among the clan members. So he refused. The captain threw a violent tantrum, but Kampembe did not budge a single millimetre from his stand.

The next morning, all Kampembe's military gear was left neatly folded on the step at the entrance to the captain's *basha* (quarters), his spotlessly clean rifle lying on top. That was Kampembe's way of bidding farewell to Fort Doppies.

The captain searched high and low for Kampembe, but he never found him – the Bushman trackers did not offer much assistance in the search. Kampembe had slipped back into the savannah forest dressed only in his loincloth and carrying his bow and arrows. When Dewald returned from leave, he found to his intense disgust and sorrow that his friend and mentor had gone for good.

Many years later I tracked Kampembe down to a small, typical *kimbo* just north of the cutline inside Angola. He was content and had no intention of ever being a soldier again. Of course he also hunted game inside and outside the reserve but in the old traditional Bushman style. He was once again in complete harmony with his environment and hoping that the outside world would forget him.

Among the young there was an outstanding individual by the name of Shuffle Foot. He was fairly well educated, a product of the Fort Doppies primary school and in due course, he became a corporal, the only Bushman to actually attend and pass a proper promotion course in Pretoria.

Shuffle Foot was reasonably at ease in western society. He had the strength of character not to be consumed by its materialism and useless trappings, but nevertheless, he still hankered for the old days of the Bushman hunter-gatherer.

The two of us had long discussions on the future of the Barakwenas, especially their very valid claim to the western Caprivi as their own homeland from which they did not want to be forced by the large-scale migration of "long feet". We even planned some political action, but I was ejected from the area before our plans could take shape. No one stepped into the breach to take up the Bushmen's cause.

I shall never forget Shuffle Foot's intelligent, but sometimes also sad face, as long as I live. Unlike most of the other Bushmen, he could appreciate – with fearful clarity – that the future existence of the Barakwenas hung on a slender thread.

In spite of being drawn by the bush, and his undoubted adequate knowledge of bush lore, tracking and so on, Shuffle Foot had already lost that bushwise sharpness so characteristic of the older generations. He tried his best to recapture that former harmony between the hunter-gatherer and the environment, but the prevailing conditions were really not conducive to success.

It is extremely difficult for a Bushman, even one as knowledgeable and dedicated as Shuffle Foot, to live with one foot in the western materialistic world and with the other in the old Bushman world of Stone Age man.

A Bushman had to be one or the other. He could never be both.

The Bushmen were still under the fatherly control of Delville Linford, the one officer who really could relate to his "bushies", when both of us returned to South West Africa from Angola after our victorious campaign during Operation Savannah in 1975. I brought with me my battalion of black FNLA soldiers.

Delville went back to Alpha Base and I, after many trials and tribulations, settled my close on 2000 troops and their dependents on the east banks of the mighty Okavango River.

It was the beginning of 1976, and a new chapter in my love affair with the Caprivi and Cuando-Cubango was about to start.

FIVE

A Short Spell of Rest in Paradise

The Cuito River is a major contributor from south central Angola to the Okavango River's flow of water into the Okavango swamps.

At Cuito Cuanavale two rivers, the Cuito and the Cuanavale, join up to form one mighty stream which flows all the way south as far as Dirico, where it spills its clear waters into the Okavango.

The Cuito is second only to the Cuando in its wildness and pristine beauty.

The waters of the Cuito and Cuanavale rivers rise on the southern edge of the Angolan central highlands. Rainfall is high and vast, spongy swamps ensure a constant flow of the crystal-clear water so characteristic of all rivers rising in the southern highlands.

I came to know the Cuito intimately as far as Vila Nova D'Armada in 1976, and reasonably well as far north as Tempue during an abortive attempt by Unita to take Cuito Cuanavale ten years later.

Towards the tail end of Operation Savannah, after they had been sent on leave to recuperate from their highly successful but extremely stressful battles against the MPLA, I gathered all my FNLA troops together.

This is not the place to describe the really hard-fought conflict we were involved in, but I will say, without fear of contradiction, that Operation Savannah laid the foundations for the best infantry unit on the South African army's active list since the end of the Second World War.

Admittedly, my men did not look like the cream of our

fighting troops when I concentrated them once again at Mpupa, from where our war had started a bare four months earlier. Then they had looked even worse. They trickled in from all over southern Angola, bringing their families and all their wordly goods which gave the impression of nomads or gypsies on the move rather than battle-hardened soldiers.

Feeding the vast hordes of dependants severely undernourished from the ravages of civil war was to be one of my biggest headaches.

Eventually I had a company deployed at Vila Nova D'Armada, about 200 kilometres upstream from Mpupa, a company at Baixo Longa about 80 kilometres north of Vila Nova, a company at Luenge 180 kilometres north of Mucusso and a platoon at Mavinga 120 kilometres north of Luenge.

The main body of the battalion and all dependants were based at Mpupa.

All the troops had to be fed, but I was desperately short of transport. The answer was to "liberate" as many trucks as possible from better equipped South African units, which we did with great success and much hilarity among ourselves and to cries of rage from the victims.

Another partial solution was presented by the discovery of two magnificent river patrol boats at Vila Nova D'Armada. They were quickly commandeered into service by South African naval personnel.

The Cuito was easily navigable between Cuito Cuanavale and Mpupa, but further south the impressive Mpupa falls made progress impossible unless the boats could be winched over dry land and past the falls to the foaming waters rushing downstream in a narrow gorge before levelling out into a slow-moving, meandering river.

However, for the moment I could rely on my own little navy to get supplies to the troops at Vila Nova and from there by truck to Baixo Longa.

Unfortunately, there was never time for me to go on the river, but I assigned a small section of young national service engineers the pleasant task of operating the boats.

It must have been one of the finest river voyages in all of Africa, and probably the best job any national serviceman ever had.

The boats were substantial craft, built of steel, and were about 18 metres long. One of them had quite comfortable cabins obviously designed to take on passengers, or for the use of senior members of the Portuguese marine crew.

The youngsters took three days on the upriver leg and two days to get back to Mpupa. They sailed only during daylight hours and tied up on the river bank at night.

From the elevated bridges and former gun decks, they looked out over the many islands dotting the swampy flood plains teeming with thousands of red lechwes, as the boats twisted and turned to follow the meandering main stream of the Cuito.

Occasionally they passed herds of hippo basking in the shallows or snorting and blowing in the deep channels. Huge crocodiles slid into the water from the sand banks the moment they heard the throbbing engines. From time to time, the crew spotted the elusive sitatunga or the bobbing heads and tails of reedbuck running through the long grass.

The western bank of the Cuito is fairly heavily populated, with dilapidated little *kimbos* at regular intervals. Game on the western side was therefore scarce.

But wherever the main stream touched the unpopulated eastern bank of the flood plain, the lads could expect to see herds of elephant disporting themselves in the shallows or huge herds of buffalo staring at them from the shadowy fringes of the riverine forests.

The eastern bank was completely wild. This was Africa in the raw, untouched by human hand and therefore undisturbed by man's destructive influence.

At night, the boats moored at an island or among riverine forest trees close to the bank. After a leisurely meal, the crew could sit and listen to Africa's nightlife taking centre stage.

The elephants, of course, were ever present, loudly breaking off branches, trumpeting and growling at each other or noisily splashing in the water nearby.

Hippos chuckled at their own jokes from the various pools as they prepared to move out into the flood plains to graze.

As the night wore on, the drawn out "whoooop!" of scavenging hyenas could be heard, perhaps even the distant roar of a lion announcing a kill in the early morning hours.

The islands and east bank of the Cuito River provided an incredibly rich display of African wildlife as animals, including birds of all shapes and sizes, grazed or browsed, killed each other for prey, fought for territory, vied for space at drinking places, procreated, fought desperate duals or simply hid from all the turmoil and noise around them.

It was a feast for city-weary eyes, a magnificent display that was, alas, soon to disappear under the onslaught of Unita hunting rifles.

Our stay in Mpupa, and other points further north, was cut short when several Fapla brigades decided that B Group – as my unit was called at the time – had to be pushed out of Angola.

With overwhelming force they launched separate advances on three fronts. After some strenuous fighting, especially near Mavinga and Baixo Longa, we were forced to withdraw. In the process a Unita combat group joined the fray and decided to attack my company at Baixo Longa. The company withdrew with Unita in hot pursuit, only to run up against a small ten-man patrol of Bravo Group from Vila Nova.

The confrontation that ensued was like a scene from a farce. The entire Unita force, including 13 French mercenaries from Bob Denard's organisation, were captured by the white South Africans and eight black FNLA troops. The loot was spectacular, and included trucks, four-wheel-drive vehicles, an armoured car, Savimbi's personal Citroen sedan, 106 mm recoilless guns, heavy .50 Browning machine guns, Entac anti-tank guided missiles and even some Strela anti-aircraft missiles and launchers. This was the first time the South Africans had ever clapped eyes on the notorious Strela, with which Joshua Nkomo's guerrillas had shot down two civilian Viscounts during the Rhodesian war.

Our transport pool welcomed the new additions and many of the Unita troops promptly decided to join B Group. The defectors included a troupe of strippers from Lobito, who had evidently been entertaining Bob Denard's mercenaries at Gago Coutinho in between their "battles" with the MPLA.

Unfortunately, in the face of overwhelming odds stacked against us, we had to vacate the Cuando-Cubango.

By Easter 1976, my troops and their families were squatting miserably in pouring rain under tarpaulins and some moth-eaten tents on the east bank of the Okavango River, much further to the south in the western Caprivi.

Malaria was rife and we were losing at least one infant a day, and adults too, particularly among the dependents.

The troops were well fed after their months of training and campaigning and had a fairly high resistance to the disease. The families, however, had always been short of food, particularly protein, as a result of Angola's ongoing civil war. It was a gift from heaven when their husbands fetched them from wherever they were living in abject misery and brought them into the welcoming arms of the battalion.

But there was a lot of leeway to be made up and the constant rain did not help.

Our malaria victims were laid to rest in 32 Battalion's rather extensive cemetery, the only war cemetery in the entire operational area. Unfortunately, the first to be buried there were not fallen soldiers, but little babies and, sometimes, their mothers.

We had to start a building programme as a matter of urgency, and found a suitable spot on high ground above the clouds of mosquitoes from the Okavango's swampy banks. We pitched our tents all over the place, using the dense stand of red syringa trees as overhead cover for camouflage purposes and to provide shade once the rains stopped with the sun once again beating down on us.

From Dirico we "liberated" a huge 600 KVA generator, and

built a bush power station with enough electricity to supply a town the size of Rundu.

There were some electricians among my troops, especially among the captured Unitas, and we soon had a Heath Robinson-type power supply system going that made our South African signallers and engineers responsible for providing the army with electricity go pale around the gills when they inspected it. Nevertheless, it worked extremely well and no one was ever electrocuted.

When we first settled in the area, wildlife was largely absent. Fortunately, the frequent and defiant *makorro* crossings by Mbukushu poachers from the Okavango side, to the proclaimed game reserve of the western Caprivi, came to an abrupt and very dead halt.

Our presence in the western Caprivi was meant to be secret, and using this as an excuse, we gleefully took appropriate steps to get all the *makorros* confined to the western bank of the river.

The Hambukushu complained bitterly to their tribal chief, who went, in turn, to sector headquarters. Sector headquarters took matters up with us, insinuating that we were using unnecessary force and blood-curdling threats to keep the poachers out of the reserve.

We ignored them. After a few "sinking" incidents – usually leaving a poacher minus his expensive hunting rifle and desperately swimming for the western shore – the incursions ceased and the game began to return to the east bank of the Okavango.

Soon trumpeting herds of elephant swept majestically through the middle of the main base and the training camps to get to the water. Thundering herds of buffalo crashed in dust clouds through the reeds of the flood plains. At night prides of lions casually strolled our sandy streets, vehicle parks or parade grounds. Inside the flimsy canvas tents, families cowered in terror at the unusual experience of coming face to face with the king of the savannah, his harem and offspring, with only a tent wall separating them from the dreaded fangs of these powerful beasts.

My troops and their families spent many nights under their army beds instead of on top of them.

Hyenas loped through the base to inspect the contents of rubbish bins, the kitchen area and other promising spots for bits of juicy offal. Their approaching whoops could be heard miles away, while their excited maniacal cackling at cornering an interesting morsel of melodious refuse chilled the blood in the veins of the superstitious listeners hiding behind their canvas walls.

The hyena has always held a particularly sinister niche in African folklore.

It was, all things considered, the most splendid place in which to live.

We had brought with us one of the river boats from Mpupa after manoeuvring it around the falls. It was now tied up alongside a steep embankment where it floated serenely on the wide Okavango River.

The other and more luxurious boat sank at the foot of the Mpupa falls when my impatient senior engineer stupidly decided that it would be quicker to take it over the falls instead of winching it over dry ground on wooden rollers before launching into the turbulent stream below.

So he nonchalantly pointed the boat straight at the falls and stepped into a rubber duck at the last possible moment. He was just in time to see the stern disappear over the edge with a grinding noise as the steel plates of the hull were torn apart by the sharp rocks forming the lip over which the water plunged into the depths below.

The boat tumbled down in a cascade of water and wedged firmly among huge boulders at the bottom, a heap of mangled iron and splintered wood, a spectacular but inglorious end to a brave little boat that did its bit for the South African war effort in Angola.

I was furious. My vision of sundowner cruises on the placid Okavango while viewing game from the top deck, one hand holding a glass of whisky, the other trawling for tiger fish over the stern, was shattered. I had dreamed of tying up to a couple of trees in one of the side streams at nightfall and waiting for darkness to descend over the Caprivi with the sun sinking in a blaze of colours to the west. One could then sleep comfortably in a luxurious bunk in one of the four cabins with the night sounds of primeval Africa all around but held at bay by a stretch of water and a solid steel bulkhead.

However, all was not lost. There was a serviceable river tug upstream from Rundu at a place called Cuangar. This boat used to pull, and often push, freight and passenger barges up and down the Okavango between Calais, opposite Rundu, and Caiundu, hundreds of kilometres upstream and deep inside Angola.

I managed to acquire the tug and had it taken downstream, with a freight barge in tow, as far as Rundu, where a splendid eight-passenger barge was added to our little flotilla for the next part of the journey, as far as Andara, just above some rapids.

Here the engineers came to my assistance. Using one of their low loaders, used for transporting their gigantic bulldozers, they transported the tug and its barges in separate loads to Bagani, where they were placed back in the water and sailed downstream to our new base.

The tug was a splendid "Saunders of the River" type vessel. It had an impressive marine diesel engine, housed below the raised bridge in a spacious engine room. The bridge itself was enclosed in glass and contained all the engine controls, the ship's wheel, light controls and a very nautical-looking engine-order telegraph, made of solid brass.

Aft of the bridge and a step down were the crew's quarters, basically a roomy cabin with two bunks.

The passenger barge had two large cabins, each with four bunks in two tiers. In the centre, between the two cabins, was a shower on one side and the heads on the other, with a passage in between.

Aft of one of the cabins, or ahead (because it did not matter much with this snubnosed vessel in which direction it was pulled or pushed) was quite an adequate little galley with a generator compartment at the opposite end.

The roof of the cabins formed a spacious sun deck with an all-round view over river, swamps and forests.

My dream of sundowners on the water would become a reality after all. Turning in to the sound of snorting hippos and splashing fish in some isolated little creek deep inside the ancient heart of Africa is the best tonic for insomnia I have ever tried.

This vessel became my place of abode each time I came to the now base from our headquarters in Rundu.

Charlie Hochapfel arrived to take up the position of commander of the base. He had a rather sharp, reddish nose and soon acquired the nickname of Pica Pau, the Portuguese for woodpecker. Quite logically, the base also became known as Pica Pau, an indication of Charlie's energetic and successful attempts to make it viable and comfortable for troops and their families.

Meanwhile, the Fapla brigades decided that their supply lines to the north were becoming far too tenuous as they were forced to rely on some of the most atrocious tracks to be found anywhere in Africa. They decided to turn their tanks and armoured cars around, and return from whence they came.

Like little terriers at the heels of a cumbersome rhino, my troops followed up, moving back into the vacated bases while the dust of Fapla's departure was still visible on the northern horizon.

We also opened a new theatre of operations inside Angola, just north of Ovamboland. These operations, conducted with up to seven or eight independent platoons, were directed at Swapo forward bases.

Young second lieutenants and corporals, straight from the infantry school, were placed in command of battle-hardened platoons in which each and every former FNLA soldier had more firefights under his belt than his young commander had breakfasts. The kingpin in the platoon was always the hard-bitten sergeant, usually a former FNLA commandante. To get my rank structure right I had to promote the white corporal "platoon leaders" to sergeants, without authority from the army, of course, as they would never have understood my man management problems.

These young South African lads were sent into areas teeming with hundreds of Swapo guerrillas for up to three months at a stretch, with orders to harass the enemy with ambushes, mines, hit-and-run attacks and any other tactics they could think of.

It worked like the proverbial charm. With few exceptions, the youngsters enthusiastically got stuck into the war, were accepted by their veteran troops and started to give Swapo much larger doses of the horrid medicine they were trying to dish out to us and especially to the civilian population.

Small-scale actions flared up all over the territory just north of the border. We started to record "kills" daily, when other units went for weeks, sometimes even months, to get a single kill.

We reoccupied our former bases in Luenge, Mavinga, Baixo Longa, Vila Nova D'Armada, Caiundo and Savate, and I also took over a base by the name of Omauni, inside Okavango, and west of Mpungu Vlei. Eddie Viljoen became the base commander and also the commander of all operations west of Katitwe.

We were deployed over a 500-kilometres front, a gigantic area to control but, fortunately, it was mostly just empty space.

In the area newly opened up to the west, the wildlife had been under tremendous pressure for a considerable time, though some elephants were still to be found in and around Omauni and to the north towards Savate and beyond.

The Savate area used to be well known for its herds of sable antelope and some remnants were still about when we moved in, but they have since disappeared.

Elsewhere, the African savannah had been turned into sterile bush, empty and brooding in the hot tropical sun with scarcely a bird to break the oppressive silence.

North of the cutline, the most common sound was the rattle of AK-47s, the deeper and more business-like crack of the R1s, the thump of mortars being fired and the thud of their shells exploding.

The only animal life found there was in the shape of wandering donkeys. My troops soon trained them as pack animals, so that they, too, could do their bit in fighting off Swapo incursions into Ovamboland and the Kavango.

Over such a wide front, things were always simmering, and I had my hands full just keeping the lid on while at the same time holding Task Force Headquarters at Grootfontein at bay.

Things really started to boil when Fapla suddenly decided that another push southwards would be in order. This time, it was a much heavier three-pronged attack that came rolling south. The Fapla brigades were considerably bolstered by Cuban forces, large numbers of tanks and close air support in the shape of MiGs to drive us from our positions.

Battles flared up north of Mavinga, where I had only a platoon, and at Baixo Longa, which housed a raw FNLA company, to face the heavily reinforced Fapla advance.

Task Force Headquarters quite sensibly ordered a withdrawal from all my forward positions except for those platoons operating against Swapo bases north of Ovamboland.

The troops withdrawing from Mavinga and Luenge ran into a strong cut-off force at their rear and suffered some casualties. I subsequently lost all three of my Portuguese platoon leaders in a fluke contact, a loss that is felt in Special Forces and 32 Battalion to this day.

The troops from Baixo Longa and Caiundo came back in good order, however, bringing with them more women and children whom they had rounded up in a final sweep through southern Angola. They had some close calls and the Savate and Cauindo groups managed to get themselves into a situation worthy of an old-fashioned, British slapstick comedy. I will not enlarge on this episode, as it is extensively covered in my book, *They Live by the Sword*.

Suddenly, across the border stepped the emaciated and exhausted Dr Jonas Savimbi and four or five of his high command. I rescued them, just in time, from being lynched by one of my FNLA patrols. Perhaps I should have arrived an hour or two later, because Savimbi was destined to become a big, and very bad apple in the future conservation barrel, exerting a baleful influence on rhino horn and ivory smuggling in particular.

He and his staff were whipped off to a secret training base and Military Intelligence imposed on me to lend Unita some instructors to retrain Savimbi and the remnants of his guerrilla army.

These Unita stragglers were filtering out of Angola with the help of my unit, but there were numerous firefights between my troops and Unita before I could convince the former FNLA soldiers that we were now supposed to fight alongside Savimbi's men and not against them.

In one contact, my troops shot more than 80 Unitas, at no loss to themselves, under the pretext that Unita was as bad as Swapo, or even worse, since they had always collaborated with them. This was a known fact.

The Fapla brigades reached the SWA-Angolan border and began to dig in at Cuangar, Calais, Dirico and Mucusso.

I was ordered to move my base from Pica Pau to somewhere else in SWA since some were of the opinion that we had become a magnet for the Fapla forces.

A location in Bushmanland, far to the south, was suggested. I had no intention of going there, and set all the bureaucratic machinery in reverse pitch to postpone the inevitable move for as long as possible. To stall a cumbersome bureaucratic machine is, in any case, one of the easiest things to do, so that was no real achievement.

Finally, we loaded all our gear and moved the combative part of the unit, without dependents, some eight kilometres upriver and closer to the nearest Fapla garrison at Mucusso, instead of away from them as we were ordered to do.

The new site was an absolute Eden, with huge fig trees on the river bank interspersed with gigantic knobthorns, camelthorns and extensive stands of Rhodesian teak.

With a clear conscience, I informed my general that we had removed ourselves from Pica Pau, as ordered, and that we were settling down in our new location.

He never asked where this was and only discovered much later, when the danger had passed, that we were somewhat closer to Fapla than he had intended us to be.

Our name was changed from Bravo Group to 32 Battalion – to confuse the enemy, I suppose.

Meanwhile, the wild animals increased as soon as they discovered that there was a sanctuary for them away from the hunting rifles of poachers and legitimate trophy hunters in Botswana to the south.

Elephants in particular became so numerous that we became blasé about their presence. In winter they were always there as part of the landscape and barely worth mentioning over a beer or two in our primitive bush pub.

We were just beginning to prove that we were the best fighting troops in the South African army when I was rudely and expeditiously plucked from the African bush to be dumped, protesting bitterly, on the campus of the Army College in Pretoria, to do a staff and command course.

SIX

Back in "Civilisation"

For almost a year I sweated it out in lecture rooms and fought a paper war, pushing mechanised brigades and divisions around on maps that covered entire walls at times.

Admittedly, I learned more in that time about all the aspects of the theory of war than during any other period of my life. Being a soldier with more combat experience than any of the other students on the course helped a lot. I could discourse about practical problems in the field with some degree of authority, having already experienced most of them. But a soldier never stops learning and honing his craft and the Army College was then one of the best institutions in the western world for turning out senior staff officers and formation commanders. Soon my knowledge of warfare was being widened in a most satisfactory manner and my initial resistance turned to enthusiasm.

Nevertheless, I felt good when the course ended, but discovered that instead of going back to 32 Battalion, I was being posted to Northern Transvaal Command and a dreaded staff job.

Fortunately, the commanding officer delegated everything that smacked of operations to me as the senior staff officer operations. This meant getting away from Pretoria and spending as much time as possible in the Transvaal bushveld, the lowveld and even in the then Rhodesia, where the war was still firing on all cylinders.

During this time, I also had the unexpected honour of leading paratroopers from the three parachute battalions in an airborne assault on the main Swapo base at Cassinga. We killed more than 600 guerrillas and wounded another 1000 in a base that was brimming with between 2000 and 3000 armed Swapo cadres.

Afterwards, the international media, the World Council of Churches, at least one of the bishops of the Anglican Church, Swapo, the Cubans, the Angolans and the Russians were not exactly standing in line to congratulate us on conducting the most successful airborne assault since the Second World War. Condemnation was heaped upon our heads for attacking a so-called refugee camp.

They were certainly the best armed refugees I have ever come across. They put quite a number of shots through us, myself included, and also through some of the aircraft.

From the moment we stepped into the slipstream from our lumbering C130s and C160s, we encountered heavy but inaccurate ground fire. We jumped almost on top of the target and I felt extremely vulnerable suspended in the blue sky above, at the end of a parachute that had opened almost directly over our objective, which was seething with terrorists taking pot shots at us.

The preliminary air strike silenced the defences initially, but our difficulty in regrouping on the ground after the landing gave the enemy enough time to reorganise and to meet us with heavy machine-gun, AK-47, light machine-gun and mortar fire.

However, 370 paratroopers tore into the massive guerrilla base as soon as we had oriented ourselves and we soon began to get the upper hand.

From the south, a Cuban-Fapla mechanised battalion attacked with tanks and armoured personnel carriers. Between my anti-tank platoon and the supporting aircraft, we soon brought them up short, knocking out all but one of their tanks and all their armoured personnel carriers.

We found a number of women, much discussed in the media, in the camp, and some of them were unavoidably shot. They were holed-up in a huge brothel area where Swapo cadres indulged their sexual urges at will.

The women had been schoolgirls when they were abducted

by Swapo from Ovamboland. We found the latest batch there, about 70 young girls (future prostitutes) and young boys (future guerrillas) who had been snatched just three weeks before from an Anglican mission station. They begged to be taken back to their homes, but this was impossible. The helicopters used to extract the airborne assault force were already overloaded and the abductees had to stay behind to face their grim future alone, while a self-righteous Anglican bishop condemned the operation as a despicable war crime against the blacks of Ovamboland.

Perhaps as a result of the Cassinga operation, I was subsequently given the mission of getting 44 Parachute Brigade off the ground. Elements of the brigade were involved in all the wars raging around southern Africa, including the conflict in Rhodesia, South West Africa and Angola. An airborne assault on the scale of the Cassinga operation was never repeated, much to our disappointment. The army top brass still did not grasp the significance and advantages of the surprise factor inherent in the deployment of paratroopers, in spite of our proven success at Cassinga.

Small sub-units took part in various operations as so-called fire forces, particularly in Rhodesia, where the concept brought satisfying results, or as semi-independent raiding forces in Angola, where we successfully knocked out rather large Fapla combat groups and teams with few casualties on our side.

I found myself operating in areas which had become completely sterile as far as wildlife was concerned, especially in Angola. Obviously, the war had taken a devastating toll, not so much in terms of operations conducted by South African forces, but in the form of plundering by roving bands of Fapla, Unita and Swapo troops, all of them at near-starvation level and therefore stripping the bush of everything edible, from plants to almost all its animals.

The locals had to eke out a miserable existence, dodging marauders from all three of these forces by trekking deeper into the bush. Every time we stumbled across these little settlements in our wide-ranging operations we were welcomed with open arms as liberators. The local population could never comprehend that our sojourn had to be only temporary.

Sadly and glumly they saw us on our way after each incursion, fully expecting bloody revenge from Fapla or Swapo the moment we had vanished into the thick bush of southern Angola.

The area had become a war-shattered and miserable land for its few surviving occupants, man and beast alike, thanks to selfish, treacherous and manipulating political leaders playing their deadly chess game in a part of Africa that had become the last outpost for creatures of the savannah.

When I left 44 Parachute Brigade in 1982 for another staff job – this time at Military Intelligence – I thought I would never see Angola again. I was left with my rather morbid memories of a "dead" Angola, at least that part of it stretching westwards from the Cuito River to the Atlantic Ocean. These thoughts were somewhat tempered by the false impression that at least the Cuando-Cubango was still teeming with wild animals and in the same pristine condition as when the creator had shaped it.

But these comforting memories would soon be shattered.

SEVEN

Terry – The "Terrorist" from Fort Doppies

Against all expectations, my new job took me back to my old stomping grounds. My assignment was to open a guerrilla school where we could train allied forces and our own in guerrilla warfare in suitable surroundings. It didn't take much brainpower to figure out that the most suitable location for such a school would be on the banks of the Cuando River, not far north of Fort Doppies.

The school opened soon afterwards and our first students arrived within weeks of the first sod being turned. Fortunately, guerrilla warfare training is about 80 per cent dependent on the natural environment and only 20 per cent on human-made training aids and other artificial devices and I intended keeping the school's infrastructure as basic as possible. Students moved into an operational base deep inside the bush, dug slit trenches and bunkers and stayed there for the duration of the course. There was no electricity, refrigeration, kitchens, vehicles or other facilities normally found at military training schools.

The area was rich with game – elephants, a few rhinos, buffaloes, lions, leopards, hyenas and, near the river, hippos and lurking crocodiles, all inadvertently contributing to making the training realistic, interesting and tinged with danger.

Any disturbance of game was, of course, strictly prohibited. The game always had first priority and rite of passage under all circumstances, especially during field firing exercises.

For instance, no one was allowed to scare elephants away from a base by firing shots into the air. If an elephant herd decided to wander through a base, daintily plucking pods from the camelthorns while training was in progress, all the students could do was grin at them and be prepared to make a dash for the nearest tent or hut.

This approach resulted in some amusing incidents, but not once was a student attacked by an enraged animal. In fact the animals soon learned to accept our presence as normal and part of the local scenery.

To the south, Dewald de Beer was still ruling the roost at Fort Doppies. While I was reconnoitring a suitable area for the school, I made it my business to renew my acquaintance with Fort Doppies, its associated training area and, of course, the resident wild animals.

A newcomer at the camp happened to be a fellow called Terry who stayed in the base from time to time and had the disconcerting habit of appearing at the most inopportune and unexpected moments from the depths of the forest.

Terry was a fully grown lion, who had a pride of lionesses and cubs that would have made Solomon green with envy.

On my first visit to Fort Doppies after an absence of several years, I was sitting in Freedom Square outside the pub and chewing the fat with Dewald while, most appropriately, having a Lion beer, when Dewald suddenly interrupted.

"There he is!" he exclaimed, pointing to the pub entrance behind me.

I turned around and looked straight into the eyes of the biggest lion I had ever seen. I had heard of Terry, of course, but the size and majesty of the animal took my breath away when we finally came face to face.

Terry looked at me unflinchingly with his warm, amber eyes, his tail up, to indicate his friendliness, and decided that I was part of the group. He ambled up slowly and rubbed himself against me, almost pushing me off the bench. Apprehensively, I stroked the iron-hard muscles on his back while Dewald looked on with amusement, no doubt expecting his former commanding officer to bolt swiftly for the nearest tree.

Terry found me acceptable and flopped down at my feet. When we moved into the pub as darkness descended on the base, he followed us indoors and stretched himself out below the dart board.

The troops ignored him and carried on playing darts, stepping over him every time they had to retrieve their missiles.

After a while, however, Terry decided that enough time had been wasted, and it was time for dinner. Unerringly, he walked to the cook who was deeply engrossed in his beer. He grabbed him by the leg of his trousers and without further ado pulled him to the walk-in refrigerator in the kitchen next door to the pub.

The cook's keys were hanging above the door. He had to unlock the fridge, step inside and bring out a huge, frozen quarter of beef which he handed to Terry.

Terry took it, moved out onto the lawn and for the rest of the night dined noisily off prime beef courtesy of the army quartermaster.

The next morning he was gone. He had returned to the pride where he was lord and master of about 20 lions, lionesses and cubs.

Terry originally belonged to a safari company which did some hunting in the Lianshulu area to the south of Fort Doppies. He had a little sister called Liza. Both came from the Kalahari and were therefore endowed with genes which would make them stand at least a hand taller than the lions of the Caprivi. Both were also coloured a lighter shade, in keeping with the Kalahari sand dunes to the south.

They had the run of the Lianshulu safari camp and grew up among the admiring clients and an indulgent staff. Like all lion cubs they were, of course, extremely mischievous and very lively at night. They were never locked up, restricted to a compound or fenced in any way.

This created problems as they grew older. A small lion cub, romping with a human playmate, can be easily handled. As they grew older, however, their increasing size made playtime a painful and tiring experience.

The lions had no way of knowing that the same human beings they so happily played with as cubs would become less tolerant as their claws became sharper and their fangs got larger, not to mention the tremendous increase in their strength and weight.

One day, the safari company fetched a wealthy Italian client from the airfield at Mpacha and by the time they got their guest into camp, night was falling. They were just in time for sundowners and the usual splendid braai that followed.

The Italian downed his whiskies and sat down to succulent mutton cutlets and beef steaks, the best the safari company could offer, washed down by the finest South African wines. Around him was the darkness of the African bush and above the leaping flames of the campfire the star-studded expanse of an African night sky.

No doubt a nightjar was trilling away somewhere in the vicinity. Further away he probably heard a hyena whooping it up on the way to the hunt. To the west, he could doubtless hear the naughty chuckling of a hippo or two.

What he did not see, and was not told about, were the two lions lurking in the darkness beyond the firelight. The safari operators probably just forgot to warn him of the presence of Terry and Liza who were, by then, regarded as part of the permanent staff.

It was the Italian's first night in the African bush and he was most likely apprehensive about the unusual darkness, the absence of city noise, electric lights and all the other comforting paraphernalia of civilisation to which he was accustomed.

He was not the most robust of people and the trip from Italy to South Africa and on to Mpacha, in the distant Caprivi, had been tiring. He decided to turn in early and made his way to his rondavel. The ablution block was some distance away, but with the others still gathered around the campfire the Italian had no qualms about going through his preparations for bed. He was soon snug and warm, listening to the mysterious sounds of an African night.

Gradually the camp quietened down as everyone turned in and the fire burnt down to glowing embers. However, the Italian was beginning to feel distinctly uncomfortable. The heavy meal, wine and whisky were beginning to play havoc with his digestive system. The excitement and unusual feeling of remoteness, out in wild, savage and primeval Africa, contributed to the onset of an uncontrollable attack of what the army used to call "gyppo guts".

Outside, it was pitch-dark. The fairly short distance to the ablution block now seemed endless and, in the apprehensive Italian's mind, became a perilous journey beset by the threat of attacks by hyena, leopard, lion or a roving hippo.

But he had to go. There was no question about it. Finally, he decided that the nearest bush would have to do.

He rushed out of his rondavel with great urgency and squatted behind the first bush he could find.

Meanwhile, Terry and Liza had been playing their own nocturnal game and were not far from the Italian's rondavel when he scampered for a bush.

Terry could not believe his luck when he saw the Italian squatting down, his back towards him. He went into an immediate stalk and, with Liza following, closed the distance between them and their "prey".

The Italian was at the most critical part of his mission when a snarling lion suddenly pounced on him from the rear, its claws grabbing his shoulders and its fangs digging into his scalp. Almost immediately, the lion was followed by a second, equally ferocious beast, trying its best to effect a quick and easy "kill".

The Italian screamed in terror, his shrieks catapulting the entire staff from their beds and towards his hut.

They could hear the noise of the struggle, but the screams had stopped. They found the Italian almost passed out, his pants twisted round his ankles, beneath the pair of lions. The two boisterous cubs were having the time of their lives.

The Italian suffered a fit of near hysteria. He refused to stay one minute longer in Lianshulu and a hasty night drive to Katima Mulilo, some 200 kilometres away, ensued. The safari leader tried to restore the dignity of the intrepid big-game hunter, but to no avail. The Italian was a shattered man.

On arrival at Katima, he recovered sufficiently to insist on an immediate flight to Johannesburg and from there back to Italy. He never again wanted to set foot in Africa.

Back at the safari camp, the safari leader contemplated the future of his mischievous cubs. He could not give them to a zoo because there was no zoo in the area, and zoos are always overstocked with lions. He could not abandon them to the wild, because they were still too small and helpless. He certainly did not want to shoot them, so he summoned Dewald who, after doping them, bundled the cubs into his Land Rover and took them to Fort Doppies.

He was happy to have the lions and the troops were ecstatic at having two real lions as playmates.

The lions were equally happy, particularly Terry. They would have ample opportunity to practise their stalks and "kills" on a larger number of human beings and would never go short of rations. The quartermaster general, in his ignorance, would supply ample quantities of meat and milk to build two Kalahari lions up until they were big enough to stake their claim by taking on the Caprivi lions in the area.

The introduction of Terry and Liza into the story raises a sensitive issue, which necessarily implies some criticism of others, but also makes the sad point about Liza's fate.

Certain people persist in keeping wild animals as pets, usually acquiring them when they are quite small. As they grow bigger, the animals become unmanageable – and in some cases downright dangerous – to handlers or owners. At this point, the owner decides to either get rid of the animal by passing it on to someone else, or to kill it.

In Namibia (South West Africa) there was, probably still is, at least one organisation that breeds lions to be hunted and killed by overseas clients. A trophy hunter will pay a fortune to hang a generously maned head on the wall of his study or trophy room among a display of horns, heads, tusks and other visible results of his addiction to the "chase".

When they reach a certain age, the lions are sold to game farmers who run hunting safaris on their farms. There is one farm, near Otjiwarongo, where surplus and elderly lions from

136

zoos or circuses are kept in a fenced camp to be shot by intrepid big-game hunters from America, Germany, Japan and other affluent societies. The whole experience is conducted in a highly artificial atmosphere. The hunter has only to take a shot at anyone of the old lions lounging about in a lazy torpor, usually in the heat of the day when lions are notoriously reluctant to exert themselves.

After the shot has been fired, the lion is prepared for the customer as a trophy, thousands of rands change hands and a satisfied customer is homeward bound with a big story to tell to his credulous mates.

Terry and Liza were born on the property of such a deliberate breeder of lions and they were destined for the shooting gallery, but somehow the deal fell through while they were still quite small.

The breeder decided they were a waste of rations and was about to kill the tiny cubs when a soft-hearted fellow from Katima Mulilo heard about them and decided to rescue them from certain death.

He offered to take them, but the heartless breeder refused, insisting on killing them – unless, of course, the misguided Samaritan from Katima was prepared to fork out a large amount of money.

The man from Katima paid the ransom and the two cubs were soon ensconced in a cage in the back yard of his home.

The lions grew bigger and soon became quite a handful. The back yard of a house is not the ideal place to keep lions.

Neighbours started to complain that the cubs would soon be able to gobble up their youngsters, some of whom had been scratched by the cubs during boisterous play sessions.

The indigenous people in the vicinity predicted that the two lions would raid their scrawny stock and, perhaps, even their kraals for a bit of human *yama* (meat).

Everyone stared at these innocent looking, but potentially dangerous, lion cubs, not seeing the wild beauty in them but only cattle killers and maneaters on the prowl.

The lions had to go.

The first step was evacuation to the safari company at Lianshulu. The second was to Fort Doppies and into the heart of Special Forces.

At Fort Doppies, the lions were prepared for the third and final step of their journey back to the bush where they belonged.

The bottom line was that the lions had to return to their natural habitat. This meant that they had to be taught to hunt and had to sever all ties with human beings.

Both objectives were difficult to attain. Unlike leopards and other cats, lions rarely hunt alone. They always hunt as a pride, with the lionesses doing most of the killing. They work as a team.

A lion's method of hunting is a highly complicated process of stalking, followed by a short charge and a kill, or it may be a question of the males stampeding the prey from upwind, while the lionesses wait to leeward in ambush.

The cubs are taught the intricacies of these hunting methods by their mothers over a long period of time.

It comes fairly easily to a lioness to teach her cubs to hunt, but it is almost impossible for a human being to assume this vital role of the mother.

How, after all, do you teach a cub to stalk, charge and finally smother the prey to death, or break its neck in the case of larger animals such as buffaloes?

I think lion cubs would roll around laughing if they saw a human being pretending to be a lioness going through all the motions, including the blood-curdling growl preparatory to the charge.

But Dewald had to teach the youngsters how to hunt. Until then, they had eaten frozen meat to titillate their tastebuds, Dewald shot an impala and, for the first time in their lives, the cubs were offered warm, fresh meat with the blood still oozing from the wounds in the buck's sides.

They played around with the entrails after Dewald had slaughtered the buck, but still preferred the frozen meat from the kitchen. It was going to be a long process to wean them from the sophisticated rations of civilisation back to the gory hunks of meat which must be their normal fare in savage Africa.

One of Dewald's men, "Dowe" Grobbelaar, was appointed as keeper of the cubs. All he had to do was follow them around wherever they went to ensure their safety against attacks from other lions and to prevent them from straying too far from the safety of Fort Doppies.

"Dowe" Grobbies followed them everywhere. During the heat of the day, he and the cubs could be found sleeping under a tree for hours. Grobbies had to adopt the habits of the lions, which he did with gusto.

Slowly, the cubs began to adjust. Time moved on and Liza started to become more and more independent. As is the case with most wild animals, she was approaching sexual maturity long before her male sibling. Terry was still happy enough chasing after rugby balls and wrestling with the troops, but Liza began to wander off on her own for considerable periods of time.

Like human beings, each animal has a distinct personality. Terry was the extrovert, supremely happy in the company of people, while Liza barely tolerated anyone near her, except Grobbies and Dewald.

At the age of about 15 months she decided to seek her fortune among her own kind in the immediate vicinity, leaving Terry, the clown, to fool around with his human pals until he, too, heard the call of the wild.

Liza set off one afternoon and did not return, as she usually did after a night out. Terry called her all day long, wandering disconsolately around Dewald's house, but there was no sign or sound of Liza.

Disaster had struck. One of the troops returned later that afternoon from a supply run downriver to report that he had found a badly injured Liza lying under a sickle bush.

Dewald immediately set off to investigate. He found her barely alive, torn to pieces and with her back broken, probably by adult lionesses. She had to be shot. There was no other way.

Dewald backtracked her drag marks and found the place where she had tried to join a pride of eight lions consisting of an oldish male, a young male and six lionesses. Upon her approach the lionesses immediately tore into her, mortally injuring her with the initial attack. Thereafter, her back probably already broken, they played with her as if she was a rag doll.

Poor Liza. Her first introduction to wild Africa proved fatal, a penalty she had to pay after being forced by the unthinking human race to grow up outside the closed community of a family. From the start, she was considered an outsider by the pride she tried to join.

The fact that lions are group animals makes it much more difficult to return domesticated specimens to the wild.

Leopards are solitary animals by nature and this makes reintroducing them much easier. A leopard simply pushes off at the right moment of maturity and will establish his own territory, hopefully without having to fight for it. He normally lives happily ever after and will almost always ignore his former human friends.

Not so with lions. A strange pride will not easily accept a lion trying to join it. The lionesses resent the competition if the new arrival is a female, as do the older males if the new arrival is a cocky young bachelor. Almost invariably, the procedure ends in a bloody scrap, which often turns out to be fatal for the new arrival. Sadly, this was the case with the bewildered young Liza.

Terry settled in much more easily than Liza. He became a favourite with the young troopies and the Special Forces operators, but was less popular with the Bushmen.

Fort Doppies was run by a staff consisting mostly of young national servicemen, a base commander, a platoon of Bushman soldiers who provided local security, and some Bushman labourers who worked in the kitchen and carried out general camp maintenance.

The various reconnaissance regiments would send their operators to Fort Doppies on courses ranging from bushcraft and survival to minor tactics, Sabre operations and demolition. They reported to the base camp, drew rations and equipment and disappeared into the bush for the duration of their training.

As Terry grew older, he had many places all over the bush where he could visit and bask in the warmth of human company.

He started to wander away from the base camp and often pitched up unexpectedly at the temporary base of one or other training group and was always welcomed by the Special Forces operators.

Sometimes, however, the members of a particular group did not know about the lion and their initial contact could become the basis of a comedy act.

When I was still at 44 Parachute Brigade I sent a group of pathfinders to study minor tactics in the Fort Doppies area. The group consisted almost entirely of foreigners from England, Wales, Ireland, Scotland, Germany, Rhodesia, America, France and Belgium. There was even a lone Russian. It never occurred to me to warn them about Terry.

The instructor who went with them was a South African who had served in the Rhodesian army. They established a comfortable little training base some distance from Fort Doppies and set about their business.

The instructor, as demanded by his status, had a small patrol tent and a proper stretcher to sleep on, while the students were uncomfortably ensconced in their shell scrapes or slit trenches.

Terry, by this time about two years old, no doubt caught a sniff of this new base in his wanderings through the bush and decided to pay the occupants a neighbourly visit.

The pathfinders and the instructor were going about their business in the base when a huge lion suddenly materialised from the depths of the forest around them and calmly strolled into their midst.

Fortunately, they had been briefed that under no circumstances were they to shoot at any animals, including lions, that they encountered.

As one man they took to the trees, while a disappointed Terry looked on. Just wanting some human company to pass the time of the day, he decided to explore the layout of the base, sniffing at the equipment scattered about as the owners watched anxiously from their perches in the trees encircling the camp.

Most of the pathfinders had never seen a lion outside a zoo or a circus before. But they had heard plenty of stories about the ferocious lions of Africa and perhaps some were already pinning the sinister label of man-eater on the magnificent animal below.

Terry gnawed a parachute helmet for a while then decided to retire for a nap. The most inviting spot was the instructor's tent, so the lion duly entered and clambered on the inviting stretcher with its sleeping bag comfortably spread out on top.

The stretcher immediately collapsed under Terry's weight, but unperturbed, he went to sleep quite happily in his new surroundings.

Up in the trees the pathfinders took stock of their situation. The lion had taken over the base and they were stranded uncomfortably in the trees. When the beast would depart was anybody's guess since he seemed to have settled in for the day and the men were unable to retrieve their equipment or carry on with their daily training.

As they discussed the problem among themselves, it slowly dawned on the group of foreigners that this was quite an unusual lion. One or two had heard stories about a tame lion at Fort Doppies, some kilometres away, and they eventually arrived at the tentative deduction that the lion meant them no harm.

They decided to take a chance and gingerly climbed down from the trees to the camp below. Terry, too lazy to move from under the canopy of his tent, took no action apart from watching with interest as the pathfinders sorted out their gear. The instructor made no attempt to reclaim his tent and stretcher. Terry was welcome to both and could stay as long as he liked.

The pathfinders gradually gained more confidence, eventually deciding it would be in order to prepare their first meal of the day, a braai.

The truck with their rations and other heavy equipment on board was parked next to the camp and the necessary equipment was offloaded, a fire laid and lit. Soon the coals were ready and the cook for the day spread the steaks out on the grill, where they began to sizzle away merrily.

Terry, of course, caught the delicious aroma of meat being grilled from where he was still reclining, like a king, on the instructor's stretcher. He rose languidly, poked his huge head out of the small patrol tent and zeroed in on the steaks sizzling away on the grill.

The pathfinders were also eyeing the steaks with keen anticipation as Terry calmly strolled over and plucked a juicy steak from the grill, while the cook watched in dismay. He did not dare to remonstrate with the gigantic animal, and one by one, the steaks disappeared down Terry's throat until he had scoffed the lot.

About 20 pathfinders watched every piece of meat vanish, their stomachs rumbling in protest. Terry thought his newfound friends most considerate and decided to extend his stay.

With empty bellies, the pathfinders endured a full day's training, while the cook tried to find a way to sidestep the raging appetite of the unexpected guest. Finally, he found an empty drum, which he placed on the back of the truck, once again lighting a fire while Terry lay some distance away watching with keen interest the activities of the cook.

Terry always did have a great fondness for army cooks.

Once again the coals were ready and the meat was produced. With an effortless leap, Terry launched himself into the back of the truck, and with the cook watching helplessly, started to wolf down the fresh batch of steaks, depriving the pathfinders of their supper as well.

Soon after dark Terry strolled off into the bush on his own secret errands while a hungry bunch of pathfinders contemplated their misfortune. They were literally starving in the midst of plenty.

Rations were issued on a daily basis so they would have to wait until the next day to still their hunger pangs. However, it seemed the lion had gone, so the cook decided to take out some meat to marinade overnight for their first meal the next morning.

Early the next day, while still in the process of preparing the coals, Terry reappeared to spend another day in camp with his new friends. Before they could snatch away the bowl of marinated meat Terry was already at it, investigating his "breakfast".

This time, however, he turned away in disgust. Marinated meat was not to his liking and the pathfinders had found a way to keep him from their rations.

He stayed for almost a week before deciding to move on. He became very friendly with all these strangers to Africa and the instructor obligingly made arrangements with Fort Doppies to get meat for Terry so that he would not go hungry.

Rubbing elbows with a wild lion left an indelible impression on the Europeans and Americans in the company. From almost the moment of their introduction to the savage African bush, they had been privileged to meet and befriend the king of the savannah in a most unusual manner. Afterwards, they looked at the wildlife around them with a lot more comprehension and, in the end, a great deal of affection.

For a king, Terry had a decidedly non-regal demeanour. He was completely at ease among the human race, though he loved to terrorise the Bushmen, and was quite at home with the residents of Fort Doppies. He never lost his temper, growled in anger or deliberately hurt them in any way, which is amazing, since he was a very big animal with massive paws, a frightening array of claws and a set of teeth and fangs that could frighten the hell out of anyone.

But he never extended his claws when roughhousing his human playmates and he never used his fangs for anything other than holding someone or something, like a rugby ball, in a firm grip as he played.

One of his greatest joys was to play rugby with the troops in the late afternoons, when it was cool enough for him to exert himself. The troops used to kick a ball around in an *omuramba* just south of Fort Doppies, near the chopper pad, to get rid of their excess energy.

However, Terry had the distressing habit of cutting rugby practice short. As soon as the ball was kicked he would chase after it, a string of troops in hot pursuit, hoping to get to the ball before Terry could sink his fangs into it.

Sooner or later Terry always succeeded in beating the troops. He would clamp his steel jaws around the ball and set off with all the troops chasing him. This always ended with lion and troops in a tangled heap, engaged in a frantic wrestling match in the middle of a dust cloud, with the troops desperately trying to wrench the punctured ball from Terry's jaws.

If they succeeded in retrieving the ball, it was usually found to be useless for further kicking until repairs had been effected.

Dewald had a lovely family, consisting of Dorothy, his wife, and three small daughters plus a cat or two. They lived in Katima Mulilo but often came out to share Dewald's bush house, especially over weekends and during school holidays.

The girls were young, one in junior school, the middle one just at preschool age and the youngest still a toddler.

Like trusting small children everywhere, they had no fear of a lion even after it became a fully grown adult. Terry would lie down on the lawn in front of the house, staring speculatively across the hippo pool at the lechwes on the island beyond. The girls played around him and over him, scrambled onto his muscular back, dug their fingers into his mane and sometimes went to sleep against his powerful flank.

Terry endured all of this with utmost tolerance. He never snarled or even played roughly with them. It was as if he instinctively understood the relative frailty of the little girls, and was gentle with them.

Dorothy (or Dot as she was known) had a sister who lived in Pretoria, but visited from time to time. She got quite a fright the first time she saw the children swarming all over a wild, adult lion. Being unmarried, she was extremely fond of Dot's offspring and visualised the three little blonde girls ending up as dainty snacks inside Terry's stomach. She insisted that Dewald had to shoot the animal because sooner or later, but inevitably nonetheless, the lion was going to take one of his daughters for a meal.

Terry did have his little snack in the end but it wasn't one of Dewald's daughters, only their beloved kitten.

One of the little girls had dressed her kitten in a tiny knitted dress and bonnet which Dot had made. Terry was lying on the lawn taking an afternoon nap when the little girl snuggled up to his flank, cuddling the well-dressed kitten.

She was stroking her pet when Terry suddenly awoke from his slumbers. He yawned, looked over his shoulder and saw a beautifully dressed snack in the hands of the little girl. He opened his huge jaws and snatched the kitten from the surprised child's hands and swallowed the kitten, knitted dress, bonnet and all.

The little girl burst into tears and belaboured Terry's flanks with her small fists. Terry, of course, took no notice and promptly dropped back into his somnolent posture.

Dot was upset, but Dewald thought it all a huge joke. The little girl was inconsolable, but the incident did not put her off Terry.

Only once did Terry actually bite someone deliberately, though not with malice. He had got one of his claws stuck into somebody by accident before, but had never used his armoury in a deliberate attempt to grab a troop. One day, however, Terry was passing the time down at the horseshoe lagoon with some operators who were on a survival course. They had decided to go swimming and Terry went with them. He loved swimming with the troops.

One of the operators thought he'd take a closer look at the underwater flora and fauna, and was floating face down in the water, not far from the river bank, where Terry sat watching the proceedings with great interest.

In that part of the world swimming costumes are not necessary, so Terry could see the white buttocks of one of his human pals turned skyward. This mate of his was floating motionless in the water, face down and therefore obviously in distress.

Terry decided to go to the rescue.

He waded into the water and sank his formidable fangs into

one soft buttock and started to pull the screaming operator ashore, where he released him, task accomplished.

It is, of course, incredibly painful to be bitten by a fully grown lion. It can also be rather messy. There was blood all over the place and the operator was taken to the sick bay at Fort Doppies to be stitched up by the resident doctor.

The operator was quite understanding about the whole episode and attached no blame to Terry. Nevertheless, the story spread that a soldier had been attacked by Terry. The lion, according to the deduction of some, was obviously getting out of hand, reverting to his savage inbred habits.

Soon, 1 Reconnaissance Regiment's commander and Special Forces Headquarters insisted that Terry had to be shot. He was posing an unacceptable danger to the troops and sooner or later, someone in authority would be called to account by an irate parent whose son had been killed or maimed by a savage beast kept within the confines of a military establishment.

A battle of wits ensued between the Special Forces hierarchy on one side and Dewald de Beer, the operators and the national servicemen on the other. The outcome eventually determined the fate of Terry, for better or for worse.

The first attempt to get rid of the ferocious lion was an expedition mounted by a would-be big-game hunter, fresh from his plush armchair in Pretoria. This man, who shall remain nameless, was not a Special Forces operator, but armed with one of his big-game rifles, he winged his way northwards to shoot Terry, presumably in comfort and style within the gentle surroundings of the Fort Doppies base camp.

However, he had to inform Dewald of his movements, since the intrepid hunter had to be fetched from the nearest airport.

Dewald immediately detailed Grobbies to take Terry for an extended holiday in the Caprivi bush and they disappeared towards the Botswana cutline.

When the hunter appeared, salivating at the prospect of a lion in his sights, he found that Terry had inexplicably absconded the day before his arrival.

The Bushmen were despatched to find his spoor but, on strict orders from Dewald, not a sign could be picked up, except that Terry had moved south into Botswana.

No one, not even the hunter, was allowed to cross into Botswana, so he sat at Fort Doppies, consuming beer to hide his irritation and waited for Terry to return.

Meanwhile, Terry and Grobbies had a great time wandering through the bush, living off what Grobbies shot and, at times, what Terry had begun to catch for himself. They stalked game together, slept together and fed together from the same carcass.

The two were perfectly happy in each other's company. Every day, Grobbies reported back to Dewald to give him a position report, a "locstat" in army slang. Dewald, in turn, reported back to Grobbies on the situation regarding the hunter.

After two weeks, the hunter's patience finally ran out, and he flew back to Pretoria, extremely disgruntled.

He was scarcely gone when Terry and Grobbies strolled back into the base to the delight of the men, the Bushmen excepted. The Bushmen could never really understand the white man's insistence on making wild animals, particularly dangerous ones such as lions, part of their family.

Several more attempts were launched to shoot Terry, but they were thwarted every time by the men at Fort Doppies. Finally, it sank in at headquarters that the Doppies men would never cooperate in having Terry taken out of circulation permanently, so a compromise was suggested: Terry would be presented to a zoo.

Dewald immediately objected. Terry had never been restricted. To have him confined in a small enclosure or a steel-barred cage would be worse than having him shot. He stated unequivocally that he would never cooperate in having Terry transported to a zoo.

It was then arranged that Terry would be flown to the estate of a well-known circus, somewhere in Natal, where he could while away his remaining days watching other lions and lionesses being bred and trained for a life in the sawdust ring.

This was an almost equally obnoxious proposition, although he would, at least, have some space in which to wander around. But Terry was a bush animal, a king of the savannah, already in his own way in contact with some wild members of his own species. He would not fit in with a bunch of lions in civilised, rural surroundings.

Nevertheless, preparations were made. A robust cage was obtained, the necessary drugs were prepared and a Dakota once again winged its way northwards to take a comatose lion back to its new home in Natal.

This time Terry, already two years old, decided to go walk about on his own. When the Dakota landed at Immelman airstrip, Dewald could say, with his hand on his heart, that Terry had taken to the bush, hopefully for good.

The lion "capture team" stayed for a few days and then departed without having seen their quarry.

Terry, meanwhile, was having his own problems. He had picked a tremendous fight with the leader of a pride when he tried to gate-crash this fellow's particular domain. Being still a youngster he was soundly licked by the wily old-timer.

Terry slunk into the small hide, on the Botswana cutline, of Captain Didis (Diederichs) and his sidekick. They were preparing for a deep penetration operation into Angola but Terry, badly mauled, felt very sorry for himself and needed all the comfort and sympathy his human friends could give him.

He stayed with his two companions for several weeks, waiting for his wounds to heal under the expert supervision of Didis. Didis copiously applied the necessary ointments, disinfectants and antibiotics and, from time to time, also provided excellent sustenance for a voracious young lion in the shape of a buck or two.

Soon Terry was back on his feet and as good as new. He left Didis and his buddy and strolled back to Fort Doppies – for the moment putting an early return to the African bush out of his thoughts.

Meanwhile, Dewald had been pondering the lion problem. There was no doubt in his mind that sooner or later Terry would be shot. A plan had to be made to keep Terry out of the Fort Doppies base camp.

Dewald mustered as many Bushmen as he could find, armed them with saucepans, dustbin lids, sticks, drums and anything else with which to make a racket. The idea was to drive Terry out of the base with shouting and screeching, accompanied with a cacophony of percussion sounds which no self-respecting lion would tolerate.

Terry always announced his imminent arrival at Fort Doppies from some distance away with a series of roars. This was the signal for the Bushman choir and their steel band to turn out for the confrontation.

The first time, they met Terry just outside the base. The terrific din sent him scampering for cover in the bush growling in fright.

He soon returned for a second and third attempt, only to run into an impenetrable wall of noise.

The strategy seemed to work, but Dewald still felt uncomfortable about Terry's welfare. He was not sure how he would cope hunting on his own.

So Dewald shot a duiker or steenbuck from time to time to feed Terry, luring him away from the base camp by dropping the kill as far away as possible.

One day, when duty prevented Dewald from going into the bush to look for Terry and give him his dinner, two national servicemen played waiter to the lion and set off in the Land Rover up the nearest *omuramba* with careful instructions about where Terry could be found.

The national servicemen drove along, stopping from time to time to call for Terry as they proceeded up the *omuramba*.

There was no sign of Terry anywhere near the base, but after much searching and calling, they finally spotted him lying under a tree against a slight incline. They stopped the Land Rover and one of them hoisted the freshly killed steenbuck on his shoulders and they approached the lion lying blissfully at ease in the heat of the day, in the ample shade cast by the tree.

They dropped his lunch at his feet. The lion looked at the

two national servicemen with every sign of boredom, sniffed at the carcass and started to eat.

The two drove back to Fort Doppies, satisfied that Terry had been fed.

Several kilometres on, and not far from the base, they pulled up suddenly. The real Terry was blocking the road. He had been eagerly awaiting their appearance, and his meal.

Terry finally got the better of the Bushmen. Once again he announced his approach with a roar and once again the Bushmen mustered to drive him off.

However, they had become overconfident at Terry's obvious fright every time he came face to face with them and only two Bushmen turned out for the confrontation, the rest lolling about in the vicinity of the kitchen.

Terry was met by Langman (the old tracker) and Tokoloshe (the inveterate poacher), each armed with a saucepan lid and a stick.

For a while, Terry stared at his puny reception committee and then he let out a blood-curdling growl. The men dropped their saucepan lids and sticks and bolted as fast as their old legs could carry them, a snarling and angry lion close on their heels.

They saw the golden blur of the king of the bush rapidly descending upon them in full fury, his frightful fangs exposed and snarls and growls reverberating through the peaceful Fort Doppies base.

They scampered for the roof of the kitchen, jabbering and squealing like a troop of monkeys.

Terry jumped for the roof, sending shivers of fear through the Bushmen with his snarls, his fearfully extended claws gouging deep scars in the walls of the kitchen roof.

It was a show of force to intimidate the Bushmen. For a while Terry strutted around the building, each approach initiating a fresh torrent of squeals and jabberings from the men huddled on one side of the kitchen.

Finally, he walked away and stretched himself out on the lawn in the shade of a tree, confident that he would once again be master of Fort Doppies.

From time to time a Bushman tried to sneak down from the roof, only to be promptly chased back by a snarling, charging animal.

Only after Dewald took Terry away to be fed did they venture down from the rooftop.

From then on it became routine for Terry to chase the Bushmen onto the kitchen roof every time he returned from the bush. He no longer paid any head to the drums, sticks, lids and other noisy paraphernalia the Bushmen used to keep him at bay.

He never physically harmed any of them, however. To him, the psychological warfare he was waging was quite sufficient.

Dewald decided to make another attempt to get Terry out of the base and out of the area. He began to look for a distant place where the lion could be released without any possibility of returning to his human friends at Fort Doppies.

A place was found on an island roughly 100 kilometres south, deep inside the Linyanti swamps.

Two adjacent islands provided a remote refuge for large numbers of lechwe, buffalo, warthogs, baboons, some lions and other game species. Here, Terry would be isolated from both friend and foe, with plenty of water as a natural barrier and a well-stocked larder at his disposal. There were also other lions with whom, it was hoped, he could come to an amicable agreement about who would be the boss around the place.

Terry had killed one of Peter Quando's cattle on the east bank of the Cuando River. Peter Quando was highly upset, but it was his own fault. His herdsmen chased his cattle into the western Caprivi, across the bridge, in spite of the fact that domestic animals were not allowed west of the river. Dewald shot some of these cattle and Terry happily feasted off the unexpected succulent beef steaks. Unfortunately, it gave him a sweet tooth for cattle, and later on, he made his way across the river to get his fangs into some more of Peter Quando's beef burgers. Cattle were much easier to catch than buffaloes. Terry was on his way to becoming a problem animal.

Manie Grobler, the local biologist from Nature Conservation, agreed to assist in Terry's relocation. A helicopter was laid on and the necessary drugs were procured for the translocation of a large carnivorous animal from one part of the African savannah to another. In other words, they were going to deal with Terry in the prescribed and preferred method designed by Nature Conservation for dealing with problem animals.

Terry was injected with the drug and was loaded into the helicopter. They set off for Nkasa and Lupala islands in the middle of the Linyanti swamps. Dewald went with them to stay with Terry during his period of recovery and adjustment.

The lion was completely unconscious when they landed on Nkasa, and it was with great difficulty that they managed to get him out of the chopper. The helicopter then took off, leaving Dewald alone with his sleeping lion in one of the remotest spots in the whole of Africa.

Dewald made himself at home next to the sleeping Terry, his rifle at the ready to keep other lions away from the helpless newcomer in their domain.

The Nkasa lions stayed away that night. By the next morning, Terry was on his feet and he and Dewald began to explore the island. Later in the day when Dewald was certain that the drug had worn off he called in the helicopter to come and pick him up.

He left Terry with a freshly shot buck to start his new way of life, far away from his Fort Doppies pals.

Dewald left heavy-hearted and fully expecting never to see Terry again. He had made his final farewell to an unusual but true friend.

Two weeks later, a puzzled Dewald heard Terry's distinct and unmistakeable roar during the night, drawing closer from the south. He felt certain that Terry would clock into Fort Doppies early the next morning.

He was right. Out of the bush strolled Terry, majestic king of the bush and all the territory around him, announcing to the great delight of the troops and the utter dismay of the Bushmen, that he had returned to what he considered his real home. His first task was to chase the Bushmen on to the roof.

Then he was taken to the hot showers by the troops and happily stood under the jets of warm water splashing all over his body while the troops carefully shampooed and washed his coat and luxuriant mane.

The shower became a ritual, a treat eagerly awaited by Terry whenever he emerged from the bush. Like any wild lion, the results of his hunting habits and lack of fussiness over the state of the meat he ate left him smelling less than pleasant.

One wonders what the lionesses thought of Terry's morals when he returned from each visit to Fort Doppies smelling as sweet as a rose ...

Terry had now proved incontrovertibly that there was no solution to his particular problem. He just could not be weaned from the company of men in man's own time. He, not man, was going to decide when the time was ripe for him to break his ties with homo sapiens.

The mystery of his return from Nkasa island remains to this day. He left Fort Doppies in a deep coma, to be dumped, still in a stupor, in a remote spot at least a 100 kilometres south of Fort Doppies. Dewald left him there tucking into a freshly shot buck.

To get back to Doppies he had first to figure out what direction to follow. Then he had to swim across the various streams of the Linyanti swamps in a westerly direction, in order to reach dry land on the west bank inside Botswana. From there he had to make his way northwards, through several hunting concessions, thus taking his chance against the hunting rifles of a number of safaris.

Given his friendliness towards human beings it was indeed a stroke of luck that he did not stroll into a safari camp. He could have ended up as a stuffed head on the wall of a trophy room in some American, German or Italian home.

How did he know where Fort Doppies was? That remains the question no one can answer but, after his amazing return, Dewald gave up trying to coax Terry back into the bush. He was allowed to come and go as he pleased.

As the months passed, Terry grew in magnificence until he was the biggest lion most people had ever seen.

In spite of his size he remained, as always, a jovial fellow, except to the Bushmen, of course. He became well known throughout the army. Articles appeared about him in the national newspapers, but none of it went to his head. On the other hand, perhaps it did, considering his distinct lack of respect for the leaders of the land.

It was the custom of the South African cabinet, under the leadership of then prime minister P.W. Botha, to retreat into one of the remotest areas of southern Africa, for a week or so, for so-called "team-building" sessions. Later, this process became known as a *bosberaad* or bush conference.

Places such as Fort Doppies and Buffalo where 32 Battalion was based, became attractive venues for civil servants entrusted with organising a team-building exercise for South Africa's political and military leaders.

Fort Doppies inevitably became the prime location. It had strict security, was virtually inaccessible to outsiders, intimately close to an abundance of game, located on the banks of perhaps the most scenic river and swamp system in Africa and yet had excellent radio communication with the outside world.

More than once the Fort Doppies personnel had the presence of almost the entire cabinet inflicted on them. This meant the staff had to scurry around to provide the civilised amenities the visitors were accustomed to in order to soften the harshness of a primitive African savannah environment.

There had to be a selection of the best whiskies, wines and brandies. Only prime steaks and the best cuts of meat were allowed. Accommodation had to be comfortable and at least warm enough to keep at bay the cold winter nights which are a feature of the Caprivian winters. Suitable vehicles had to be provided for game viewing and boats had to be laid on for excursions on the river and swamps.

Fort Doppies was, in fact, turned into a five-star safari camp during these visits.

It was almost inevitable that one of these visits would coincide with one of Terry's visits to the Fort Doppies area. What made such a visit potentially more interesting was that Terry, at the time, was in the process of shedding his loyalty to his human buddies in favour of a more satisfying relationship with the lionesses in the vicinity. He had, in fact, become the dominant male of a pride of about 20 animals, including a few males, a nice harem of lionesses and a nursery of small cubs, all of them Terry's offspring.

He was not "at home" at Doppies to meet the cabinet, including the prime minister, but he continued to pay unexpected visits. Usually he would leave his pride on the outskirts of the base while he came in to say "hello" to the chaps.

The cabinet knew about the lion from a previous visit, but Terry was still a cub then, and no threat to anyone, just extremely – and occasionally painfully – playful.

The cabinet members settled in for their stay on this particular visit by kicking off with a party in the mess, then turned in after a long day's travelling.

The next morning, the late Louis le Grange, the most distinguished-looking of the ministers, a tall, straight and handsome fellow, decided to start the day, as men often do, with a visit to the latrine.

The latrines at that time consisted of so-called long drops. A deep hole was dug into the ground on top of which was placed a plastic toilet seat. We used to call these toilet seats "go-karts" because of their shape. Around the hole, with its go-kart, a hessian screen was erected to afford some privacy, but hessian is translucent, so that anyone squatting on the go-kart is clearly silhouetted to the outside world.

Terry had the uncomfortable habit, like all lions, of stalking and pouncing on anyone seated with his back towards him.

As luck would have it, Terry had brought his pride into the vicinity of Fort Doppies early that morning and decided it would be in order to drop in on his pals for a bit of a chat, a quarter of beef and the usual shower and shampoo. He was about three years old by then, fully grown and the most powerful lion in the western Caprivi.

He approached Fort Doppies from the toilet end and soon had the hessian screens in sight.

The honourable minister of police was squatting on his go-kart, his trousers around his ankles, listening to the enchanting chorus of the myriad of birds perched in the luxuriant vegetation bidding welcome to another beautiful Caprivi day.

When Terry saw the silhouette etched on the hessian screen, he came to a stop, stalked up to the screen, carefully crawled under it and pounced on the unsuspecting minister's back with a ferocious growl.

Le Grange found himself in the clutches of a 200-kilogram lion, with huge paws on his shoulders while sharp fangs prepared to attack his scalp.

He screamed and somehow found the strength to forcefully shrug off the attentions of the ferocious monster. With his trousers in one hand, the honourable minister flattened the screen on the other side in his haste to get out of the latrine. He legged it for his room with Terry in gleeful hot pursuit, his gaping jaws snapping at the minister's bare buttocks.

Dewald and his men came to the rescue and after a while the commotion died down and the ragging started. Le Grange took it all in good spirit once the fright had worn off and even made friends with Terry who had settled in for the day.

Towards afternoon, Terry disappeared and everyone relaxed. Although he was quite harmless, the sheer size of the animal tended to make people feel uncomfortable.

After the day's team building, the cabinet adjourned to the pub, playing darts, fooling around and generally behaving like schoolboys away from mother while supper was being prepared on the barbecue outside.

Excellent food and wine followed and afterwards the ministers returned to the pub to carry on drinking. The winter night was beginning to bite a little, and Dr Dawie de Villiers, who never was a partying man, decided to turn in for the night.

He had a hot shower and slid in under the thick blankets topping the envelope of cold, crisp sheets, to luxuriate in the warmth building up in the enclosed space. However, he had left the door open.

Terry decided to investigate the source of all the noise emanating from the pub and possibly reconnoitre a suitable place to doss down for the night. He was not averse to making full use of human luxury when it was available, so it was never wise to leave one's door open when Terry was around because he had a tendency to take over the sleeping arrangements.

De Villiers, a former Springbok rugby captain whose cabinet portfolios included trade and industry as well as environmental affairs, was at peace with the world in his darkened room, out like a light after a long day, when the huge shape of Terry materialised in his doorway.

Softly, Terry padded to where the sleeping minister was stretched out on his back under the warm blankets, clambered on board the sturdy army cot and collapsed on top of De Villiers with all his weight. As a friendly gesture, the lion decided to bestow on the minister a sloppy and rasping lick with his rough tongue.

De Villiers woke with a start, pinned down by a fully grown lion belabouring his face and hair with rough, wet licks.

He screamed at the top of his voice, but the party was in full swing, and no one came to his rescue.

Once again, fear injected incredible strength. With a display of muscle power not entirely unexpected in a superb athlete, he managed to extricate himself from the bed and heaved himself onto the metal wardrobe, where he sat for the rest of the cold winter's night shivering in his pyjamas.

Terry, meanwhile, snuggled down in the warm blankets on the vacated bed and peacefully went to sleep.

Of course another campaign to get rid of Terry was launched. He could, after all, have killed two cabinet ministers in a row with "dire consequences for the country's leadership and future". Once more there was talk of shooting him, since all other measures to remove him had clearly failed.

Fortunately, nature was taking its course and Terry became a less frequent visitor to Fort Doppies.

Dewald helped to defuse the situation by clamping strict censorship on Terry's movements. Operators and national service men were barred from talking about the lion or writing home about his exploits. Dewald also kept Terry under control by detailing one of his men to accompany him and his pride on a full-time basis.

The caretaker did not, of course, move in the pride himself, because that would have been suicidal. However, he had a close enough relationship with Terry who often preferred his keeper's company to that of his harem.

The next step was to spread the rumour that Dewald had reluctantly been forced to shoot Terry. This story went around Katima Mulilo for quite a while, and even I was taken in at first. I was disgusted with Dewald when I heard that he had thrown in the towel.

As time went on, Terry and his pride moved closer to the Botswana cutline, and soon began to move back and forth across the border without the caretaker being able to accompany him into a foreign country.

Lions, of course, do not need passports.

Finally, Terry kept his pride permanently on the Botswana side of the border and he was never again seen at Fort Doppies, not even in the training area. A most incredible chapter in the history of Fort Doppies and Special Forces had come to a close.

Many people's lives had been profoundly enriched by their close and friendly relationship with the king of the bush. There had never before been such a lion as Terry and there probably never will be again.

Whatever his ultimate destiny, it was best for Terry to spend his adult years back in the African bush, the undisputed leader of a pride, in firm control of his own territory: a supreme, majestic ruler, happily ensuring that his genes would live on in his numerous offspring.

EIGHT

The Guerrilla School

Terry's saga was drawing to its final conclusion when I began another period of intimate association with the Caprivi bush.

Gradually, my various training bases took shape and students from far and wide came to be initiated into the secrets of guerrilla warfare and related subjects.

Accommodation for the students was deliberately basic. A group earmarked for guerrilla training would move into the depths of the forest, removed from any luxuries or the slightest whiff of civilisation and told to establish a temporary base. This formed the central point of all their instruction for the next few months. From there they radiated out to undergo training in guerrilla tactics, bushcraft, survival, navigation, weapons, demolition, signals and other subjects.

Every night they returned to their base to have a meal, prepare for night training and, afterwards, rest in the few hours left to them before "stand to" at first light.

The animals of the bush wandered all around them, grazing and browsing, hunting, fighting, mating, digging, growling, squealing and generally going about the business of eating, survival and reproduction without taking too much notice of the men in their midst.

Heaven help anyone rash enough to interfere in any way whatsoever with the basic flow of life in this last outpost of primeval Africa. Punishment was both swift and severe.

This led to some unusual relationships and often comical confrontations between man and beast. We took in a group of black soldiers who, strangely enough, had never before been face to face with any of the citizens of the African savannah.

They arrived late one night by aircraft at our isolated airstrip and were taken over indistinct bush tracks into their own remote little corner of the training area.

It was dark and quiet all around when they were dumped unceremoniously and ordered to make themselves comfortable in a circular defensive perimeter for the night.

Fearfully, they stared at the black shapes of huge trees surrounding the area, not a single distant light in sight to indicate some comforting pinprick of civilisation. They started digging shell scrapes in complete silence, hardly daring to breathe.

Suddenly the silence was shattered by the angry trumpeting of an elephant close by. The recruits had no idea what it was, but they started digging faster and deeper.

The cracking of breaking branches could be heard as something huge moved through the forest. The almost continuous growling and snorts, punctuated by an irritated trumpeting from time to time, left no doubt in their minds that, whatever it was, it was much bigger than they were and also very angry.

The elephants moved off towards the river in the east and silence fell once more. The troops tried to go to sleep in their trenches. For a while all was peaceful and then they heard it: the unmistakeable roar of a lion.

I have always liked the way George Adamson described the roar of the king of the beasts:

"Who is the king of the bush? Who is the king of the bush? Who is the king of the bush?"

"I am! I am! I am! I am!"

The roar was drawing closer to the base and the troops began to sit up, trying to penetrate the deep darkness of the trees with fearful eyes.

Eventually, the roar could be heard just outside the base. They could hear the lion grunting as it moved around the periphery of the base before settling down to the north, from where it kept up its roaring throughout the night.

From time to time, another lion answered from the south, distant, but close enough to aggravate the fit of jitters among the young black soldiers.

They could not sleep. They squatted in their trenches, eyes watering with fatigue as they peered into the dark, sweaty hands grasping their rifles.

The instructors had made themselves comfortable in the middle of the base. Unperturbed by the nocturnal racket, they were sound asleep.

The returning elephants passed by with the customary breaking of branches, crashing of trees, trumpeting and general mayhem. Hyenas whooped it up as they trotted down the nearby *omuramba*. The lion and his mate roared to keep in touch with each other.

Finally, the first grey light of dawn appeared in the east. From the river the recruits could hear hadedas in early-morning cry. At least that was a familiar sound that they had heard before.

Gradually, the night retreated from the lip of their trenches to five, then ten and finally about twenty paces away. For the first time, the nearest soldiers could make out the indistinct silhouette of something lying in the short grass, its regal head erect, the unmistakeable fringe of a mane confirming its identity as a male of the species *Panthera leo*, an animal of vast reputation and the source of many stories, fables and superstitions among Africans through the centuries.

As he roared from deep inside his chest to greet the new day, the recruits could see the king in all his majesty, his yellow eyes staring unflinchingly as the receding darkness trailed its grey skirts through the distant trees.

The lion yawned, his huge fangs gleaming in the dawn light, and then looked at the frightened troops cowering in their trenches with careless disdain.

With a supreme show of indifference the lion rose to his feet, gave a final full-throated roar to his mate in the south, then strolled off without as much as a backward glance at the thoroughly cowed human specimens he was leaving behind in their miserable, temporary base.

This particular lion was second only to Terry in size. He ruled a territory north of the Golden Highway stretching some distance into Angola. Terry's territory was south of the Golden Highway, towards Botswana.

This was an old lion, comparatively speaking, his body dark grey with age, his mane showing touches of black.

I met this lion unexpectedly a few times while strolling through the bush or along the river.

One day I was walking along the edge of the swamp, rifle slung carelessly over my shoulder, with a perpendicular earth bank about a pace away to my right, when a ferocious growl just above my head brought me to a dead stop.

I looked up into the yellow, flashing eyes of a lion only about two metres above, crouched menacingly on the bank. My reflexes took over and I scampered back around the nearest corner, desperately trying to unsling my rifle.

About 20 paces away I came to a standstill, heart throbbing like the base drum in a military band. Carefully, I scrambled up the vertical bank. I had to get the lion within my sight to prevent him stalking me along the top of the bank. I was just in time to see him disappearing among some sickle bush as he hurried away from the river. Evidently, his fright was just as big as mine.

He had probably been dozing in the shade of the trees when I came blundering along, unannounced, around the corner.

I shall never forget that growl. It froze me in my tracks as effectively as a bullet would have stopped me in battle.

About a week later, I went for another walk, this time into the bush away from the river. Once again I bumped into this fellow, this time lying at the base of an ant hill about 15 paces away. With an angry growl he rushed off while I stood there, slack-jawed, gaping at him, astonished by his impressive size, which I saw fully exposed for the first time.

We were becoming acquainted with each other on at least a nodding basis when I met him for a third time, out on the flood plain as he moved with flowing grace through the tall grass.

This time I was in my Land Cruiser so, with a show of bravado, I stopped my vehicle right next to him. He looked me right in the eyes, his fierce yellow orbs drilling through me and,

I swear, with disgust written all over his face. Slowly he sank down on his stomach, tail twitching, then looked away from me into the distance, his whole attitude showing imperious disapproval at my rude intrusion, lack of manners and crass stupidity.

I looked to my left and saw a small herd of majestic sables, their heads turned towards me, not more than 30 paces away. The lion had been stalking them when I blundered upon the scene in my noisy and foul-smelling vehicle.

I have been put in my place before by my superiors, but never as effectively as this. I felt like jumping out and going on my knees to beg his majesty's forgiveness, but thought better of it. The king would no doubt mete out suitable and much more painful punishment than I had bargained for.

So, red in the face with embarrassment, I drove off, mumbling my apologies to the stiff, unforgiving back of the king. The sables cantered off to the east, towards the river.

I saw that lion a few times more, sometimes with a female and sometimes with his whole pride. He and I also had a difference of opinion at a later date when I tried to introduce two young males into his territory. More of that in due course.

The lion was not shy of human beings, but he treated us with supreme indifference. I think he tried to intimidate us on purpose.

One of my officers was sleeping in his tent on a hot summer's night in one of the training bases on the banks of the river.

The tent was three metres by three metres with canvas sides that could be partially rolled down to allow fresh air to circulate through the dank interior.

The young officer, recently promoted to lieutenant, was dead to the world, in a dream world no doubt populated by luscious young girls, when he was awakened by a tremendous roar in his left ear, from the other side of the thin canvas wall.

Fearfully, he lifted his head to peer out into the dark. The moon was shining brightly and he found himself staring at point-blank range at the mighty flank of the old lion himself.

164

His majesty, of course, was fully aware of the presence of the mere mortal almost touching him, but ignored him completely as he stared across the eastern flood plain in the direction of a distant island. Then he roared again, sending a nocturnal royal communication to the Cuando swamps.

The lieutenant carefully slid off his army bed and crept to the open doorway of the tent. Carefully, he did up the canvas cover and then proceeded to pull an empty bed across the entrance to keep the lion out. It was just a gesture, just something to do because he could not think of anything else.

The lion, of course, had no intention of wasting his time on a puny man.

For a while, the lion's roars continued, reverberating over the camp and the vastness of the swamps. The lieutenant crouched in the furthest corner of the tent and listened apprehensively.

After a while, the roars stopped and silence descended over the camp once more. Cautiously, the lieutenant lifted his head above the top of the canvas wall.

The king had vanished without a sound.

The next morning, the lieutenant and the other instructors examined the huge pawprints in the sand, about a metre away from the lieutenant's bed. The gigantic spoor was the only evidence of the lion's visit and there was a distinctive and noble lineage of royalty captured in those impressive marks in the sand.

And so there were the two leonine extremes. Terry ruled in the south, a friendly, warm fellow, a jovial companion completely at ease with his human comrades. The lion of the north was never given a proper name and treated us disdainfully, with an utter disregard for our human pride, and it somehow reduced us to our proper size.

The elephants were another experience altogether. They wandered wherever their fancy took them and we could not stop them from roaming through the camps, browsing or grazing as they went. Not that we really wanted to stop them, but it was somewhat disconcerting for the more civilised among us to be having afternoon tea on the lawn while a huge bull placidly pulled up prized garden plants, almost within arm's length, and scoffed them with a great show of savouring the unusual flavours with contemplative appreciation.

My main base was called Fort St Michél and this was where officers, instructors and administrative personnel had their very comfortable quarters. Proper houses were eventually built for the married men and they were well furnished and fitted with hot and cold running water, gas or electric stoves and every other facility that could make a stay in the depths of the bush, 200 kilometres from the nearest town, acceptable to the rather frail and well-groomed wives of the rough soldiers under my command.

Thanks to nature's relentless bounty, these young mothers had a clutch of crawling, toddling and bawling infants, who caused me some anxious moments. I had to keep in mind the towering hulks of elephants moving around at will across lawns, pathways and roads, lions, leopards and servals scavenging among the refuse at night, troops of baboons rampaging through the area and, not least, dangerous snakes of every description sometimes finding their way indoors.

No human was ever mauled by any of the animals, although they were in almost daily contact with each other. Being so small and young the children had no fear, even of the largest elephants. Mothers became hysterical when a little one decided that some wild animal had to be investigated at close quarters, but only once did I have to take steps to prevent a child from being hurt, in this case by a lion, and even then the situation only developed because of the stupidity of the parents. This was a marvellous place for youngsters to grow up. They became accustomed to elephants, hippos, buffaloes, impalas and other animals in the same way that city children get used to cars, buses, motorbikes, trains, bicycles, discos, television, pop concerts or any of the other trappings of civilisation.

Some elephants were resident throughout the year, all bulls. The breeding herds disappeared as soon as the rains came and pans, away from the river, filled with water. They returned in winter to feed along the river banks and in the swamps and to luxuriate in lagoons and streams. Most of the unattached bulls went too, but a handful always stayed behind.

We had a resident bull, advanced in years but, fortunately, with quite insignificant tusks, who took up his abode among the houses, stores, workshop, offices and transport park. He had been there ever since I came to the Caprivi, his mediocre ivory his passport to a long life.

When we built St Michél base he watched the unusual activity unperturbed, but with interest, and decided to stick around. After all, it was his territory. He came first and we had to fit in with his routine, not he with ours.

This is what we did. Everyone had express orders not to disturb the bull, or any of the other elephants for that matter.

If he wanted to push down our beautiful pub, that was his prerogative. We could always build another pub elsewhere.

In spite of dire warnings about the destruction the elephants would cause, none of our installations suffered the slightest damage. The elephants pushed down reed screens to get to the camelthorns or enclosed gardens, but they never touched any of the structures, apart from a few dents on the roof of the mess hall where they placed their mighty forefeet on the iron sheets while going after dropped camelthorn pods.

The resident bull moved around without restraint but had the strange habit of unexpectedly materialising right in front of one, usually while walking from one place to another with one's mind in neutral and at peace with the world.

Despite of their huge bulk, the elephants could be almost invisible until you literally bumped into them among the profusion of trees and shrubs that covered the whole base.

I had a cook, a short, fat, round and jolly little fellow by the name of Thomasie. He was a Shona from Umtali, trained in the Cecil Hotel there and one of the best cooks I have ever come across. He was worth his considerable weight in 24-carat gold.

One day Thomasie was on his way to the store to get washing powder, a walk of about 200 metres through the bush along a track bordered on both sides by trees and shrubs.

Thomasie waddled along, quite happily, and was close to the store when there was an ear-splitting, trumpeting blast from close quarters on his right. He looked up, startled, into the probing end of an elephant trunk, just millimetres away from his face.

Thomasie went into top gear, his short legs a blur under his bloated, rotund body as he made for the open door of the store.

The bull was in hot pursuit, trumpeting and flapping his ears, almost treading on the heels of the puffing little man.

Thomasie crashed through the doorway and disappeared behind the shelves. The bull skidded to a halt, his bulk blocking the doorway as he tried to explore the interior with his trunk.

After a while, he withdrew a short distance into the cover of a nearby stand of sickle bush.

Thomasie, sweating profusely, got his washing powder from the storeman and carefully spied out the lie of the land outside. There was no sign of the bull.

Apprehensively, the cook stepped out into the sunlight to make his way back to the kitchen. Suddenly, the huge bulk of the bull burst from the sickle bush, trunk raised, ears flapping and shrieking raucously. Thomasie hastily sought safety inside the store again and the bull retired into the bush once more. After a while, Thomasie ventured forth gingerly. He had the evening meal on the stove and it had to be attended to before it burned.

Again the bull charged, and again Thomasie beat a hasty retreat.

This went on for two hours while the mechanics, "tiffies" as we called them, formed a group of interested spectators in the nearby workshop. They enjoyed every minute of it.

Of course, the bull knew they were there and seemed to be encouraged in his antics by their presence, as if he was playing to an appreciative crowd.

Finally, the bull relented, or got bored, and trundled off. Thomasie, after waiting quite a while to make sure his tormentor had gone, hastened back to his kitchen to try and rescue our meal.

This bull had reached an understanding with the "tiffies", which meant that he never disturbed them and they left him alone. The workshop was a high-roofed, open-sided, small hangar, in which the vehicles were parked for maintenance or repair work. Like most of the other buildings, it was surrounded by camel thorns and therefore a favourite spot for the bull and also for the other elephants when they returned to the river line.

The bull would stand there, crunching pods, swinging his trunk, snorting from time to time while the "tiffies" worked on their vehicles, almost under foot. He took no notice of the clangs, epithets, oily smells and test running of engines and carried on feeding, quite at peace with the world.

Of course, there were certain unwritten rules which we all adhered to. If one met the bull anywhere along a track or footpath, one would step aside and wait for him to pass. If in a vehicle, one would stop and wait for him to cross or move leisurely around the vehicle and on to wherever he was going.

The same applied to other elephants roaming through the base. My house was a good two kilometres from the main base, beautifully situated on the edge of a large, forest-fringed lagoon. I had resident bulls as well, including one with the biggest tusks I ever saw on any elephant from that part of the world. In winter, a herd of younger bulls, ranging in age from five to twenty or more, moved in to tear down the bush, pull up the few plants I tried to cultivate and flatten the reed screens I erected to keep lesser animals at bay.

Every night was noisy, with the crackling sounds of tree limbs being torn off, the dull thuds of elephant feet digging up roots, angry trumpeting as rivals contended for a choice morsel of bark or twig, and incessant snorting and growling as they fed and moved about.

Often, the elephants would move into the lagoon and have a noisy, splashing bathing session that would last for hours.

On winter nights, we were almost always hemmed in by elephants. To reach my Land Cruiser to drive to supper could be quite an experience. There was one bull in particular that was fond of guarding my vehicle, as if it was his very own. I could not get near it until he moved off to feed or became bored with the game of trying to provoke me into doing something stupid.

The two-kilometres drive from my house to the base often took more than an hour. The track was frequently blocked by a horde of feeding elephants, usually on their way to or from the water.

From our verandah we could see an elephant drinking place up the river, about 800 metres away, which was frequented by breeding herds. It was not unusual to see several hundred of them hastening to the water in a heaving mass of grey, barely discernible through the dust clouds. They usually arrived in late afternoon and one could then be assured of an interesting night, filled with trumpeting, snarls, growls and snorts inbetween the splashing of giant bodies as they refreshed themselves in the waters of the Cuando. The usual snorts and grunts of the hippos were completely drowned out by the hordes of elephants.

One day, I sat on the bank of the lagoon in front of our house watching 13 bulls from "my" herd, enjoying themselves like a bunch of overgrown schoolchildren. It was a very hot day and the bulls were making good use of the cool waters to overcome the heat.

One bull squatted down in the water on his rear end like a fat old lady, rose up and crashed down on his side to disappear completely, in a sort of sideways dive, with a tremendous splash. The tip of his trunk appeared above the surface like a snorkel, and he stayed down for long moments, letting the water wash over his thick hide. After a while, with a mountainous heave, the bulk of the bull appeared above the surface with much snorting and spraying of water. The whole sequence was repeated, almost monotonously. Many of the others joined in and the pool became filled with "diving" elephants.

This went on for at least half an hour, until finally the elephants decided to leave. As the last bull emerged from the water the one ahead of him, already clear of the lagoon, turned around and pushed him back down the bank. The bull sat down on his fat behind as if submerging in a bathtub, while the second bull kept on pushing, until the first had completely disappeared under the water. The rest of the herd came to an abrupt halt when they saw the two bulls in the muddy water, ducking each other like naughty schoolboys. They pondered the situation and decided that they had left the lagoon a mite too early, turned around and charged, en masse, back into the mêlée in a mighty phalanx of huge, grey bodies.

The playing and splashing went on for another five or ten minutes before the waves subsided, with all the elephants immersed up to half their height in the cool water. One bull then placed his forefeet on the back of the animal in front of him and this led to a chain reaction.

Thirteen elephants finally formed a line, each one with its forefeet on the back of the elephant in front, a perfect chain of interlocking elephant bulls.

The only other time I have seen this was in a circus, when Indian elephants carried out a similar stunt to much cracking of their handler's whip. Yet here, in the middle of Africa, a herd of wild and untrained elephants did exactly the same thing without coercion. It seems to be a natural game played by elephants, so their circus performance may not be so remarkable after all.

Unfortunately, I did not have a camera with me, and an extremely rare opportunity was missed. Moments like this can only be savoured occasionally and by a privileged few, and are to be cherished.

Other elephants also made their presence felt up and down the Cuando River. I have already mentioned the tusker who was a sedate and even stately fellow, always accompanied by a brace of younger bulls known as "askaris". This name, taken from the many books on big-game hunting in Kenya, means "soldier" in Swahili.

Dewald always maintained emphatically that sooner or later, the majestic old elephant would be shot for its tusks.

He was right. I knew the animal well, and so did Dewald. We had seen him frequently for years wandering around the Fort Doppies and St Michél areas. Every winter he came back to the same location on the Cuando River, but in the end, this was not far enough away from the Golden Highway to keep him safe from some greedy, poaching bastard.

Dewald and I both left the Caprivi under duress and under somewhat unusual circumstances. The bull was still around when we shook the Caprivi dust from our feet, the only bull with such magnificent tusks in an area stretching over several thousand kilometres. They formed a magnificent matching pair, curving away with a perfect sweep like two giant sabres.

Not long after my departure, a truckload of ivory was confiscated on a farm near Okahandja, just north of Windhoek. The truck belonged to a Portuguese man from Windhoek, who ran a transport business to supply Savimbi and his army with victuals and other commodities in south-east Angola.

Photographs appeared in newspapers of a policeman holding up a perfectly matched pair of giant-sized tusks. They were almost as long as the man was tall. Dewald and I recognised those tusks immediately. They could only have come from the placid and friendly old bull that used to wander around between my home and Fort Doppies with his small escort of askaris.

His mild-mannered temperament cost him his life. A grasping Portuguese in Windhoek, a greedy Chinese in Pretoria, and finally a stinking-rich tourist in Hong Kong had to satisfy their all-consuming lust for blood-stained money and useless ivory baubles. For this, a monarch of the savannah had to be slaughtered in faraway Caprivi.

There were other elephants, however, who weren't so placid.

One of them was a tuskless old cow, the leader of a breeding herd further to the north. Her gaunt old body towered above her daughters and granddaughters when they moved in a grey phalanx through the bush. No one dared get between her and her herd. Her temper was fearsome and her charges awe-inspiring. It was best to get out of the way and watch her from a distance, guarding the flank of her herd while tossing her head in anger, ears flapping, until all her descendants had passed safely.

Somebody once told me that tuskless elephants are always ill-tempered. Evidently the lack of tusks prevents them from stripping bark off trees, a large part of their diet when the trees are bare and devoid of foliage in mid-winter. The tuskless ones then have to fight other, more fortunate elephants for the strips of bark they have torn off with their tusks, and this constant fighting makes tuskless elephants irascible and extremely aggressive.

Three young bulls always moved into one of my northern training bases for the winter. This base was usually filled with troops rotating through it on a regular schedule and the elephants enjoyed chasing them whenever the chance came their way.

They waited patiently until the troops left one lecture room and were on their way to another, then all three would suddenly burst from cover in a sudden spasm of violent activity. With deafening shrieks, much dust-kicking and ear-flapping, they would charge the wildly scattering students. Afterwards, much time was spent by an instructor coaxing students from the trees and other hiding places inside buildings before training could resume.

One of these young bulls chased me into the ration store one day. I managed to stay ahead of him by only a short head. He stayed outside screaming, kicking up dust and tossing his head while daring me to put my head outside the door. Fortunately, being young, his patience soon wore out and he ambled off to join the other two to plan their next escapade.

An older bull used to frequent our outdoor parachute training area. We had set up flight training swings, aircraft drill mock-ups, parachute landing ramps and even an impressive jump tower in the middle of the African bush, where black soldiers were put through their paces to qualify as paratroopers.

This bull enjoyed parachute training as much as the students hated it. He would watch from a short distance away while the "sticks" were being instructed in the intricacies of parachute landings, flight and safety drills, slowly rocking from side to side while idly swinging his trunk.

Now and then he got it into his head to introduce some life into the proceedings, especially when the heat of the day became a bit much for the students.

Flapping his ears and kicking dust, he would suddenly utter a terrific scream and go into a thundering mock charge.

Invariably, students scattered in all directions and the instructor would have to get them down from the trees while the elephant moved back to his favourite tree to continue drowsing in the shade, idly flapping his ears to cool off.

But once was never enough and the "game" was always repeated several times during the course of a day's parachute training.

We had no real problems with elephants getting violent or aggressive, at least partly because we kept out of their way and avoided taking any action that could make them feel threatened.

Once or twice I had to severely reprimand someone whose unthinking actions could have led to distressing the elephants and endangering his own life.

When I caught one youngster teasing the resident old bull at St Michél, I gave him all sorts of hell. It could have been fatal, especially for children, if the old bull had taken a dislike to the human species and the youthful culprit never teased any wild animal again.

Another young lad, not a member of my unit, decided one day to take close-up photographs of a breeding herd, gathered around a water hole close to the Golden Highway.

While one might take chances with a bull herd, it is highly dangerous to try one's luck with a breeding herd, especially if it includes unweaned calves.

The young man, a second lieutenant, got out of the army truck and calmly strolled into the herd to take his photographs. One elephant, more than likely a cow, eyed him from the rear and decided that the lieutenant represented a threat to the calves.

This elephant went into a real charge, not a noisy and spectacular mock one.

A real charge is always carried out in deathly silence, the ears pinned back and the trunk rolled up under the chin. A mock charge is accompanied by much screaming, head tossing and flapping of ears amid clouds of dust.

The elephant bore down on the unsuspecting officer, skewered him on the end of one of her tusks, then shook off the mortally wounded man before disappearing rapidly – with the entire herd – into the bush.

The death of the young officer was extremely unfortunate, but the reaction of certain people who should have known better greatly angered me.

A major at Fort Doppies, one of the base wallahs who claimed that he had been a big-game hunter in Kenya before joining the army and that he knew all about "jumbos", decided, after this incident, that there was a rogue elephant bull at large in the Caprivi Strip. Before the animal could kill again, it had to be destroyed. The major started oiling his large-calibre hunting rifle in preparation for a Kenya-style expedition that would climax in a confrontation with the mad killer. He probably saw himself on the front page of a newspaper posing heroically with the impressive tusks of the rogue monster that gored a young South African national serviceman to death. You can imagine how well that would go down with the young man's parents and the public back in South Africa.

When I heard about the major's plans from Dewald, I rushed to Fort Doppies and I confronted the intrepid big-game hunter, demanding to know how he was going to identify a killer bull among several thousand elephants roaming the Caprivi bush.

This big-game "expert" was evidently unaware of the fact that the elephant in question was more than likely a cow and probably the leader of the herd.

Dewald and I were concerned for the safety of our carefully observed and surreptitiously guarded tusker bull and I suspected that the major was after him, whether he was rogue or not.

I peremptorily ordered him to put his rifle away and threatened him with dire consequences if he should go after the so-called killer.

Later, I had good reason to get this particular officer banned from the Fort Doppies training area forever.

Of course, life with elephants was not all pleasant adventure, comical episode and symbiosis between man and beast. There were tragedies and there were scandals.

We had to shoot elephants limping along, their bodies riddled with lead, usually AK-47 bullets fired by Unita hunters north of the Angolan cutline. We also found .303 bullets embedded in their skins. Several elephants had been moving targets for years, judging by the old wounds, scars and bullets found in them.

Nature also played its cruel role. One day we found a starving young calf that had strayed from the herd. It was in obvious distress, but there was nothing we could do. We simply could not catch it. In the end, I ordered my troops to let it go, knowing that its weakened condition would soon make it easy prey for the lions.

Another time, we found two young bulls, one about three years and the other about two years old, firmly trapped in mud. They had been stuck for days, and one was already dead. It was the gathering vultures that led us to the scene of the tragedy in the first place.

The bigger bull was still alive, but very weak and dehydrated. We finally got it out of the mud, but we could not get it on its feet. The shock was too much and it soon died.

In retrospect, I think I was in too much of a hurry to get it free of the imprisoning mud. I should have built up its strength first – while it was still stuck – with copious amounts of water, and pacified it before attempting a rescue.

Some idiot caught a young calf one night on the main road to Katima and handed it over to a local resident, who tried to raise the little elephant on bottles of pasteurised cow's milk. The calf developed a loose tummy and made a mess of the man's house and outbuilding and he sent me a desperate request to get the calf off his hands. However, before we could get there, the calf died.

So much for people who cannot keep their meddling hands off young wild animals, be they vervet monkeys, lion cubs or elephant calves.

It is generally accepted that when an elephant lies down, it is either in the process of dying, or already dead.

One of the wives at St Michél was therefore extremely concerned when she found a young bull, perhaps eight or ten years old, lying on its side in thick bush no more than 50 metres from her house. She was already anticipating the stench of a huge carcass rotting on her doorstep, to say nothing of nocturnal visits by hordes of cackling hyenas and daily forays by clouds of vultures, probably using her roof as a perch and leaving behind the inevitable bonus of fresh "whitewash".

She dashed off to the duty officer, Major Frans van Rensburg, and asked him to do something about the potential problem.

Frans strolled across in execution of his duties to assess the situation. The woman, a petite blonde by the name of Florine Williams, wife of one of my lieutenants, watched from the front porch as Frans fearlessly approached the young elephant.

Frans was a recent arrival at Fort St Michél and had never been in close contact with elephants before. He grew up in Robertson, a typical Boland town as far removed from the depths of the African savannah as the posh suburb of Sandton is from a squatter camp.

He knew that I insisted that every carcass found in the bush had to be reported to me and that I would want to know the probable cause of death.

So Frans approached the elephant to determine whether it had been shot recently and perhaps died of its wounds, a stone's throw from Florine's house. The carcass looked remarkably healthy, even from close up.

Frans stood between the elephant's stumpy legs, his eyes searching the thick hide for a bullet mark.

There was none.

He leaned forward to get a better look at the animal's head, placing his hand on the elephant's flank to keep his balance.

To his surprise, he saw the elephant's eye slowly open, then it was as if the young bull had been injected with a dose of adrenalin as it heaved to its legs with a frightening scream.

Frans took off as fast as he could, but there was no way he could execute the sharp 180-degree turn needed to reach the safety of Florine's porch, so he ran in a wide circle through the thick bush, a bad-tempered young bull hot on his heels.

Suddenly, Frans stumbled over another grey hulk, also reclining on its side. The second elephant heaved itself to its feet just as energetically as the first, and Frans now had two young bulls in hot pursuit.

Florine, meanwhile, was doubled up with laughter as she watched them disappearing towards the nearby house of Major Willem Rätte.

Zaanzie, Willem's wife, heard the commotion and came rushing out to save her children. She was just in time to open the door for a frenzied Frans van Rensburg who gratefully dashed inside leaving two furious young bulls going through the entire range of their impressive power display while shattering the silence of the winter morning with their trumpeting.

Elephants, of course, sometimes do lie down to sleep, particularly when it is cool. But they have to flap their huge ears constantly to keep their body heat radiating effectively from the veins that run close to the rear surfaces of their ears, which means they doze mostly on their feet.

When the weather is cool, elephants take the opportunity to get their considerable weight off their long-suffering feet and will then lie down, taking advantage of the fact that ear flapping can be dispensed with for a while.

Driving to work along the sand track from my house to the base one morning, I came across a similar situation.

At a T-junction, where I had to turn right, there were two soldiers from an organisation which habitually ran out of fuel when they got near my base approaching on foot from the left, carrying empty jerry cans. Each base had its own meagre allotment of fuel and I was tired of these guys sponging off us.

They waved to me to wait while they broke into an unhurried shuffle. Angrily, I ignored them and drove off. A few hundred metres further I passed a breeding herd of elephants, most of them peacefully lying on their sides like so many dead hulks, while three or four remained upright, facing outwards and acting as sentries. Cows and calves were all in a deep slumber, scattered haphazardly across the terrain. I drove past slowly, so as not to disturb them. They were no more than 20 paces from the side of the road but the sentries, being used to my Land Cruiser, simply ignored me.

But I knew what would happen when the two troops with the jerry cans came trotting down the track.

Some distance along, I stopped, waiting in anticipation for the drama to unfold.

The two sweaty soldiers stumbled into the herd unexpectedly, and all hell broke loose. There were angry trumpetings, a crashing of trees and branches, dust rising above the tree canopy and two little figures legging it madly down the track, back to their stranded vehicle, with a couple of cows thundering behind. They dropped their empty jerry cans and left them lying forlornly in the middle of the track.

The herd moved off to a more secluded place where they were less likely to be disturbed and I drove on, happy in the thought that I had deterred a certain organisation, at least for a while, from draining our limited fuel supplies.

A paratrooper's greatest fear in the Caprivi is to land in a crocodile-infested pool or on top of an elephant or buffalo during a parachute descent. The latter finally happened to a paratrooper during a night jump near Katima Mulilo.

It was pitch-dark and the jump was over an *omuramba* fringed with the usual savannah woodland.

One paratrooper came down, tensing for the landing, without having the slightest idea how far he still had to go before hitting the ground. This is normal for any night jump conducted when there is not even a sliver of a moon.

The paratrooper landed on what he thought was terra firma, except that his "landing zone" suddenly took off in panic. There was a high-pitched squeal as he and the elephant crashed through the bush, the soldier still strapped into his "chute" and trying to get some handhold on the broad bouncing back of the charging animal. The parachute soon dragged him off and he landed, without mishap, on the sandy soil. All around him the bush was crashing and snapping as a whole herd of elephants got under way in a hurry, their irate trumpeting proclaiming their strong protest at the intrusion of the paratroopers.

Gradually, some animal species increased, while others went into a decline. When I arrived back in the Caprivi, I settled down at first in a small riverside camp on the banks of the Cuando. I was completely alone, which suited me fine. I could stroll through the bush, rifle slung over my shoulder, to become acquainted with the various animal species, the intricacies of a swamp ecological system and the luscious islands covered in dense riverine forests that dotted the blue-green expanses of reeds like coral atolls standing out in a tropical sea.

These islands are often fringed with the so-called wild date palms which grow quite tall if the elephants stay away from them and their delectable bunches of fruit. The palm trees reinforce the coral island impression.

Around this time, the Department of Nature Conservation was conducting a game capture operation to remove sables, roans and tsessebes thought to be threatened by unacceptable poaching pressure in both the western and eastern Caprivi. In the eastern Caprivi they had already been hunted to extinction.

There were still some herds of these animals left in the western Caprivi and I tried to convince the department that it would be better to leave them there where I could keep an eye on them.

One afternoon, the leader of the capture team landed at my small camp in a helicopter to discuss the matter further. When I met my visitor at the chopper he was almost incoherent with excitement and said he wanted to show me a most unforgettable sight from the air.

The helicopter swiftly climbed away and tilted westwards, away from the river.

There, stretching for kilometres into the interior and kilometres up and down the edge of the flood plain, just beyond the riverine forest, was the biggest concentration of elephants I had ever seen.

The bush was covered in thousand upon thousand of grey humps, feeding, moving, no doubt trumpeting at the helicopter and generally milling around in an area that was about five square kilometres in size. We started to count and got to 1000, then estimated the size of the herd.

At least 5000 elephants were gathered in one massive, moving and feeding crowd.

Obviously, the herd was made up of hundreds of smaller breeding herds, some bull herds and perhaps a number of loners, and this singular gathering of the clans was of a temporary nature only.

I don't know why they decided to congregate in such a mass. Perhaps they were having a convention to discuss elephant problems, or perhaps it was a festival of some sort.

The bush had been burnt down shortly before by the Bushmen, so it could be that the concentrated minerals in the ash attracted them from far and wide. I am no fundi on elephants, but that sight was enough to take my breath away and I consider myself very fortunate indeed to have witnessed one of Africa's most impressive spectacles.

The tsessebes had decreased alarmingly ever the years. There was a time when they were the most common antelope, but they are now seen only rarely. One of them, a lone bull, joined a small group of blue wildebeest and seemed quite happy with his new and unusual associates. In that particular area there were no other tsessebes he could team up with, anyway.

The same applied to the roans, probably the fiercest of all antelopes. Only occasionally did we see small herds of them venturing out of the bush into the flood plain and their days in the western Caprivi are almost certainly numbered.

Blue wildebeest also became scarcer as the years went by. Although not strictly a plains animal like the black wildebeest, the blue wildebeest does like wide, open spaces. Bush encroachment, possibly as a result of an overall decline in elephants to act as bulldozers, has changed the habitat for the worse as far as the blue wildebeest is concerned.

The 5000 elephants I saw upon my reintroduction into the western Caprivi were strictly a one-day show. The elephant population declined alarmingly over the years, until the thousands eventually dwindled to only a few hundred along the Cuando River.

Zebras, like blue wildebeest, were beginning to fight an uphill battle, as were the giraffes. They were under intolerable hunting pressure from the Bushmen, virtually all armed with R1 military rifles and using military ammunition and often hunting on horseback.

I found the remnants of my old herd of buffalo again, roaming around between Angola and the Caprivi. Watching them one afternoon, crossing the track in front of me, I counted every one, arriving at a total of 273.

These were the only survivors of the herd of 1000 or more which gave us such anxious moments in 1970 when they went into an uncontrollable stampede as we tried to escape them in our Sabres.

The buffaloes had been ruthlessly hunted by Unita troops in the north, biltong hunters from Katima Mulilo and other opportunists drifting carelessly through the Caprivi, blazing away with scant regard for hunting permits or the fact that they were hunting in a game reserve.

I gave special attention to the buffaloes and by the time I was unceremoniously kicked out of the Caprivi, the size of the herd had grown to well over 400.

My favourite antelopes were the sables. The few small herds gradually increased during my tenure as commander of the guerrilla training school until one herd numbered 35, another 27, a third 19 and a fourth 17. All were in prime condition, flourishing in a habitat that became more and more appropriate for sables while less acceptable to blue wildebeest.

One of the most majestic animals I had ever seen, the kind

that brings a lump to one's throat, was a huge sable bull with horns sweeping back over its shoulders and clearing its rump when it held its head erect by no more than 50 centimetres.

This bull was often on his own, though at times accompanied by two younger bulls who were magnificent in their own right. The majesty of the old bull, however, detracted somewhat from the nobility of the younger specimens.

Dewald was convinced that this bull carried a record set of horns. Manie Grobler, the resident biologist at Katima's conservation office, was almost certain that he was a royal sable which had somehow made its way south into the Caprivi from among the few specimens still left in south-central Angola.

However, it was definitely a "common" sable, as found in southern Africa. It had the distinguishing white markings around the muzzle and a blaze, whereas the royal sable has a completely black face.

It was a treat to see this animal. Every time I came across it I forgot all about work and sat watching it for as long as possible, time which I could ill afford as commander of a guerrilla training school.

A sable on the run, with its tail switching, head down and the horns sweeping back in an arc, is a wonderful display of controlled energy and flowing grace. A herd on the run is a simply awesome sight. No wonder these noble animals are used to prop up the coats of arms of several countries and organisations.

The impalas increased to a satisfactory level. They are specially protected game in Namibia because of the threat to the endemic black-faced impala, found only in the Kaokoveld and south-western Angola. Our local herds of common impala increased to the extent that after the lambing season, it was not at all uncommon to see a herd of 50 or more ewes with bouncing lambs running close to their mothers.

The lechwes on the islands were under tremendous pressure from the Mafwe tribe east of the Cuando until intensive patrolling put a stop to their poaching and the lechwes gradually began to pick up in numbers.

However, the animals under probably the most pressure were the African savannah's dredgers, the hippos. The Mafwes hunted them mercilessly, sometimes using methods which can only be described as barbaric. My almost single-handed patrolling also put a stop to this slaughter but inevitably led to voices being raised in protest by, particularly, the headmen of Mafwe villages. A coordinated campaign got under way to banish me from the western Caprivi back to South Africa.

But this still lay in the future. In the meantime, far more sinister characters were lurking in the wings: the ivory- and rhino-horn barons who, in the end, succeeded in getting me removed from the scene of slaughter that was poised to engulf not only the Caprivi, but also the Cuando-Cubango, Zambia and the Zambezi Valley.

In the interim, I had been landed with two lion cubs who took up all my spare time. I was also appointed as a nature conservator by the Department of Nature Conservation, my conservation duties being performed over and above, and often in conjunction with, my military ones. Inevitably, this conflict of interest led to some unpleasant clashes with my bosses on opposing sides of the fence.

NINE

Rufus and Dayan

I became a surrogate father to four lion cubs when one of our trucks returned from 32 Battalion at the other end of the Caprivi Strip with the tiny creatures on board. The cubs had been picked up by a well-meaning soldier taking a leisurely stroll through the bush, probably because of their piteous cries for their absent mother.

It was fortunate for the soldier that the mother was not in the immediate vicinity. It's possible that she had gone off on a hunt, leaving her cubs hidden in a den. Lionesses have been known to stay away for up to two days while ranging far and wide looking for a kill.

On the other hand, the lioness might have come to grief somewhere, although this was a fairly remote possibility, or simply abandoned the cubs.

Nevertheless, we now had four mewling cubs on our hands. The first priority was to feed them, the second to figure out what to do with them.

Piet Brink, one of my sergeant instructors, improvised a bottle and they were soon sucking away for dear life. Their bellies swollen, they went to sleep peacefully in a box lined with a blanket.

From then on, Piet had his hands full to satisfy their almost continuous demand for milk.

The cubs were so small that they could only waddle around the floor of the hut, still pretty weak in their hind legs, but they soon attracted attention from all and sundry, including nature conservation officials.

It wasn't long before Nature Conservation informed me that they would be coming to remove the cubs.

Alan Celliers, a nature conservator from Rundu, duly arrived and took the cubs back to Rundu, where they were placed in a small park with other animals.

We thought we would never see them again, so I was greatly surprised some months later to find Alan and the Rundu game park owner at St Michél on my return from an operational excursion into Angola. They had brought the two male cubs back with the request that we look after them and, if possible, reintroduce them to the wild.

The cubs, by then eleven months old, were lying on their sides in a rather comatose state in the shade of a sausage tree. They had been tranquillised for the journey. The one who became known as Rufus looked pretty thin while the other, then called Ogies, appeared somewhat more robust.

The park could no longer afford to feed them. They had been raised on dog biscuits, which is not the usual fare for growing lions.

The park owner approached Nature Conservation with the problem and said he was willing to keep the two lionesses, but the males had to go.

Windhoek headquarters, in its infinite wisdom, decided that the cubs had to be donated to a certain gentleman who had a hunting farm near Otjiwarongo and specialised in offering lions to his overseas clients, for which he charged an exorbitant fee. It was the same farmer who had almost got his hands on Terry and Liza. His custom was to collect unwanted lions from zoos, at a minimal price, and release them into an enclosed camp to await a bullet between the eyes from a fancy, high-powered rifle in the hands of an intrepid big-game hunter. Amongst his victims had been the entire unwanted lion population from the Cape Town zoo.

Rufus and Ogies were therefore destined to become trophies on the walls of overseas hunters, and Alan, true conservator that he was, vehemently objected to the prospect. Without further ado, he brought the cubs back to us, Windhoek being none the wiser.

Fortunately, I had already built a small enclosure where any wild animal that reached us in distress could recuperate before being returned to the bush. The enclosure was at my house, allowing me to keep an eye on the occupant for at least part of the day.

The still sleepy lions were taken to the enclosure and one of my national servicemen, an armourer by the name of Pine Pienaar was assigned to be their nursemaid, and "officially" dubbed "keeper of the lions".

Alan and the previous owner stayed at my house for a few days to make sure that the transition would run smoothly.

Ogies had a continuous discharge of tears from his right eye, hence his name.

When he was small, a dog had bitten him in the eye and the tear duct became blocked though, fortunately, this had no adverse effect on his ability to see.

We renamed him Dayan, after the famous one-eyed Israeli general. It seemed more appropriate for a lion to bear the illustrious name of a man who was a lion in his own right, rather than the somewhat insipid name of Ogies.

Our immediate problem was to wean the two cubs off their beloved dog biscuits and on to proper lion fare.

Initially, we mixed the dog biscuits, of which we were given a couple of bags, with carefully hidden morsels of meat but both lions turned up their noses at our offering.

Dayan turned out to be less fussy than Rufus and after several more attempts, he started to nibble at the meat and, eventually, to wolf it down with relish. We cut out his dog biscuits entirely.

Rufus preferred crunching away at the biscuits, leaving the meat strictly alone. Finally, we were forced to let him starve for a while in order to arouse the pangs of hunger and persuade him to eat meat as any self-respecting lion should.

I had visions of a full-grown lion wandering through the African bush feeding on dog biscuits, regularly supplied by the army. It would certainly not contribute to the regal image of the king of the beasts.

So we persisted in our efforts and he finally took to meat, but never as wholeheartedly as Dayan, always remaining a somewhat fussy feeder.

Consequently, Rufus was always a few kilograms lighter than Dayan but, on the other hand, a lot more energetic and intelligent. He always took the lead in devising a new set of tricks with which to torment his human companions.

We augmented the meat diet with copious amounts of milk, mixed with Pro Nutro and rations designed for Special Forces operators as a mineral and calcium supplement.

From the first day, Pine and I got on extremely well with the two cubs, which accepted us as if we were long-lost friends.

Alan and the previous owner left for Rundu, the latter sobbing openly over having to leave the youngsters behind.

During the next few days we worked out a routine and the cubs rapidly began to gain weight and became more boisterous. We covered the top of the enclosure with corrugated iron to keep out leopards.

There is a deep and instinctive sense of distrust between different members of the cat species. Lions are inclined to go for leopards, cheetahs and any other cat lower down on the carnivorous ladder, while leopards will attack cheetahs, servals and so on down the line, the process being repeated at every level until the bottom rung is reached, where the small spotted cat is wise to keep out of the way of all the others.

The reverse also applies. A leopard will go out of its way to kill unattended lion cubs and so, no doubt, will cheetahs.

It all has to do with competition for the same food source. Lions eat anything, including mice and rats, and will therefore take out a house cat if one can be found.

We had a huge and highly intelligent house cat, a ginger male by the name of Recce. I took him down to the lion pen while the cubs were still comatose, to introduce him to his cousins. He sniffed them thoroughly, but did not appear at all impressed by the newcomers in his own back yard.

Some weeks later, I started releasing the lions after their morning feed, first making sure that Recce was nowhere around. The cubs showed a keen interest in the cat and there was no doubt that Rufus, at least, harboured a burning desire to sink his huge claws into Recce. Recce generally managed to stay one jump ahead of Rufus and seemed far too agile for any blundering lion, but one day, when Rufus had already grown to a respectable, sub-adult size, Recce was caught off guard. Rufus and Dayan had more or less settled into their environment by then, but had the disconcerting habit of unexpectedly paying a visit to our house at the most inopportune moments, much as Terry had been wont to do.

The two lions strolled into the clearing surrounding our house while Recce was out in the surrounding bush, trying to get his little claws into a bird or any of the smaller mammals. Rufus suddenly spotted him and turned in a heartbeat from a rather indolent creature into a highly strung, lightning-fast streak of buff-coloured fur.

He descended on Recce like a ton of bricks, but Recce was no laggard when it came to split-second reactions. He took off like a little ginger rocket, an equally fast yellow monster pounding along in hot pursuit.

Recce could not manage the sudden sharp turns required to reach the safe interior of the house through a door left slightly ajar and secured on a chain for that very purpose but, fortunately, my Land Cruiser was parked in his path and he leapt through the open window into the cab, then crouched in the farthest corner.

Undeterred, Rufus went after him, but because of his size, could get only his huge head through the window. His shoulders got firmly stuck.

By this time, Recce was a ball of ginger fury, spitting and growling as if possessed by a thousand little demons. He lashed out at the nearest part of the lion's anatomy, which was its glistening black nose, with his outspread paws, the claws cruelly extended. With a few lightning swipes he opened up a number of deep scratches on Rufus's nose.

Rufus jerked his head back, nose dripping with blood, and sloped off in a stupefied daze to rejoin Dayan who had been watching the fun and games from a distance. His ego had been thoroughly deflated by the smallest of the cats in the family.

In the evenings, my wife and I would sit in the lounge, reading or talking, with Recce lying on the carpet on one side of a diamond mesh screen and the lions on the other, staring longingly at Recce. Because of the heat during summer, and even on winter days, the entire front of the lounge was a wire-mesh screen, a diamond-mesh gate filling in as a door. The result was a sort of cage in which Recce, my wife and I were on nightly display to Rufus and Dayan. They loved to lie on the verandah watching us, for all the world as if they were on a visit to the zoo, until the time came to turn out the lights.

This entailed a stroll to the generator, accompanied by the boisterous lions, to switch off the engine, then returning in the dark and trying to get into the house without the lions forcing their way inside.

It was fine going to the generator, but not so on the way back, knowing that Rufus was waiting in ambush around the corner.

I was inevitably met by a several-hundred-kilogram body launching itself at me with enough momentum to floor me if caught unawares. The fat would then be in the fire. Invariably I ended up under a heap of struggling lions, but they would lose interest in me after a few seconds and go for each other, using me as a wrestling mat in the process. It was always with some difficulty that I managed to disentangle myself from the heaving mass of lions and sneak into the house while they were still fighting.

Rufus and Dayan spent the first few months in their small enclosure and around the house. Pine Pienaar brought their rations from the mess every morning and evening and we let them out for a while in the late afternoon, but found that it was better to feed them in the enclosure. It was the only way we could get them back into captivity for the night.

I disliked the enclosure and, in any case, wanted them to get used to the bush around them. As they grew bigger and more capable of asserting themselves, especially against the ever-present hyenas or a marauding leopard, I decided the time had come to allow them the free run of the area around the house, at least during the hours of darkness.

The drill changed to feeding them in the evening, inside the enclosure, and then releasing them after my wife and cat had been duly secured inside the safety of the house.

My wife is not exactly the tough athletic type one would associate with a bush wife. She is, in fact, rather petite and slightly built and certainly no match for the massive energy locked up in the muscled bodies of sub-adult lions. Once, in a friendly but typically robust fashion, Rufus jumped up against her and she simply collapsed under the onslaught, with a slightly astonished and bemused Rufus on top of her.

So it was a nightly ritual to ensure that my wife and Recce were safely indoors before letting the lions out. We would then observe one another through the wire screen of the lounge until bedtime, switch off the lights, and, after I'd been suitably mauled by the lions, we would turn in.

Lions are particularly active at night. The house I had built was constructed of wooden panels scrounged from 32 Battalion, and it trembled and shook with every onslaught from the lions, charging round and round the house, chasing each other and frequently bumping into the flimsy structure with their full combined weight.

This went on for hours while we were trying to get some sleep, the wrestling matches accompanied by much "fierce" growling and panting. After a while, they would refresh themselves with loud, wet lapping from a zinc bath filled with water, which I had placed right under one of our bedroom windows. A short pause would follow, and the whole process would start anew.

Then, in the small hours of the morning, a sudden quietness would indicate that they had gone to take a nap in the vicinity of the boats tied up in the lagoon a short distance away.

At first light every morning, I rose to carry out my first task of the day: take the lions for a walk through the bush so that they could become familiar with the early morning wildlife.

I dressed in long pants and a thick parachute smock, in preparation for the inevitable mauling.

The lions never meant any harm, but they simply could not comprehend that, unlike them, I was not covered in thick fur, and that my fragile human skin was no match for their claws and fangs. I bled a lot for those lions!

The first part of our morning regimen was a walk to the rear of the house, 50 metres or so along the access track. Then I would stop and call them from wherever they were lurking in the bush near the boats. To go and look for them in the thick scrub was to invite an unexpected ambush and I preferred to see them approaching. It gave me time to take the necessary action to steel myself for the ferocious assault.

After a while, I would spot a slight rustle in the tall grass. To pinpoint their positions I always shouted their names, followed by "Come along then, my beautiful little babies!"

Invariably, their tails rose up above the grass as they responded to my call. Of course, by no stretch of the imagination, could they be described as "beautiful little babies", but one does tend to get a bit soppy about animals.

They certainly were magnificent and exceedingly affectionate into the bargain.

I followed their stalking progress by keeping tabs on their tails. For them, this was the first game of the day. They stalked in single file, Rufus always leading, until they reached the edge of the track.

Here, they hunkered down side by side, back legs drawn up under their bodies, bellies close to the ground, yellow eyes firmly fixed on me, every muscle tensed for the final charge.

I didn't want to spoil their fun by acknowledging that they had been spotted. They would simply subside into a heap unless I could induce them to charge. The whole idea was to get them mobile so that we could take our daily constitution, so I had to sit down in the track with my back turned towards them. For reasons best known to itself, a lion cannot resist charging when one turns one's back.

I would go down on my knees, every muscle tensed for the impact. The sudden rustle of the grass behind me would in-

The author in front of his Sabre during Operation Protea. The others in the picture are, from the left: Sgt Major Dennis Craukamp (ex-Selous Scout), Cpl Price (driver and ex-RLI), Cpl David Barr behind the guns (ex-Marine, ex-Israeli paratrooper and ex-RLI) who lost his legs in a mine blast about a week after this photograph was taken.

The resident pack of wild dogs near Fort St Michél.

Poachers were an ongoing plague. A few Bushman troops from Fort Doppies with confiscated game meat. Shuffle Foot is on the right.

Some poached elephants, one with only one tusk removed.

A young elephant getting out of a river.

Two young elephant bulls near Buffalo Lodge.

Playing games with an adult lion can be a frightening experience!

The author relaxing in the lounge of the house that he built himself in the Riverine forest, Buffalo Lodge.

Ros laying out Sunday breakfast.

Buffalo Lodge nestled in the shady trees.

Bull elephants on an island across the lagoon from Buffalo Lodge.

Going "walkies" with the young cubs Rufus and Dayan.

Dayan inspecting the rations prepared by Pine Pienaar.

Rufus and Dayan exploring their surrounds.

The Zambezi River as it meanders by Katima Mulilo.

Lechwes grazing on Lupala island.

Taunu doing his "morning business".

Taunu checking out a Unimog.

The author with the fully grown Taunu.

dicate the start of the charge, followed by the heavy thud of pounding feet as the lions bore down on my inviting back.

First one, usually Rufus, then the other hit me with tremendous force. I always ended up underneath them, being rolled around in the sand while they went for my head and shoulders with jaws wide open, terrifying white fangs glistening.

A nibble here and a nibble there – always painful – was followed by rasping, wet tongues covering my face and arms in a show of slobbering affection.

Fortunately, the urge to wrestle quickly turned to a contest between the brothers and I could wriggle out from under them to commence the morning stroll.

We would walk up the track, the lions either next to me or slightly ahead. Every time Rufus lagged behind I could expect him to pounce on my back, so I preferred to keep him at my side.

Almost every morning, as we moved away from the lagoon and the river, we could expect to encounter the resident troop of baboons. These fellows became stressed and almost hysterical when they saw us approaching, with a tremendous amount of barking and threatening gestures from the males and much frightened screeching from the juveniles.

Rufus displayed great interest in the antics of the baboons and would stand below the tree while they chattered incessantly in the branches above. However, he never growled at them, they were just an interesting curiosity. Dayan always stayed with me, showing his disapproval that Rufus was holding up our walk.

At the first turn in the track, Pine would be waiting with their morning rations in the Land Rover.

They loved Pine and another round of ecstatic greeting and wrestling followed until finally it was time to get back to the enclosure and to their meal.

Once the lions were safely back in their cage, my wife and Recce could venture forth from the safety of the house and I could go to work to perform my soldierly duties, without fretting about what the lions were up to.

However, the morning walks were just one small step towards moving the lions back into their own environment. The next step was to have them stay in the depths of the forest all day, bringing them back at night to the vicinity of the house, where they were reasonably protected from hyenas, leopards and other lions, especially my savage friend and his pride to the north.

So the morning walks were extended to coax the lions to a particularly idyllic spot situated away from the river and deep inside an extensive stand of *Burkea africana*, commonly known as red syringas.

It was a much longer walk and I had to get up earlier each day.

On the first morning, I met Pine halfway with his bucket of meat. We took the lions deep inside the forest, past a troop of protesting monkeys, and settled them in a grassy glade, each with a huge pile of meat in an aluminium bowl filled to the brim with a delightful mixture of milk, Pro Nutro and some of the Special Forces' concentrated vitamins and minerals. As we slowly made our way back to our vehicle, the lions tucked in.

For the rest of the morning I worried about the two youngsters, picturing them at the mercy of a marauding lion, on the receiving end of a concerted attack by baboons or wandering around completely lost, while trying to find their way back to my house and their human "parents".

Eventually, I could take it no longer, and halfway through the day, I went back to where we had left them.

They were nowhere in sight.

Thoroughly worried, I began to call them, but there was neither sight nor sound of the missing lions.

I covered the entire area, becoming more and more frantic and visualising them at the mercy of the less than friendly neighbouring pride of lions. I was thinking about deploying all my available troops to carry out an extended line sweep through the forest, when I was suddenly bowled over by an attack from the rear, and ended up as the wrestling mat for Rufus and Dayan who had been stalking me for the last half hour or so, while I wandered around calling them.

Notwithstanding the discomfort of their robust attention, I was delighted to see the lions and happily walked them home, to the consternation of my wife and, no doubt, Recce.

Of course, the next day I had to take a firm grip on myself. We could not keep the lions forever and I simply had to go through the whole exercise again. I tried hard not to think of all the dangers lurking in the deepest recesses of the forest.

It was always astonishing to see the absolute trust these wild animals showed towards their human mentors. They were quite happy to leave Pine and me to determine their daily routine and future, showed no signs of anxiety, and happily fell in with whatever we had in mind. This made me doubly aware of my responsibility for their safety and wellbeing.

I knew virtually nothing of lions and had not much more than a rudimentary knowledge of the African savannah. So, with deep concentration, I read all the lion books I could lay my hands on, including everything written by George Adamson, the lion man of Africa, a book written by Dr Smuts and, of course, the excellent volume by Smithers and his team, *The Mammals of Southern Africa*.

It was no use seeking advice from the local Bushmen about the lions, because to them the animals posed a threat, were viewed with superstition and were generally considered a menace to God's creation. Bushmen tend to steer clear of lions.

The same applied to the members of the Mafwe tribe, just across the river, except that their solution to any lion problem was energetic extermination the moment one came anywhere near their cattle kraals.

After their first full day in the bush, Pine and I anxiously went out to find the lions, taking with us their meat and milk rations to entice them back to the enclosure at my house.

They came bounding out of the forest, clearly happy to see us. We were even more pleased to see them. We took them home along an elephant footpath and the edge of the lagoon to where Pine's Land Rover was parked near their cage.

The walk was punctuated by much stalking and ambushing, but we finally got them home and safely ensconced inside their enclosure, tucking into their food.

This procedure was followed for several months, by which time both lions were showing the first signs of sprouting manes. They were becoming quite big, bigger, in fact, than other lions of their age, probably because of the excellent rations they were getting.

Around this time, I received visitors from Pretoria, two of whom stayed at my house, while the rest were accommodated in the St Michél mess. My house guests were long-standing friends and therefore more than welcome.

Pine assumed full responsibility for the lions, my commitments to the visitors preventing me from caring for them temporarily. It never occurred to me to inform our guests that lions lurked around my house at night, as by then Rufus and Dayan were less playful, though they continued to prowl around the grounds, terrifying the baboons in their perches downriver, but generally making less noise than previously.

After a splendid dinner and a few bottles of good wine one night, I took my mellow guests home, where they soon settled down in the quiet and darkness of an African wilderness night.

The next morning they rose bright and early, refreshed after the tedium of keeping their noses to the grindstone in bureaucrat-ridden Pretoria.

Sybie van der Spuy, a spic-and-span soldier, liked his boots to be polished and buffed in keeping with the age-old infantry tradition, so, armed with a tin of polish, a battery of brushes and his boots, he found a spot on the verandah and proceeded to coax a glass-like sheen from the well-polished leather.

Rufus and Dayan had been nestling near the boats, but when they heard the early morning movement at the house, they decided to start the day in their customary fashion. They set about stalking the house, their ultimate target the man on the verandah happily shining his boots.

Sybie looked up just as Rufus raised his head above the furthest end of the verandah, his polishing halted in mid-stroke as he stared in amazement at the huge creature glaring at him with yellow eyes just over the concrete surround of the verandah floor.

"Jan," he said, "this dog of yours looks just like a lion."

The next moment, Rufus charged with a growl.

"It is a lion!" shouted Sybie as boots, polish, brushes and other cleaning paraphernalia flew in all directions.

Dayan added his considerable weight to that of Rufus and a comical struggle ensued, with Sybie desperately trying to fend off the concerted attack of two ferocious man-eaters.

I rushed out to rescue Sybie but, as usual, Rufus and Dayan had already turned their attention from Sybie to a wrestling match between themselves, the struggle for possession of Sybie's discarded brushes, highly polished boots and an open tin of brown polish, adding fresh interest to the bout.

It was with great difficulty and amid much growling that I retrieved Sybie's boots and returned them to him, by which time he was safely behind the wire screen of my lounge.

On another occasion, one of my majors, the proud father of a young toddler, had visitors from the Republic.

Pine and I were on the way back from the forest with Rufus and Dayan when the officer and his visitors came upon us as we crossed the access track to Fort St Michél. They had been game viewing and were returning to the base and the lions suddenly found themselves the main attraction of the day.

It had been my policy to keep the lions away from people, except those who worked with them. But I felt duty bound to interrupt our walk, so that the "rubbernecks" could take photographs of "wild" lions at close quarters.

Dayan was most unhappy with the attention, refusing to co-operate and lying down in the long grass where he tried to stay out of sight.

Of course, the major had to come across to pet the more amenable Rufus and everyone else in his party followed suit. Rufus became confused by all the people milling around, sank down ominously on his stomach and flattened his ears.

The major's wife, however, decided that the picture of the day would be a snapshot of her toddler sitting with his arm around the lion's muscular neck.

Without as much as a "by your leave", she deposited the infant on the ground, within easy range of Rufus's jaws. I could see that the lion was getting agitated, and I heard a soft growl forming in his throat.

Quickly, and rather rudely, I grabbed the child and pushed him into his indignant mother's arms. Incredibly, seemingly not the slightest bit perturbed, she again propped the child against the lion's flank, whereupon I lost my temper.

"Take your child away and stop pestering my lions!" I shouted at her.

"I want a photograph of my son with the lion!" she retorted.

"If you want a photograph of a lion with your badly mauled and dead son, say so, but I refuse to have my lions upset by you, your child or your friends."

The major, now also highly indignant, chipped in that all they wanted to do was take some photographs.

With a complete lack of diplomacy, I ordered him to take his guests and to get the hell out of my sight within seconds.

Rufus and Dayan were as taut as bowstrings and I fully expected to see two ferocious animals tear into the ill-disciplined mob wandering around the two terrified lions. Keeping them under control under impossibly difficult circumstances would not be easy.

In a huff, the major ushered his guests into his Land Cruiser and drove off, wheels spinning in a cloud of dust. It was an inauspicious end to their game viewing, but it took us almost an hour to pacify the lions and get them on the move again to my home and safety.

Some months later, I was guilty of a serious misjudgement when I decided to get my own back on a corporal who had given me good reason to discipline him.

My British brother-in-law had come all the way to the Caprivi to visit and I decided we would take the short cut through Botswana when travelling to South Africa on my annual leave. This meant I had to travel on a false passport, as the Botswanas would have liked to get hold of me and hand me over to the

Zimbabweans. I had escaped a Zimbabwean hit-squad in Francistown some years before with only hours to spare.

To enter Botswana, we had to pass through the South African customs post at Ngoma Gate, on the Chobe River, just inside the eastern Caprivi where the barrier was manned by members of 701 Battalion.

We duly parked our vehicle and checked through immigration and customs. I had parked in front of the customs building, as no other parking area was indicated.

As we were getting back into the car, a corporal from 701 Battalion came strutting over and rudely ordered us out. Then he ordered me to park my car elsewhere. I was on the point of departing, anyway, and I told him so. He started to berate me and threatened that he would shoot me unless I moved the car.

My habitually short fuse ignited and I told the corporal what I thought of him as a soldier, that I took an extremely dim view of his bullying manner when dealing with the public and promised I would make it my business to sort him out after my return from the Republic.

He, of course, had no idea that I was a colonel in the army and bemused by my violent reaction, made no response.

I drove off, fuming in anger.

Three weeks later I returned through the same border post, this time with my wife. I sought out the corporal, informed him of my real identity and assured him I was looking forward to having him all to myself in my Caprivi base, so that I could sort him out as I had promised.

In due course I prevailed upon his commanding officer, a friend, to post him to me for two weeks.

The corporal spent his time digging ditches in the heat of the day, laying pipes and generally being given a hard time with little respite from dawn to dusk. In between he had to write essays on how to deal with the public, a soldier's niche in serving the community and good, old-fashioned manners.

Towards the end of his time with us, I decided to teach him a final lesson by bringing him face to face with the lions. I hoped to scare the daylights out of him.

He did not know about the lions as they never came near Fort St Michél, so it was with unconcealed disbelief that he heard me inform him that he and I were going into the bush to feed the lions.

By this time, Rufus and Dayan were staying in the vicinity of their feeding area on a permanent basis. I had stopped taking them home every evening, much to the relief of both my wife and Recce.

We drove into the bush with the meat ration, the corporal clearly apprehensive about the unorthodox exercise, refraining from comment.

The lions were not at their usual feeding site, so I divided the rations in two and posted the corporal to guard the food while I went out into the bush to call the lions. I also informed him that should the lions appear while I was gone, he was to make sure that each lion went to its own pile of meat to prevent them from fighting each other.

He looked at me with wide-eyed incomprehension and misgiving, but in utter silence. He was unarmed.

I moved to the river and soon disappeared from sight, calling loudly for two virtually fully grown lions. "Come on then, my beautiful little babies! Come on then! Come and get it, baby boys!" I don't know what the corporal thought of a colonel wandering through the bush calling lions as if they were helpless little kittens.

I soon found them, or rather, they found me after the usual lengthy stalk and we wrestled on the river bank for about half an hour.

When they had had enough of the horseplay, they began moving to their feeding site.

We strolled along placidly on the well-trodden elephant footpath and as we approached the shady glade, my vehicle became visible through the shrubs. I could also see the corporal, staring at me incredulously as I rounded the bend. The grass was fairly tall and the lions were quite close to him before he saw them for the first time.

Rufus, as usual, led the way, and he saw the corporal almost at the same moment the corporal saw him. The lion's demean-our changed instantly from that of placid playmate to the high-ly strung tautness of the predator. He sank down and, his eyes fixed firmly on the frightened face of the corporal, advanced in a low crouch. Dayan was right behind at first, but slowly, with sinister intent, he moved off to a flank. They were going to at-tack the corporal from two sides.

The corporal found his voice. Trembling with fright and in an unnatural, high-pitched voice, he pointed a shaking finger at a pile of meat. "This is your meat. This is your meat," he said to Rufus, almost pleadingly.

Rufus had no interest in his supper. His attention was riv-eted on the corporal, at whom he suddenly launched himself with a blood-curdling snarl.

In a panic I rushed forward to grab the lion and pull him off the now petrified soldier. Rufus had him by one arm, sharp fangs sinking into his flesh.

I shouted desperately at Rufus, injecting all the anger I could muster into my voice. He relaxed his hold and I managed to pull him clear, only to be confronted by Dayan attacking from the other side. Another struggle followed with the corporal sobbing and pleading. "Please, Colonel! They will kill me! They will kill me!"

My first priority was to get the corporal to the nearby Land Cruiser. "Walk to the Cruiser!" I shouted above the tumult of growling lions. My final lesson in manners was backfiring hor-ribly.

But the corporal was frozen to the spot. "They will kill me!" he wailed.

"Walk to the Cruiser!" I shouted again, pushing him towards the vehicle, despite the fact that Rufus had the corporal firmly by the other arm. "Colonel!" he wailed "I promise you, I will never be rude to you again."

This was no time for apologies. "Walk to the Cruiser!" I shouted, by now desperate.

After what seemed an eternity, I managed to get him into the back of the Land Cruiser, where Rufus promptly joined him. Another struggle developed between Rufus and me, until I finally had the corporal sitting in the cab, both windows rolled up, grey with fear and sobbing uncontrollably.

As soon as their prey was out of reach, the lions lost interest, calmly strolled over to their respective piles of meat and started feeding. I swore at them for a while but they took not the slightest notice. Then we returned to St Michél. I was feeling pretty shaky myself.

The corporal was subsequently posted to Kongola, just across the Cuando from our training area. There he manned an internal control point with his section of men. Once in a while, I used to drive to Katima for business or to do some private shopping and passing through the control point was a tedious business. Logbooks were inspected, forms were filled in and sometimes vehicles were searched from front bumper to rear.

After the first turn from the bridge over the Cuando, the road stretched straight and level for about two kilometres before reaching the control point.

On my way to Katima one morning, I was therefore somewhat surprised to see the boom being raised long before I reached it. I was even more surprised to see the entire infantry section formed up next to the control point. I almost fell out of my vehicle when they smartly presented arms as I passed through.

A broadly smiling corporal, now thoroughly imbued with good manners, waved me through without stopping.

Although the lions had now been weaned as far as human companionship was concerned, they were still not independent. They persisted in their habit of paying unexpected visits to my house, much to my wife's discomfort, and I was ambushed more than once by Rufus returning from the mess. He would wait for me in the dark, just around the corner of the house. It was a nerve-wracking business to climb out of the Land Cruiser and make sure that the coast was clear before my wife would budge from the safety of the cab.

Pine and I therefore decided that the next step in their education was to take them to a place from which it would be too difficult for them to return to my house and their familiar stomping grounds. We decided on an area north of St Michél, which was to act as a barrier between the lions and the Breytenbach family, including Recce the cat.

For some reason or another the lions were wary of St Michél and the strange noises emanating from there.

On the night of the exodus, it was arranged that St Michél would shut down. All lights were switched off and everyone in the camp confined to home or quarters. Not a sound was to be made by any machine or generator.

Pine and I took the track leading through St Michél and further northwards. It would have been impossible to transport the lions in the Land Cruiser, as they were not accustomed to riding in a vehicle, having last done so when they were much smaller, and heavily sedated.

The moon was shining brightly and it took a great amount of coaxing to get the lions on the move. They were nonplussed by the unusual activity but at the same time quite curious about the fresh terrain opening up before them as we headed north.

With some reluctance and trepidation, they gingerly made their way through a deathly quiet St Michél, situated on the slopes and crest of a thickly wooded sand dune. They glanced at the few buildings they could see from the road, no doubt taking in the strange smells of the vehicle park, workshop and refuelling point, and moved off into the more acceptable flood plain beyond.

I left Pine north of St Michél to carry on alone to the lions' new home. There was already a tent in the area which Pine would use, so that at least someone whom the lions knew and trusted would be on hand to help them through that first night in unfamiliar surroundings.

About three kilometres north of St Michél, the man and the lions turned off to the right, through a vast flood plain to a dense, far distant riverine forest. The forest ran down to the Cuando mainstream and was a well-used drinking site for all sorts of game. It was, therefore, a place where their education would enter a whole new phase.

I dearly wanted them to start hunting on their own, but I had not the foggiest idea how to go about it. Not even George Adamson could give me much assistance in this respect. All the other books I had read, except his, hammered on the fact that it was virtually impossible to reintroduce tame lions to the wild.

But, like Adamson, I remained optimistic. I had no intention of being saddled with two huge ravenous lions for the rest of our collective natural lives.

As Pine trudged through the night with the two recalcitrant lions, a herd of elephants suddenly materialised, moving in the same direction, en route to their distant but favoured water hole. As they stumbled on the modern-day Moses leading a two-lion band of Israelites to their promised land, all hell broke loose. The elephants, a breeding herd with calves, began to trumpet loudly and charge in all directions as they tried to chase the lions back into bondage.

Pine dashed for a lonely clump of combretums and scaled the biggest one he could find, though it was a rather puny one, with a tendency to droop alarmingly towards the ground.

The lions immediately took up the challenge, charging the elephants with mighty growls and snarls. They probably thought it was a game.

The last Pine saw of the herd was a cloud of dust as they disappeared in the moonlight, stampeding over the flood plain with the two lions in close pursuit.

He stayed in his little tree until long after the commotion and trumpeting had died down, then climbed down to face the daunting task of finding his lions.

Like a lost soul he wandered through the tall grasses of the extensive plain, calling the two absconders without much hope of ever seeing them again.

To his absolute surprise, and indignation, Rufus suddenly signalled his return with an unexpected attack from the rear. Pine had found his lions, after all, and they proceeded peacefully once more to the new location. Many hours later they reached the tent and an exhausted Pine fell into bed, only to be pounced on by his rambunctious companions. There would be no sleep that night.

The next morning I took a load of fresh rations to them. We fed the lions and decided to leave them on their own for the rest of the day.

Pine and a friend of his returned in the evening to be close to their charges and experienced a repeat performance of the previous night's antics. Nights were made for leonine activity and there was no sleep that night either.

Eventually, it became necessary to change their normal human habits and sleep by day, so that they could play by night.

During the day, when the lions were less demanding, Pine and his buddy did some fishing, much to the delight of Rufus. No sooner would a fish be landed and Rufus had laid claim to it. It became his habit to watch the float almost as keenly as the fisherman and from the moment an angler started to reel in, it became a race between the two to determine who would get to the fish first. Needless to say, no sensible fisherman would even attempt to snatch a delicate morsel from the jaws of an almost fully grown lion.

After a day or two, Pine's pal gave up. He had been bitten black and blue by the two lions and decided enough was enough. He trekked back to his workshop, leaving Pine alone with his charges.

A few days later, I moved Pine away as well. By then the lions were well and truly established in their new habitat and, more importantly, thoroughly enjoying it.

No one went near them except for Pine, my wife and me. I issued very strict instructions that no training was to be conducted in the area and though we did carry out some parachute jumps on the extensive flood plains, the lions stayed out of sight. The jumpers, in any case, were completely unaware of their existence.

It always amazed me to experience anew the attachment of lions to Pine and me. After being away on leave for three weeks, they were all over me when I returned. The same happened each time I visited their new locality.

From time to time, it was necessary for me to fly down to Pretoria, the mecca of moribund bureaucracy and the centre of religiously applied red tape and regulations. I am convinced that somewhere in Pretoria there is a secret factory where they manufacture the millions of kilometres of red tape needed by ardent, hidebound civil servants to strangle those who show any sign of initiative, or dare to challenge the cast-iron system, even if the protest amounts to no more than a whimper.

I always returned from Pretoria with my soul polluted by officialdom, choked by rules and regulations, dazed by the circuitous passing of the buck and frustrated by the infinite attempts to postpone the moment of decision. Looking forward to getting back to real life, honesty and genuine companionship in the company of my lions, I was never disappointed when I once again felt the dust of the Caprivi under my feet. Strangely enough, the lions normally took a long time to answer my calls, but after one of my absences, they would come bounding up within seconds, bowl me over in their enthusiasm and ply me with their rough tongues until my face and arms were raw, red and sore.

It was always great to get back and be accepted by the savage but uncomplicated soul of Africa, to be once again at one with some of its creatures. Those rough tongues soon cleansed me of civilisation's contamination.

But there was still the problem of getting my temporary charges accepted by their own ilk and affording them at least an even chance of survival. The primitive life, about which I wax so lyrical, revolves around one vital factor: survival of the fittest.

I began by trying to follow the feeding pattern of lions that roamed freely and hunted for their food. At best, they can count on a meal every second day, but normally it's every third day. Of course, once they have made a decent kill, they gorge themselves to a standstill in preparation for the lean days ahead.

I started to cut back on Rufus and Dayan's meals, feeding them only in the evening, though the daily amount of food remained the same. It was my intention to get them used to a good feed every second day.

Teaching them to hunt for themselves remained the biggest and most difficult problem.

Incredible as it may seem, lions do not, on the whole, appear to be natural hunters. To Rufus and Dayan, stalking was a game. They would view distant game with interest, but made no attempt to close in on them, at least not while we were about. In our role as "victims", we were much closer, more available and seemed to fully satisfy their instinctive urge to stalk something.

I considered the possibility of deliberately wounding an animal, perhaps an impala, and leaving it at the mercy of the lions, to "play" with, so to speak, in order to arouse their hunting or killer instincts, but before such a drastic measure could be taken, disaster struck.

I remember lying in bed one morning and listening to the incessant roaring of lions close to St Michél. From the sound, I knew something was amiss.

On arrival at the base, I was met by some very concerned naval personnel who had been erecting extra accommodation, with the news that the old lion from the north had been sorting out some young lions only a few hundred metres from the camp. The young lions had run away.

I attached no immediate significance to the information, knowing that Rufus and Dayan were a considerable distance from where this incident had taken place.

But the next day I found the lions' meat rations putrefying and crawling with flies. There was no sign of either lion. This was definitely unusual, and for the first time the incident of the previous day loomed ominously in my mind.

I went up and down the river, calling the lions as I went, but there was no response. I followed their spoor along the river bank for several kilometres, but found no hint as to their probable fate. In the end, I had to give up as darkness was falling.

Soon everyone was looking out for Rufus and Dayan. We stared into the blue sky for any sign of a build-up of vultures, we listened to the hyenas at night, we tried to interpret the roars from the northern pride, but we found no evidence on the whereabouts of Rufus and Dayan.

I was abandoning hope when one of my men reported that he had come across the northern pride and that Rufus, or at least a young lion, was among them. I knew that the pride had not previously included young lions, and this news was encouraging. After all, the objective had always been to place the lions back with their own.

A male lion cannot easily survive unless he forms part of a pride where teamwork, and the killing ability of the lionesses, form the backbone of the capacity to survive.

But the news accounted for only one of my lions.

A week later, I was driving home from work with my wife when I spotted the spoor of a lion crossing the road fairly close to my house and stopped to investigate.

It was definitely the spoor of one of my lions and it led to the reeds blanketing the swampy western edge of the lagoon.

I called and to my unbridled joy, the unmistakeable head and shoulders of Dayan emerged from the thick cluster of reeds.

He was in dreadful shape, with a stare coat. His mane was unkempt and clogged with grass and twigs, but I knelt down in front of him, put my arms around his neck and almost cried as he licked me with his rough tongue.

He was subdued and painfully thin. I sent Ros, my wife, back to the camp to fetch some meat and one of the men to help me get him back to the enclosure at the house.

Dayan, however, took it upon himself to move away, in the opposite direction from the house, and deeper into the forest. All I could do was follow him, hoping he might even lead me to Rufus. But he walked a few hundred metres before collapsing, panting like a dog. There was obviously something seriously wrong with him.

We managed to get him into the back of my Land Cruiser and then into the cage. I tried to feed him, but he would not take anything. He was panting rapidly, as if he was having trouble breathing. Eventually he did take a little milk mixed with Pro Nutro, but that was all.

I noticed some blood on one of his front paws, but at the time, its relevance escaped me.

The next day I sent one of my men to summon the vet from Katima. I sent a detailed description of Dayan's symptons and asked the vet to come and examine the animal himself.

He could not come, but sent a course of antibiotics for Dayan. According to him, the lion had some kind of inflammation in the digestive system. My wife, a trained nurse, gave Dayan his injections as prescribed by the vet.

It was heartbreaking to watch him. His breathing was shallow and rapid and he just lay on his side, unable to get up or move around at all.

I sat with him for hours, talking to him and stroking him, trying to induce some interest in the meat and milk that were always close at hand.

But he showed no interest in food and every time I tried to leave, Dayan would lift up a huge paw and place it firmly on my head, forcing me to sit down again and stay with him. He would lick my hand for a while afterwards, his paw still on my head.

The message was clear. He did not want me to leave him alone in his distress.

Of course I had to desert him from time to time. I still had a unit to run.

One incident in particular stands out clearly in my mind from this period. A delegation from my Pretoria headquarters, including a certain general, came to visit. While there, the general accompanied me when I went to care for Dayan, trying to give him at least some moral and medical support. The general stayed outside the cage, watching sceptically.

"I don't know how you can touch that thing," he said. "I will never trust a lion, no matter how sick it is."

The remark illustrated perfectly the attitude of this particular general to wildlife. His extremely capable brain was so clogged with the intricacies of the rat race and power play, the lifeblood of ambition in Pretoria, the seat of that great idol called personal achievement, that absolutely no room remained for compassion for the animals of the wild.

Some time later, this same general took a herd of elephants under fire with a 50 Browning heavy machine gun from the safety of a circling helicopter. He fired into the herd not caring how many animals were killed or wounded in the process and was immensely proud of his achievement.

Fortunately, this man had business elsewhere, so he soon left me to get on with our fight for the lion's life.

Sadly, despite all our efforts, he showed no sign of improvement. Ros had administered the whole course of antibiotics as prescribed by the vet, but it made no difference. All we could do was wait and hope.

On the last morning we were woken by tremendous roars from the direction of the cage. I jumped up, dressed quickly and rushed to the cage, where Dayan had reared up on his hind legs, his front paws clawing at the wire mesh as he gazed out across the flood plain and lagoon. He was roaring from deep inside his chest at Africa and the rising sun.

I rushed back to Ros to tell her the wonderful news, that Dayan was at last back on his feet and that I was going to the mess to fetch him a huge helping of meat to welcome him back to the land of the living.

When I returned with the meat, I found Ros on her way back to the house from the cage, in tears. "He is dead," she sobbed.

I rushed to the cage. Dayan was lying on his side, the early morning sun bathing his fur with a golden glow, his yellow eyes staring blankly up into the African sky.

In his dying moments, the magnificent beast had summoned all his strength to roar his farewell to Africa and perhaps to Rufus out there somewhere. He had said his farewells in his own majestic way, as only an animal of noble birth is capable of doing, then left this world as bravely as any king ever did.

It is always a tremendous blow to a nature conservator when a project, such as the one involving my lions, ends in failure. I felt I had to carefully review the drama of Dayan's last days to learn where I had gone wrong.

Firstly, I should have investigated the extent of the northern pride's territory far more thoroughly than I did. I obviously encroached on the southern limits of their domain when I moved Rufus and Dayan north of St Michél. It was only a matter of time before my old adversary from the north picked up the presence of the youngsters. Territories do not remain territories unless they are covered regularly by patrolling.

Secondly, I should have kept the lions under closer surveillance, nearer to my house, for a longer period. Incidentally, it seems my house was located in a sort of no-man's land between the territory of the northern pride and that of Terry and his pride to the south. Rufus and Dayan were much safer in the immediate vicinity of my home than anywhere else in the western Caprivi.

Inevitably, my military duties clashed with my conservation duties and it quickly became apparent that tending properly to a couple of frisky lions can be extremely time-consuming. The rule of the clock must be thrown overboard when one deals with wild animals on an intimate basis and this is patently impossible when one also has a military unit to command.

Many a day I seethed with impatience when the lions stubbornly refused to do what was expected of them, such as keep moving on our early morning walks so that I could get them to their feeding place in time for me to keep an appointment with an expectant class of eager students at one of my training bases.

It was not so much the reluctance to keep moving as their need to play and wrestle for as long as possible that made it rather difficult to stick to a schedule.

There was a heap of sand next to the track that held a particular attraction for them and where they played their version of the children's game, king of the castle. One lion kept on pushing the other off the top. If I tried to pull them off the heap they seemed to think, not unreasonably, that I had decided to join them in their fun and it became my turn to be pushed off the heap. Sometimes I could get them past the heap of sand for a hundred metres or more before one of them, usually Rufus, would suddenly remember and rush back to establish himself as king of the castle. Dayan would take up the challenge at once.

The point is one should not be bound by other commitments when working closely with wild animals.

I spent much time ruminating on Dayan's illness. It was obvious, in hindsight, that Dayan had not had gastroenteritis. I only wished the vet could have come to examine him instead of relying for his diagnosis on my description of the symptoms, which included a green and loose discharge from his bowels.

The blood on his one front paw assumed a new significance as I thought about it. There were two puncture marks on top of his paw from which the blood had been oozing, and, too late, I reached the terrible conclusion that Dayan had been bitten by a snake, probably while trying to catch it for a meal. His laboured breathing and lack of response to the antibiotics seemed to confirm that it was a cobra-type snake.

I believe that his tremendously strong heart finally packed up under the strain on that last morning when he roared his tragic last farewell.

We buried Dayan and all I had left to remind me of him and Rufus were two empty and very battered aluminium bowls. I still hoped for the best as far as Rufus was concerned and asked everyone to keep an eye out for him.

It wasn't long before a report came in that a young lion was definitely with the northern pride. Then another report reached me from one of the men who had been driving a Unimog to one of the northern bases. He had spotted a lion in the long grass and stopped the truck. The lion, a young male, approached the vehicle, in no hurry to reach it, but not wavering in his stride either. He was heading somewhere and the truck was just something he had to pass on the way.

The driver, feeling rather apprehensive, drove on before the lion reached him. He saw the animal cross the track behind him, heading for the very spot on the river frequented by Rufus and Dayan before they disappeared.

This lion's behaviour indicated that he was used to human company. A wild lion would have stopped, turned around and made a wide detour to reach its destination. Thinking that perhaps it was Rufus, I immediately went to the river to look for spoor, but found nothing.

Some months after Dayan's death, I began finding lion spoor fairly frequently in close proximity to Buffalo Lodge, our house on the lagoon. On one occasion the spoor led down to the cage where the lions had spent their youth. The imprint was too big for a lioness, but not that of a fully grown adult, either.

Later the spoor of a lioness was found with that of the young male from time to time.

For the first time, too, a lion could be heard roaring quite close to the house. Normally, their roars were some distance away to the north. They rarely ventured south of Fort St Michél.

It became obvious that a lion and his mate had taken up residence in the no-man's land between the two established territories. I dared to hope that the new resident lion might be Rufus, probably having left the old lion's pride when he began to pose a threat to his leadership. I have no doubt that Rufus would have been tolerated inside the pride only up to a certain point, and that thereafter, he would have been expelled.

Lions not strong enough or too young to assert themselves in a pride become nomadic, pinching prey from the territory of other lions or are forced into areas where game is scarce and other lions don't go. They are forced to move around a great deal, hence the term nomadic, and frequently team up with lionesses in a similar predicament.

In this case, there was plenty of prey to be had in the area that this fledgling pride, presumably Rufus and his mate, selected as their territory.

There were simply not enough lions to stake out all the available claims due to hunting pressure before we moved in to control the Fort St Michél training area.

I know of several incidents where lions were callously shot by hunters from the south who regarded them as vermin. To shoot a lion was to do the Caprivi a big favour, and of course, an enormous boost to the ego.

My wife once spotted a lioness lying out over the water on the limb of a sycamore fig tree, just below the cage Rufus and Dayan had occupied. It is not impossible that this was Rufus's mate and that he was somewhere nearby. A wild lioness would not make herself at home within 30 metres of an inhabited house, especially in broad daylight, unless she was accompanied by an animal who knew no fear of humans.

I also spotted this lioness, on her own with two young cubs, and two years later I saw her again in the same territory but some distance from the river, with three small cubs. The first two had probably grown big enough by then to set off into the world on their own.

Much later I saw her south of Fort Doppies with the same three cubs which, by that time, were as big as their mother.

But this was after the most tragic episode of all during my short spell as a nature conservator.

One day I was heading inland, away from the river towards Malombe pan, when I came across the fresh spoor of a small herd of buffalo which had crossed the road from north to south.

This herd had been under tremendous pressure from poachers and reckless drivers. There was one particular driver, who worked for Military Intelligence, who had ploughed into the herd at night on two separate occasions.

The first time he killed one cow and no doubt injured several others. The second time he killed two cows and a calf. On both occasions he was driving a 10-ton Samil truck.

The first time I reported him to his commander, but no steps were taken against him. The second time I grabbed him and threatened him with terminal consequences if I ever saw him in the western Caprivi again. Once more his boss turned a blind eye, but the driver got the message and gave the western Caprivi a wide berth from then on.

I therefore had a particular interest in the welfare of this small herd, about 30 strong, and decided to follow them. They were heading south-east along a little used track to some fairly substantial water pans not too far off the main road. I stopped short of the pans and went forward on foot.

I was not armed, having long ceased to carry a rifle, as I felt common sense and acute observation were more than adequate protection for anyone venturing into the wilds of Africa.

On reaching the pans I stood for a while, trying to decipher the deep muddy imprints of the buffaloes when suddenly there was an angry growl close by.

A fully grown but youngish lion jumped up from its lair in

the long grass fringing the pan and ran away. To my horror, I saw that its right rear leg was swinging loosely from the hip, like the empty trouser leg of an amputee.

I scrutinised the lion more intently and recognised him almost immediately. It was, unmistakeably, Rufus.

When I shouted to him, he stopped in his tracks, sat down and looked at me. He was no more than 50 paces away and I closed the distance to about 30 paces. Not once did he move or show any distress at my presence.

He was still in good condition, apart from his broken leg, but with that injury it would be impossible for him to obtain adequate food, so the accident must have been a recent one.

The reckless driver from Military Intelligence sprang to mind, and my blood boiled. I was convinced that Rufus had been run down by a night driver while crossing the nearby Golden Highway.

For a while, I talked to him, trying to decide what to do about his leg, which was obviously broken in the femur.

In spite of his past, Rufus was now a completely wild lion and to approach him and handle him would be foolhardy. I had no equipment with which to dart him and nor did any other conservation station in the northern border area. It would take time to get equipment from Windhoek and I knew, in any case, what Windhoek's reaction would be. To them, lions were classified as vermin. Even if I could have the broken limb set in a plaster cast, how do you keep a grown male lion from tearing off the cast?

Where do you keep such a lion? Will a broken femur ever heal properly?

All these questions went through my mind as I searched desperately for an alternative to what I already knew was the only possible solution.

Rufus would have to be shot. There simply was no other way.

I drove the 15 kilometres back to Buffalo Lodge to fetch my rifle, but when I returned an hour or so later, Rufus was nowhere to be seen. I got out of the Land Cruiser, this time with my rifle, and started to walk carefully in the direction of the pan.

I was hardly twenty paces away from the vehicle when Rufus calmly rose to his feet almost directly ahead of me and no more than ten paces away.

He looked at me, his regal face now framed in a splendid mane. Stupidly, I started to make excuses to him, explaining that this was the only way out. I begged his forgiveness. He still did not respond, just looked at me steadily with those splendid yellow eyes.

I lifted the rifle, my trusty FN, and looked through the sights. He looked back at me unflinchingly. I pressed the trigger and Rufus dropped as if struck by a bolt of lightning.

I have been in many battles, fired many shots at many people, seen too many dead bodies, but I have never broken down, not even when a friend fell next to me.

But the day I shot Rufus and stood over his dead body, I cried and I could not help myself. It was as though I had shot my own son.

Even in his wild state, Rufus trusted me implicitly. He probably thought I would be able to help him, as I had always done before. But, in the end, I could not.

The only help I could offer him was a bullet between the eyes. That bullet was so final and Rufus was so dead. A final, thick rod line had been drawn at the bottom of the page dealing with the life and times of Rufus. Nothing would ever be able to resurrect him. No longer would he flow along, a golden form of pent-up force under easy and relaxed control as he moved silently through the dappled shade of the African woodland savannah, his proud face framed in his magnificent mane, his keen yellow eyes surveying his domain.

Rufus and Dayan gave me one of the most precious treasures I have ever had, their genuine affection for me as a friend, perhaps even a member of their family. Only a few men in Africa have known such a privilege and I thank God that I am one of them.

TEN

Taunu – The Lone Ranger

For a while after Dayan died, I was deprived of the company of a wild animal. Savimbi did promise to send me three lion cubs picked up somewhere in the Cuando-Cubango – the guerrilla school's reputation as lionkeepers had spread far and wide – but they were killed by his own troops before they could get to St Michél.

One night the silence was shattered by gunfire from the direction of Kongola bridge. Bouts of indiscriminate shooting at marauding elephants occurred from time to time on the other side of the river and were of great concern to me, but this time the shots seemed to be coming from the guard post on the bridge. I angrily jumped into my Land Cruiser and drove off to investigate.

I found four or five black troops from 701 Battalion crouched behind their sandbagged control point, staring fearfully into the dark.

"What the hell are you shooting at?" I demanded angrily.

They looked at me apprehensively. One of them, probably the guard commander, answered apologetically that some lions had crossed the road just 50 metres away.

"But we did not shoot at them, Colonel. We only fired into the air to frighten them off. We know that all the lions are your children and we will never hurt them."

Evidently the word had spread via the 701 Battalion corporal – who had learned to mind his manners – that I had a close relationship with wild lions, which obediently emerged from the bush every time I summoned them to be hand-fed by me.

I left without enlightening the troops. In Africa it could be advantageous to have a slightly sinister reputation, and an ability to consort or communicate with lions would be an accomplishment bordering on the unnatural.

My reputation among the indigenous people, including the Bushmen, was certainly not impaired when I unexpectedly found myself playing stepfather to the most beautiful animal God has ever created, a juvenile leopard.

Apart from being the most exquisite, the leopard is also one of the most dangerous animals in the African bush.

This one arrived on the ration truck one evening, sent all the way from Windhoek to Rundu and then on to us.

During the 400-kilometres trip from Rundu over the most atrocious roads in Namibia, the animal bounced around in a small cage in the back of the truck.

A label on the cage informed me that his name was Taunu. As I looked at this lovely but despondent-looking spotted cat, covered in dust and cooped up inside a tiny cage, he tugged at my heart-strings, and I felt desperately sorry for him.

Since we had no prior warning of Taunu's arrival, we had made no preparations to receive him.

Fortunately, the former lion enclosure at my house, where Rufus and Dayan had spent their early days, was still available.

Taunu looked at me through the mesh on the top of his little cage with doleful eyes. Instinctively, I pushed my finger through the wire and he immediately began to lick it. He responded to my voice with funny noises, halfway between a miaow and a whine. He was obviously craving human company.

Later I learned that he had been kept in the back yard of a Windhoek house until he grew too large, and perhaps too dangerous for the neighbours.

Taunu was taken to my house and I arranged for a ration of meat to be made available from the kitchen. When we placed his small cage inside the enclosure and released him, he exited like a bat out of hell, tackling me with a surprisingly powerful lunge at my throat before I was ready for him. A group of my men stood outside the enclosure, probably thinking they would have ringside seats to see the old man being sorted out by a wild leopard.

But, after his introductory lunge, Taunu sniffed at his meat and attacked it with relish. Only hours after his arrival, Taunu was beginning to find his feet in his new home.

My wife was none too happy about having another dangerous carnivorous animal so close to home, especially one that we would constantly have to be on guard against, since leopards are a lot more devious than lions.

Leopards love lying in a hide, perfectly camouflaged, and pouncing when one least expects it, so a simple stroll around the house, if the leopard was not confined, was going to be an exciting experience. It was one my wife could happily do without and she made that plain.

I wanted to keep closer control over the leopard, while at the same time doing my job as commander of the guerrilla school, so I decided it would be best to erect a large enclosure around my office. Taunu and I would share the same premises so that I could keep an eye on him and my wife would be a happy woman.

Fortunately, and deliberately, my office was situated in a rather isolated spot away from the main base. I had it built under some huge monkey-orange trees, the biggest I had ever seen. Therefore, Taunu would not be in the base as such and, consequently, not in daily contact with the occupants – so I thought.

I assigned Marius Heymann, one of my instructors and a former forester, to build the enclosure. Craig Gainsford, a young national serviceman who would assist him, was duly appointed keeper of the leopard, following in the footsteps of Pine, the keeper of the lions.

The enclosure, triangular in shape and measuring about 50 metres along each side, was soon ready to receive Taunu.

It was a great day for the leopard when he was transferred from his small enclosure to the bigger one and he became quite ecstatic when he realised that he would share his enclosure with me. The only problem was that he persisted in trying to get into my office, so the door had to be kept shut at all times. He then took to making running leaps at the screened windows, ending up with all four paws grimly clutching the mesh. I was treated often to wonderful close-up views of a thickly furred, white, spotted tummy, and a pair of blue-grey eyes staring at me appealingly whined pitifully for attention.

I must admit, though, that the first time he leaped at the window was quite an alarming experience. I thought he had taken leave of his senses and that he was trying to take me out behind my desk. Visitors to my office, understandably, dwindled to a trickle and finally only to those who absolutely had to be there.

Taunu would lie in wait behind a log, his blue-grey eyes glittering above the rim, ready to pounce the moment someone opened the gate.

Our biggest problem was to keep him inside the enclosure. It took him only a few days to find a way out and when I arrived at work one morning, he had notched up his first victims.

The wives of two instructors who both worked in the base in an administrative capacity had been walking to their office when Marius Heymann's spouse was struck violently from the rear by the hurtling body of Taunu. He knocked her flat on her face in the sand and started to "gnaw" at her scalp, fortunately protected by a thick head of blonde hair.

The women's shrill screams were followed by a desperate sprint to the shelter of their office, Taunu hot on their heels.

He got there first, jumped onto their desks and began inspecting the contents of various files in an appallingly disrespectful manner. Only by mustering three or four troops could Marius get Taunu out of the offices and back into his enclosure. By the time I arrived, Marius and Craig were adding dannert wire (precursor of the ubiquitous razor wire) to the top of the three-metre fence, with Taunu "assisting" by pouncing on their backs.

For some weeks Taunu stayed in his pen, but he was forever inspecting the defences. It became an established drill for him to ambush me whenever I locked up for the day. From my movements and general preparations before going home, he knew precisely when to move into his ambush position around the corner of the building. Every time I opened the door, a metre or so from where he lurked, and stepped outside, he was onto me like a bolt of lightning.

No matter what I did, I could never avoid being bitten in the shoulder. I knew he was waiting, I could actually see him through the window, but his speed got the better of me every time. I had no chance of escaping that leopard's painful attention.

He was about 13 months old when he arrived at St Michél, but he grew rapidly on the excellent food he got and his weight was quite considerable as he approached the age of 18 months. He was bigger than most adult leopards.

One day I left my office through the furthest door, slipping out without Taunu seeing me. I sneaked around the back and rounded the rear corner to see him flattened against the wall, his tail end towards me, waiting in fevered anticipation for me to come through the usual door.

I approached silently until I was directly behind him. I was in two minds as to whether I should startle him, or just announce my presence quietly. Fortunately, common sense prevailed. A frightened leopard will instinctively apply survival drills and I could have ended up battered and torn to pieces by a frenzied leopard, scared out of his wits.

So I simply said, very quietly: "Hello, Taunu."

He glanced over his shoulder at me and I could swear he had a sheepish expression on his face as he realised he'd been caught out by his prey. He stood up and started rubbing himself against me as if to say, "This time you got me, but it won't happen again, so well done ..."

I would often sit by the window, just staring at him. There can surely be no other animal as beautiful as a leopard. His back, head and nose were a rich, rusty orange colour with distinctive black rosettes on his back and sides.

The colour gradually faded into creaminess and on his tummy and underbelly, his fur was pure white, studded with black spots that began where the rosettes ended.

Around his neck was a distinctive black band, like a necklace.

The softness of his fur always amazed me. The hair on his stomach was much longer than on his sides and back and it was sheer pleasure to run one's fingers through Taunu's coat. I can understand perfectly why some women lust after a leopard skin coat, but I can never condone them buying or wearing one. The leopard's fur looks much better on the animal than on a slinky woman, however gorgeous she might be.

A female leopard who had her territory to the south of St Michél in the Fort Doppies area had developed an unusual method of catching baboons at night.

She would jump up at the baboons perched in a tree, the younger ones on the lower limbs and the older, wiser ones well out of reach in the top-most branches. While making her leaps, the leopard would growl menacingly, using psychological warfare to upset the equilibrium of the younger, more excitable baboons.

A baboon is one animal that really does suffer from edgy nerves. It does not take much to drive a baboon to hysteria, with accompanying screams and shrieks setting off others in the troop, until the whole lot are screeching banshees.

At night, nothing drives a baboon over the edge more quickly than the presence of a growling leopard intent on sinking its fangs into the baboon's flesh. The less experienced the baboon, the sooner its nerves shatter, and the more likely it is to do something stupid.

The female leopard relied on this for her nightly meal and, invariably, one of the younger baboons would judge its situation to be precarious and seek safer accommodation elsewhere.

It would let go of its perch, land on the ground beneath the tree and desperately scamper for sanctuary in the nearest substantial-looking tree.

Without fail, the leopard would pounce on the errant baboon before it took the first leap, killing it with a single crunch to the head, then stalking off with the dead baboon dangling bloodily from her powerful jaws, to finish her meal in peace and quiet away from the ear-splitting racket of the surviving baboons.

Once the leopard had left the area, calm descended on the baboon hotel, but the next night, the whole performance would be repeated.

Naturally, the female leopard would go on heat from time to time, but there were no male leopards within striking distance to attend to the lady's feelings of ardour. Most of the leopards in the area had succumbed to the dual pressures of hunting and trapping for their pelts.

Almost everyone doing duty on the border wanted to return to the Republic with an illegal leopard skin. The Bushmen, especially, plied a thriving trade by trapping leopards and selling their skins to the troops.

Needless to say, the Fort Doppies female was over the moon when Taunu moved in next door. The moment she was in oestrus she decided to visit the young stud, prowling around the perimeter fence, encouraging him to escape over the top and do his manly duty by her.

Taunu was easily taken in by the first leopard he had seen in his life, and a friendly female one at that. He soon found a way to get over the top and join the amorous female, but he was still too stupid to know what was expected of him. Taunu wanted to play, and adult games were not what he had in mind.

All night long, the two wandered around the flood plain, the female desperately employing all her wiles to coax her toy boy into doing what she wanted, but in vain.

Towards dawn she moved off in disgust, leaving behind a slightly bemused Taunu, wondering what he had done wrong.

When we searched for Taunu's escape route over the fence, we found an overhanging tree limb, quite high up, and removed it, hoping for the best.

He continued trying to find a way out of the enclosure, but for a while at least, he was stumped.

I decided that we had to make a concerted effort to teach Taunu to hunt. The lion experience had taught me that one cannot sit on one's hands when it comes to making carnivorous animals self-reliant and the sooner we started our training programme the better Taunu was likely to fare.

There were numerous jackrabbits in the flood plains and as keeper of the leopard, Craig was detailed to catch at least one every night. Craig complied and each morning a live jackrabbit, firmly trapped inside a refuse bin, was delivered to an eagerly waiting Taunu.

We removed the lid of the bin with Taunu looking on expectantly. Out popped the jackrabbit to go bounding off to the perimeter fence, with Taunu in hot pursuit.

Initially, he thought this was just another game we had devised for his amusement, a way to keep him occupied chasing a woolly toy. The first jackrabbit escaped Taunu's fumbling clutches, slipping through the large-meshed Bannox wire fence.

The second rabbit Taunu literally played to death. He chased it around the enclosure while we blocked its path to the fence. When he was tired and needed to catch his breath, Taunu would lie down next to the jackrabbit, pinning it to the ground with one huge paw. As soon as he was rested, he would lift his paw to start the next round of the game. Finally, the jackrabbit just died, either from sheer exhaustion or being constantly pounced on by a heavy leopard. There was no sign of a bite or any scratchmarks on the rabbit.

I decided to leave Taunu with his dead jackrabbit and not feed him from the mess that day. After a while he realised that his "toy" was, in fact, edible, and tucked in, tentatively at first, then with gusto.

From then on Taunu looked forward to the daily game of leopard versus jackrabbit, which carried the added bonus that the victor could eat the loser.

It was interesting to see how cat-like Taunu was. He would toss the dead jackrabbit around, just as a domestic cat does with a mouse, tapping at it with his paw as it flew through the air and pouncing on it the moment it hit the ground. He repeated this endlessly, sometimes for an hour or more, before settling down to consume his prey.

We could never make the enclosure totally escape-proof and I eventually gave up on any attempts to do so. As a result, Taunu spent more time outside his enclosed camp than inside it and, inevitably, this led to dustbins being overturned all over the base. He inspected each one to see whether a jackrabbit might be hiding inside.

However, his chief prey was to be baboon. We had far too many baboons all along the river line, probably because there were no leopards in the area to speak of. The baboons, in turn, evicted the monkey troops and had an adverse effect on the birdlife by raiding the nests for eggs and chicks.

It became my explicit wish that Taunu be introduced to baboon meat. I started shooting one for him every once in a while and he began to show a preference for baboons. At last we could give the jackrabbits a respite and a chance to recover from Taunu's appetite.

One day I shot a young baboon which was duly presented to Taunu in his enclosure. He scoffed the entire animal in short order.

Not long afterwards, one of my men came around to have a look at Taunu and decided he looked a little peckish, so off he went and shot another young baboon. Taunu thought it was Christmas and tucked in heartily again.

Then a third chap came along and decided that a young baboon would be just the thing to perk up Taunu, so he, too, shot one and dropped it at Taunu's feet.

By this time, the leopard must have thought there was a festival going on, and that he was expected to take part in it. So, once again, he began to devour the baboon, but this third offering of the day proved too much for him. He ate as much as he could, then keeled over.

One of my men came running to tell me that Taunu was dying. I rushed to the enclosure to find him almost hidden behind his bloated stomach.

Bits of baboon were scattered all around. Taunu had regurgitated quite a lot of his gargantuan meal.

His eyes were closed so I knelt down beside him and lifted an eyelid. I got a bleak, bloodshot stare from one blue-grey eye, and when I released the eyelid, it fell shut by itself. I realised that Taunu was fine, that he'd just made a pig of himself.

This incident occurred before he learned that he did not have to eat everything at once, and that those parts of the kill he could not consume, could be hung in a tree to be enjoyed later.

After a while he started to hoist the occasional jackrabbit into a fork of the red syringa towering above my office. The roof also had a number of jackrabbit tails laid out on the hot iron sheets. Taunu never ate the tails, preferring to dry them in the sun, preferably on my office roof, or so it seemed.

My office and its immediate surroundings began to acquire quite a distinctive, gamey pong.

A large troop of baboons used to move through the base to and from the water, virtually every day at noon, and the members of the troop were not in the least appreciative of Taunu's presence in his enclosure.

Almost every afternoon the males perched in the trees around my office while barking at Taunu. Others charged the fence in small squads, baring their terrifying fangs at him. This always gave rise to a tremendous racket, the angry barks accompanied by frenzied squealing from the overexcited young ones.

It also offered the ideal opportunity for me to shoot a baboon or two for Taunu's "table".

The baboons endured an unpleasant time while Taunu was in residence and no doubt looked forward to the day they could corner him outside the protection of his enclosure.

This inevitable encounter between leopard and baboon took place one afternoon when Taunu was on his way to the workshop to terrorise the "tiffies". The baboons were making their way to the river at the same time and came up from the rear as Taunu skulked through the bush. The baboons could not believe their luck, and when they spotted him, the baboons set off a terrible commotion, barking and squealing as they closed in.

Baboons are extremely dangerous animals. The big males gang up, four or five at a time, and attack as a squad. They have the most formidable fangs, far more frightening than those of a leopard. They are also agile and extremely fast, and with those fangs they can tear their prey apart in seconds.

I had been on the receiving end of a mob attack on two occasions and knew all about baboons as assailants. Fortunately, I carried a semi-automatic rifle at the time of my encounters, or I would surely have been severely mauled.

When Taunu realised attack was imminent, he turned to face the troop, which was a mistake. He bared his fangs and growled, but the baboons were coming from all sides.

When reason prevailed, Taunu turned tail and dashed off, but the baboons gave chase.

A leopard is not one of the fittest animals in the bush, while a baboon, on the other hand, appears to have the stamina of a Bushman.

So Taunu ran as swiftly as he could, but the baboons were closing in for the kill and he would soon be forced to turn around, face them and fight for his life.

Fortuitously, at that precise moment, one of my officers drove past in his Land Cruiser. Unaware of the drama being played out next to the track, he was more than a little startled when the blurred image of a spotted cat hurtled out of the bush and landed squarely, with a resounding thud, in the back of his moving vehicle.

Through the rear window, he saw Taunu coughing insults from the safety of the vehicle at a frenzied mob of baboons, desperately chasing their prey.

The "tiffies" had a hard time with Taunu, who always managed to select the most awkward moments to go and pester them.

It was not unusual for a "tiffie" to suddenly find himself joined by a leopard while lying awkwardly beneath a vehicle, draining the engine oil. Taunu had been known to take off into the bush, the drain plug in his mouth, with an angry mechanic trying to catch him.

Another fellow who suffered was Thomasie the cook, who was not at all fond of the leopard. In fact, he was terrified, and on several occasions, I had to go and rescue Thomasie, barricaded in his kitchen while Taunu took running jumps at the wire screen covering the window.

Taunu was very fond of Craig and only he and I could really handle him. The rest of the personnel tolerated his unwelcome attentions with gritty smiles.

At night Taunu would play games with Craig on his bed, much to the alarm of the rest of the men in the barracks. Taunu would casually stroll into the room and while troops leapt for the relative safety of their beds, he would make straight for Craig's bunk in the far corner. Craig would start the ball rolling by whining like Taunu, which prompted the leopard to make a joyful leap onto Craig's bed, which became a tangled heap within minutes as man and beast wrestled on the bedding.

This could carry on for several minutes until Taunu got tired of the game and stalked off into the night to find another playmate.

He also had the disconcerting habit of strolling into the pub at night – always unannounced. It was incredible to hear the usual din in the pub suddenly being cut off as if some unseen hand had thrown the silence switch.

All eyes would turn to the door of the pub where Taunu would pause for a moment, as if to make sure that everyone was aware of his beautiful but slightly barbaric presence.

Satisfied that he had the full attention of the tipplers, Taunu would slink in with the flowing motion unique to leopards, leap effortlessly onto the bar counter and proceed to knock beer mugs, glasses and bottles onto the floor.

At this point it was my job to pluck him off the counter, carry him out and escort him into the dark, all the while shouting for Craig to come and get his bloody leopard and put him back in his enclosure.

One of my officers, Commandant Boet Swart, had no love for Taunu. One hot afternoon he was taking a nap when the leopard visited the officers' quarters.

The door to the screened verandah was open, so Taunu simply walked in and proceeded to where he heard Boet's snores reverberating inside one of the rooms. Boet's door was closed but not latched and Taunu had no difficulty pushing the door open.

He walked to the bed where Boet was stretched out on his back, snoring like a sawmill in full production. For a while Taunu regarded the sleeping figure, then gave Boet a painful nip on the ear.

Boet woke up with a start as the sudden pain shot through his skull and found himself face to face with a fully grown leopard, its strange, blue-grey eyes no more than a few centimetres away from his own.

Boet swore loudly, jumped up and shot out of his room in a panic, blood streaming from his ear, with Taunu close behind.

Of course this was what Taunu had wanted in the first place, a game with one of the human inhabitants of the base, someone he could chase like a jackrabbit.

Boet managed to get into another room and shut the door firmly in Taunu's face. Once again, Craig was called to coax Taunu back to his enclosure.

At night, of course, Taunu was in his true element, but his nocturnal wandering around the base took a heavy toll on the domestic cat population. The owners were none too pleased about this and complained bitterly. I assured them that a serval was actually the culprit – we had one who was more or less resident in the area – but while it no doubt did account for one or two of the missing cats, Taunu probably disposed of the majority.

I became aware of Taunu's rather unfortunate cat-culling habit when he took out one of our own kittens, a young feral cat called Recce Two. My wife was extremely angry with Taunu, and almost in tears, but accepted the fact that it was inevitable and in keeping with a leopard's nature. We simply had to grin and bear the loss of a naughty but sweet little cat.

We had lost the original Recce, our splendid ginger tom, some months before, and my wife mourned his disappearance for three weeks or more. Fortunately, I was spared the tragedy, because I was advising Savimbi on how to attack Cuito Cuanavale and was therefore far to the north of St Michél at the time. Deep inside Angola, I was blissfully unaware that my household had suffered an irreplaceable loss. No other cat has ever been able to fill the void left by Recce.

I could not ignore the fact that Taunu's unpredictable antics were beginning to put my men, and their families, on edge. He ambushed men, and sometimes women, along the track between the pub and the dining room at night, causing several people severe stress. He stalked and pounced on the troops at night when they left the barracks to urinate in the special urinals known as "lilies". One of the men almost had a nervous breakdown as a result.

Taunu even cornered my wife inside her Suzuki when she was a little tardy rolling up the window. The result was a petite woman pinned under the kicking full weight of a huge leopard, her legs waving frantically in the air.

He once pulled an already frightened black soldier upon whom Taunu had fixed his beady eyes from the high back of a Samil 10-ton truck, grabbing him by the scruff of his neck after a mighty leap from a stationary position.

A new arrival – a young paratroop officer – went into the ablution block one morning, still unaware that a "tame" leopard shared the camp. He started to shave, oblivious to the danger lurking in the rafters just above him where Taunu was readying himself for a sudden, "death-dealing" pounce.

Taunu had the habit of lying on the open beams in the ablution block, waiting to pounce on his victims as they came in for a shower or to use the toilets, a potentially highly embarrassing situation.

So the early morning shower was a source of great delight to the leopard, draped over a beam just behind the paratrooper and just above his head. He wriggled his rear legs into position under his belly and leapt, like greased lightning, onto the paratrooper's broad shoulders just as he lifted the razor to this well-lathered face.

The paratrooper stared in horror at the mirror, which reflected the image of a ferocious leopard sinking its fangs into his scalp.

He screamed and, with the unnatural strength that is born of undiluted terror, flung the leopard violently to the cement floor. Then, in total amazement, his screams slowly subsiding, he saw the leopard calmly scramble to its feet and felt it rub its soft fur against his leg in a gesture of friendship.

When Taunu frightened a little girl by pouncing on her from long grass beside the house of one of my instructor officers, I knew it was time to relocate him. All the wives had been briefed to keep their children indoors while Taunu was on the loose, but, like leopards, children are not all that easy to control. The little girl got a terrible fright, although Taunu did not hurt her physically.

Once again Marius, Craig and some of the black students had to build an enclosure, this time about 8 kilometres north of St Michél. It was a huge enclosure, about 150 metres by 100 metres built around a splendid little "island", overgrown with a tangle of trees and palms, far out in the flood plain. There were plenty of hiding places for Taunu, lots of tree limbs on which he could recline and ample space for him to wander around.

The enclosure was an elaborate structure, with a 3-metre-high fence, overhung towards the inside, topped by a barrier of dannert wire and another barrier halfway up on the inside so that Taunu could not gain enough momentum to clear the top of the fence. The fence was decked with a thick reed screen through which Taunu was not supposed to see, and entrance was via a sturdy gate, elaborately equipped with overhang, dannert wire, reeds and so on.

With a feeling of great satisfaction, I released Taunu into his new home and shut the gate behind me with confidence.

It took him exactly four minutes to escape.

I shot a baboon, placed it in the enclosure, got hold of Taunu and put him back inside – but this time I left the gate open. All Marius's work had been in vain and at that moment I gave up trying to keep Taunu confined.

A change of tactics was dictated. Instead of locking him in, I would keep him away from the main base by supplying him with ample amounts of baboon meat in his new home.

To some extent, this worked. Every day, either Craig or I brought Taunu a freshly killed baboon and before we even called him, he would appear, joyfully leaping for one's throat, whining as if it was a week or more since the last encounter, rubbing against one's leg, then standing for a while to be stroked and petted before slinking off to where the baboon was lying.

We followed this routine for some days and usually found him either in the enclosure or close by. Then he began to explore further afield. One of my senior officers found Taunu not far from one of the northern training bases, two kilometres north of his latest home, lying in ambush for any vehicle that passed. The officer stopped and Taunu jumped into the back of his vehicle for an impromptu ride back to his enclosure.

There were indications that he was beginning to hunt on his own and I once found a freshly killed baboon at his feeding place. He was extremely possessive about that baboon and snarled when I tried to approach him. Needless to say, I backed off.

One of my officers also found him on an impala kill a short distance to the north. Whether he had killed the impala or chased another cat away from it, possibly a cheetah as there was a male in the area, it was impossible to say. By then he was two years old and fully grown.

I was taking a diploma course in nature conservation when Taunu arrived at St Michél and one of my projects was the study of a large mammal. Naturally, I selected a leopard since I had almost embarrassingly easy access to one at all times.

The fact that he was "tame" detracted to some extent from my observations, but on the other hand allowed me to get much closer to a leopard in its natural habitat.

We would go for walks, just the two of us, while I tried to observe every activity and movement that he made. Familiarising myself with the way he stalked, ambushed, twitched his ears or tail, slunk through the bush, identified possible prey, reacted to baboons and other creatures was a thoroughly enriching experience.

I reached the conclusion that this leopard, at least, was far more intelligent than any of the lions I had come in contact with. He would painstakingly inspect a "leopard-proof" fence, with all the obstacles placed in his way, and then devise a successful way of overcoming it.

For example, I wrapped a tree trunk in several layers of dannert wire which should have made it impossible for him to climb up the tree, sneak along one of the limbs and jump over the fence to freedom. I watched him from my office, walking around the trunk and inspecting it closely before accepting there was no way up the tree. Then he moved back some paces, charged the tree and took a flying leap over the obstacle and into the branches. He sped along the overhanging limb and was out of his enclosure and gone before I could get out of my office to stop him.

Over a period of time I found he had widened several gaps in the double-Bannox wire in order to get out. The early episode with the jackrabbits and the dustbins also seemed to indicate that he was capable of making logical deductions.

His hunting behaviour was an eye-opener. Most often, of course, he used me as his "prey", rarely walking ahead of me, preferring to weave through the shrubs and grass while keeping me in sight from the corner of his eye. He seemed to avoid footpaths deliberately, and with his magnificent natural camouflage, it was easy to lose sight of him in the dappled shade of the bush. Whenever this happened, I knew he'd be lying in ambush for me up ahead.

Often I passed the ambush site without spotting him in the long grass. He would wait until I was well past before silently pouncing on me from the rear. He always went for my head and we brought each exercise to a conclusion with him flat on his back, forcefully thrown to the ground by me and being kicked angrily in the flank.

He would lie there, looking innocently up at me with grey eyes already beginning to turn an adult green, all four legs flopping about harmlessly. His mouth would be open, his tongue lolling, showing his obvious pleasure with a toothy grin.

He looked so harmless at such moments that I had to kneel down and stroke the soft, long fur on his tummy. He enjoyed this tremendously and after a while we would move on to the next instalment of the entirely one-sided ambush game.

Sometimes I did spot him, though with great difficulty, and only because his piercing eyes betrayed his hiding place. It is somewhat disconcerting to come face to face with even a tame leopard, staring fixedly at you with only one thing in mind: to flatten you with a display of explosive violence no other carnivore can match.

When I spotted him, I always stopped and stared back, not the recommended thing to do. Knowing that his ambush had been foiled, he would resort to intimidation. This began with the ominous drawing back of his lips, the wrinkling of his snout, the flattening of his ears and the baring of his formidable fangs. His eyes would become positively wild with a fixed angry gaze, as though he was trying to root me to the spot.

Suddenly there would be a frightening snarl and the leopard would lurch himself at me in a blur of spots and orange.

If he pounced from five to eight metres away, he would land at my feet and immediately spring upwards, the blood-chilling snarl caught in his throat and go for my windpipe.

No matter how accustomed I became to his frequent attacks, this performance always paralysed me. The sheer speed of his assault allowed only enough time to turn a shoulder towards him, which meant my shoulders became punch bags for Taunu's jaws. The attack ended with him sinking his razor-sharp fangs into my thin human skin. Like the lions, he never learned that my skin was not as tough as that of another leopard.

For years afterwards, I carried the scars of Taunu's bitemarks on both my shoulders.

His frontal attacks culminated in the same fashion as those from the rear, with him on his back, waiting for his stomach to be stroked.

I came to the conclusion that leopards prefer attacking their prey silently from the rear and from carefully selected ambush sites. Under some circumstances, I imagine that a short stalk can precede a lightning-fast, silent leap onto an unsuspecting grazing animal's back. Taunu always seemed to go for the head, to "crunch" the skull with his powerful jaws or sink his fangs into the victim's brain.

Leopards seldom prey on anything larger than an impala – this method is therefore extremely effective.

234

However, if spotted by the prey, the leopard will immediately launch a frontal attack, simultaneously snarling so menacingly that the animal freezes momentarily in its tracks – a fatal error.

Taunu was incredibly fast. From the moment he launched himself at me off his strong back legs from a typically cat-like crouching position, it was only a split second until he bit me in the shoulder.

A leopard is relatively light, compared to lions, but its phenomenal speed produces a momentum that makes it almost impossible to stay upright. Invariably, Taunu knocked his human victims off their feet, especially if the attack was from the rear.

At three paces or less, Taunu needed only a simple leap and went straight for my throat.

Experts describe the leopard as the most perfect killing machine on land, the feared great white shark holding that distinction in the ocean, and I believe them.

When Taunu started showing signs of sexual maturity, he began to stray southwards, past St Michél, into the territory of Delilah, the neighbouring female of his species. He was spotted once or twice in close company with this seductress, obviously now fully aware of the duties he was expected to perform.

From time to time, he still wandered into the pub unexpectedly and once bit a distinguished general's ankle, but his visits to St Michél became increasingly rare.

One day, an instructor from Fort Doppies went looking for me at one of the northern training bases, but took a wrong turn. The road led him to Taunu's enclosure, and he stopped his Land Rover at the open gate in the perimeter fence, perplexed by this unusual structure. He waited a while for a security guard to approach him, while the national serviceman who was with him, remarked on the lack of any sign of life at what they thought was the training base.

Suddenly there was a heavy thump on the Land Rover's roof, followed almost immediately by the sight of a leopard staring at them upsidedown through the windscreen.

They had never heard of Taunu and feverishly began to wind up their windows, but it was too late. Taunu slid into the cab and over the staff sergeant, took a seat between the two men and promptly started delivering painful nips to both the instructor and the troop.

The soldiers exited the vehicle in a hurry and jumped into the back. Through the rear window, the staff sergeant could see Taunu energetically sharpening his claws on the brand-new upholstery.

Then Taunu looked up, saw the two men gaping at him from the rear of the vehicle, and decided to join them. Within seconds, he was once again biting each of them in turn. They jumped back into the cab, rolled up the windows and drove off, with Taunu still in the back.

After a few hundred metres he jumped off, and without so much as a backward glance, disappeared into the bush.

Taunu's final appearance at Buffalo Lodge occurred shortly afterwards at about five o'clock one morning.

I was awakened by a whine coming from the verandah. It was pitch-dark, so I took my torch to investigate. I knew it had to be Taunu and that he was up to some mischief best nipped in the bud, as quickly as possible.

He was standing at the screen door, trying to force himself through the narrow crack left open for Recce Two.

One nervous major had already threatened to shoot Taunu if he ever came near his house, so I decided to get him back to his enclosure before he went for a stroll through the main base. I dressed hastily and stepped onto the verandah, straight into an attack.

A one-sided game, in which he had all the advantages, ensued. It was too dark for me to see, so he had a glorious time attacking my stumbling bulk from different directions.

His growls and my curses caused such a commotion that my wife jumped out of bed with a second torch and my rifle. She thought I might want to shoot him, because, judging by the noise, I was being torn apart by a pet leopard gone wild.

Of course, he had nothing of the sort in mind. He was just unusually rough and energetic that morning.

Nevertheless, I tried to gain the upper hand, and in the rare moments when I got him on the ground, I kicked him forcefully. He took his punishment with equanimity and would lay off for a while until my obvious disadvantage in the dark became too much of a temptation to resist. Again and again, his sharp fangs sank into both my shoulders.

At last it was daybreak, and I really laid into him. After a few more abortive attacks, he decided he had had enough and slunk off into the bush. I was certainly not going to follow him until it was broad daylight. In the meanwhile, he decided to visit the guard post on the nearby Kongola bridge.

Two troopies from the Cape Corps were sitting, at ease, listening to the new day awakening all around, when a leopard suddenly materialised right in front of them and snarled. They hastily abandoned the control point and ran, helter-skelter, for a nearby hut. From here they watched the leopard reclining at leisure, no more than ten paces away, while keeping a beady eye on the two faces peering at him from the window.

He waited a while, but when they failed to put in a reappearance, Taunu got bored and moved back towards St Michél.

I had followed his spoor to the bridge, where I found two frightened troops still inside their hut. They refused to believe there was such a thing as a tame leopard, but indicated the direction he had taken when he left.

I soon found the spoor and followed it back. Ros, meanwhile, had summoned assistance from the base and when one of my men appeared in his Land Cruiser, I directed him to where a baboon had been shot to be used as bait for Taunu.

I caught up with Taunu skulking through the bush along the track, heading straight for St Michél, and mayhem.

He came bounding towards me as if he had not seen me in months. The usual exchange of greetings followed, but then he did something he had never done before – he licked my boots. I have no idea what the gesture meant, whether it was a sign of submissiveness or simply that he developed a sudden taste for boot leather. Either way, he still had to go back to his enclosure, so I picked him up and dumped him in the back of the vehicle with his dead baboon for company.

We offloaded Taunu and his baboon inside the enclosure.

The next day I returned with another baboon, only to find him tucking into one he had killed himself. I left his second helping for him, anyway, and drove back to St Michél.

A few days later, I paid another visit, but he had gone and so had the baboons.

I went back daily, for about a week, taking him one more baboon, but he never returned.

I walked around calling him, but got no response and I finally accepted that I would never see him again.

My wife saw him once, however, crossing the track between our house and St Michél while she was on her way to work as a nursing sister. She called him and he looked back at her but refused to come near her vehicle.

Another time, she spotted him on a small island as we skimmed past at high speed in our rubber duck on the Cuando. I turned around immediately, but by the time I got to the island, he had gone.

One of my troops spotted him with Delilah and so did the Bushmen from Fort Doppies. He often came past Buffalo Lodge at night on his way to the baboon troop perched in their trees a few hundred metres downstream. A cacophony of shrieks, screams and angry barks always announced his presence and the final, bloody confrontation with his chosen victim.

During this time he also dispatched of the unfortunate Recce Two, when the lad left the safety of our bedroom to answer a call of nature outside. The next morning, Taunu's spoor told the sad story of the cat's untimely end.

Taunu had obviously settled into a new life, one he was destined for from the start. He did so with no fuss or bother and far more successfully than any of the lions had done because he was a solitary predator by nature and not a pride animal like his bigger cousins.

ELEVEN

The Rot Sets In

During my time in the Caprivi and the Cuando-Cubango, I witnessed a dramatic decline in game in one part of the region while in another, scrappy remnants multiplied and became sizeable herds. It was like a seesaw. The one moment the Caprivi was teeming and the Cuando-Cubango was all but stripped bare of wildlife. The next, the Cuando-Cubango was a conservator's dream, while the Caprivi was a nightmare. This fluctuation continued for some time and then it all changed irrevocably and with dire consequences.

During a 1968 game count on the eastern flood plains between the Zambezi and Chobe rivers, 72 000 red lechwes were counted along with vast herds of zebra, buffalo, blue wildebeest and many other species, including elephant.

In 1986 another game count, conducted from the air like the one 18 years earlier, recorded the sum total of seven lechwes. After countless hours of flying, that was the only game spotted. There was nothing else, not a zebra or a buffalo. Where previously there had been only a few head of scrawny cattle, now there were thousands.

The omnipresent dust clouds kicked up by hordes of stampeding lechwes that once characterised a helicopter flight to Mpalela island had settled forever.

The majority of the hippos that wallowed in the channels and pools of the flood plains, the sidestreams and lagoons of the Zambezi and the Chobe rivers simply disappeared. Formerly, each pool or lagoon had its herd of hippos basking in the sun or cooling off in the crystal clear waters looking for all the world like huge, plump dumplings in a deep pot of oil, when viewed from the air.

In 1987 Marolotswane, the chief of the Basubya tribe which occupied the eastern half of the eastern Caprivi, asked nature conservation officials to encourage tourism by establishing a game park on the flood plains – but his request came too late.

No tourist would travel thousands of kilometres to view thousands of hectares of reeds and papyrus with only the wind to stir the monotony. Why should they, when the game-rich Chobe National Park lay within spitting distance on the region's southern boundary and the magnificent Okavango swamps were less than a day's travel away? The best one could hope for was to cruise up the Chobe River to see the Chobe Park game coming down to drink on the Botswana side – in other words, watching another country's game because we cared too little to conserve our own.

Further westwards, the Mafwe tribe was even less concerned about wildlife, although they were endowed with far more natural riches than the Basubyas.

The Linyanti swamps form a magnificent smaller version of the Okavango swamps in the south-western corner of the Mafwe tribal lands. These swamps used to be populated by thousands of hippos, which kept the numerous water channels dredged and the Cuando floodwaters flowing through the swamps and along the Linyanti River – an extension of the Cuando – into the vast Liambezi lake.

Lake Liambezi was alive with fish and served as the happy hunting ground of numerous Mafwe fishermen who made quite a decent living from their catches. Most of the protein consumed in the Caprivi came from this lake and there was more than enough left over for export to Zambia, Zimbabwe, Botswana and South Africa.

But as the Mafwes destroyed nature's dredgers, the hippos, a vital component of the Liambezi and Linyanti swamp and river systems, disappeared.

Nature conservation officials tried to talk some sense into the heads of the two Mamiles – the second having usurped the throne of the first as chief of the Mafwe tribe – but Mamile II far exceeded the efforts of his predecessor, ordering subordinate tribesmen to significantly step up hippo poaching.

The water channels became choked with reeds and sand and the Cuando water turned stagnant. To amplify the catastrophe, the Cuando went through several years of drastically reduced flow during a dry cycle in the catchment areas. What little water managed to seep out of the Linyanti swamps was diverted into the Selinda spillway and thus into Botswana, and the Linyanti River began to dry up in its lower reaches. This in turn led to the drying up of the Savuti channel with tragic consequences for the game population.

Towards the end of 1987 the sun burned up the last drop in the cracked bed of Lake Liambezi. It had been turned into a vast dust bowl and a vital protein source had been totally destroyed. The few "dredgers" left simply could not keep the life-giving waters flowing.

In the middle of the Linyanti swamps are two huge islands, Nkasa and Lupala, where Dewald tried to resettle Terry. The islands were home to thousands of lechwe, hundreds of buffalo, some elephant, warthog, zebra, reedbuck, the few remaining hippo and crocodiles.

In 1986 a game count from a helicopter recorded a total of 4200 lechwe, a respectable number considering the size of the islands in relation to the eastern flood plains. The old Mamile was still in the chair at the time.

A year later, when the count was repeated, the number of lechwe had dropped to 1800. In just 12 months, poachers from the Mafwe tribe, spurred on by the new Mamile, had slaughtered 2400 buck.

The scope of the problem may be better understood if one looks at the number of licensed rifles available to the poachers.

In a population of about 40 000 people, there were just over 6000 licensed rifles in 1987. To this had to be added the 1000 or more G3 and R1 rifles from the Caprivi Battalion and perhaps another few hundred G3s issued to so-called auxiliary police constables.

Most of the animals were shot with G3 or R1 rifles. Control over live ammunition was exceedingly slack in the operational area, and 7.62 calibre rounds were plentiful, stolen by the crate from both the army and the police.

The nature conservators in Katima Mulilo fought a desperate rearguard action but, unfailingly, their efforts were obstructed by the brick wall of politics.

One of the influential politicians in the Caprivi was the former sidekick of the Swapo leader Sam Nujoma. He had left the organisation under an amnesty agreement and set himself up as the political wonder boy of the eastern Caprivi by joining the Democratic Turnhalle Alliance. He carried favour with the local inhabitants by thwarting every attempt by the Department of Nature Conservation to preserve what little game was left.

The Department of Nature Conservation tried to establish two game reserves, one incorporating the Nkasa and Lupala islands in the Linyanti swamps, and the other around a huge *chana* (grassy pan) west of the Cuando River. They held meetings with Mamile and his *indunas* (headmen) to hammer home the point that they would benefit financially from tourism by conserving the game.

The tribal authorities vacillated, especially after the Conservation Department turned down their application to slaughter some of the few remaining elephants and buffaloes in accordance with their "tribal traditions". The aspirant politician muddied the waters even further by suggesting that the game parks would be for the sole benefit of the white colonists from the south, who would lay claim to any money generated by tourism.

That was the end of the department's efforts and the game began to decline drastically. Elephants and hippos were killed at will. The lechwes came under fire as though war had been declared on them. The buffaloes, tsessebes, roan antelopes and giraffes were being exterminated, zebras, blue wildebeest and sables mown down in their hundreds.

The eastern Caprivi was becoming a sterile green desert, its empty forests, abandoned swamps and silent flood plains now home only to the increasing herds of cattle.

The director of agriculture, a friend of mine, tried to get the cattle herds reduced because they were overgrazing the veld, but he had no success. The would-be politician persuaded the tribesmen that the whites were jealous of the huge cattle herds owned by the Mafwes and that they should increase the size of their herds.

So the annihilation of the game continued. Complaints by conservators in Katima evoked one lame excuse after another from officials at the Windhoek head office for their unwillingness to act: the political situation was delicate, it was better to wait until the South West African situation had been resolved, or it was not the time to make waves.

While the Windhoek conservation officials ingratiated themselves with crooked politicians, the wild animals were being slaughtered throughout the length and breadth of the eastern Caprivi.

I met those men from Windhoek. They listened with great enthusiasm to one's suggestions, discussed with commendable technical expertise what had to be done, made promises that sent our conservationist pulses racing, then sloped off back to head office after spending a night in the wilds of Africa on the beautiful Nkasa island. For weeks afterwards, we would live in hope, eagerly preparing plans in accordance with Windhoek's verbal guidelines to save the remnants of the once great herds.

As the weeks became months, white-hot flames of hope turned to orange flickers of optimism, then to the embers of disappointment and, finally, to cold, black ashes of despair and disillusionment as we realised we could expect neither action nor support from the responsible officials to the south.

On the Fort Doppies and Fort St Michél fronts, we had to cope with constant incursions by Mafwe hunters who were after ivory, rhino horn and hippos.

Other game also fell in their line of fire, mostly for the meat, but sometimes for trophies, too.

The lechwes, because of their proximity to Mafwe villages on the east bank, were once again in the forefront of the hunt for meat. Further afield were the impalas, kudus and waterbuck, with the sable and roan antelopes the last in line. The sables were slaughtered chiefly for their trophy value as "capes", prepared from the head, plus horns, and the splendid, fur-covered skin of the chest and shoulders.

Poaching became endemic, especially after Dewald de Beer left, as just a few incidents will illustrate.

While Dewald ran Fort Doppies the game had increased significantly. Under the onslaught of the Mafwes and white hunters from Katima, the game in the Fort St Michél area was on a steep decline. Fortunately, I arrived at Fort St Michél in time to halt the destruction, but shortly afterwards, Dewald had to leave Fort Doppies which spelled disaster for the wildlife in that area.

The first poacher I caught was a Mafwe from the most notorious nest of poachers on the Cuando. He lived in the village of Maplanke, who was one of the indunas on the river front.

Maplanke had two ivory poaching sons, one of whom, I am happy to say, was eventually given a ten-year sentence for poaching elephants in the western Caprivi.

The poacher I caught, however, did nothing as spectacular as that. He borrowed induna Peter Quando's *makorro*, poled across to one of the lovely islands opposite Fort St Michél and snared a magnificent sitatunga bull.

I caught him red-handed, having taken to patrolling the river regularly in one of our rubber ducks.

The poacher was unpleasantly surprised to find an extremely angry white man breathing down the back of his neck, having thought himself quite safe at the end of a narrow sitatunga-made tunnel, which stretched away from the main stream through the tall reeds of the swamp. He was deeply engrossed in the process of removing the dead animal from his well-placed snare when I grabbed him, none too gently, by the scruff of his neck.

The sitatunga is one of the rarest antelopes in the world. In the early 1980s, it was claimed that there were only about 700 left. I have no idea what their present status is.

I forced the poacher unceremoniously into my rubber duck, taking the dead animal along as evidence. I was towing Peter Quando's *makorro* downstream towards Buffalo Lodge, but my speed was too high, and before long the *makorro* nose-dived into the deep water of the Cuando main stream, never to be seen again.

Peter Quando got his just desserts for lending his only *makorro* to a well-known poacher.

The case was tried in the circuit court and the poacher was given a suspended sentence of three months in jail. That was the first and last time that I took a poacher to court. The expert evidence by a nature conservator on the extreme rarity of the sitatunga and the sustained poaching pressure on the species, cut no ice whatsoever with the magistrate. To him, a sitatunga was just another four-footed animal like a cow or a donkey. After that, and in keeping with measures applied by my fellow conservators, I devised my own ways of dealing with poachers.

Sometime afterwards, the malodorous remains of putrid hippo carcasses began drifting downstream at frequent intervals. Over a period of three weeks, I counted the remains of eight hippos that must have been shot quite a distance upstream, judging by the advanced state of decomposition.

My Bushman patrols upstream could not locate the culprits or the locality of the shooting.

One day, my wife and I decided to go as far upriver as possible for a picnic on one of the isolated islands. We set off in a rubber duck with a picnic basket and some books to read. After about two hours we arrived at a beautiful island, with tall Natal mahoganies growing at the water's edge, and settled down for a relaxed afternoon, surrounded by the peace and quiet of one of Africa's most remote rivers.

Suddenly the silence and serenity were shattered by automatic gunfire and bullets cracked overhead through the branches of the Natal mahogany under which we had spread our groundsheet.

There is nothing that angers me more than being shot at recklessly, so we jumped into the rubber duck and, to my wife's consternation, I dashed upstream in the direction of the shots.

I finally drew level with the gunfire and found a narrow side-stream which led into a placid lagoon snuggled under the Angolan bank of the river. Four Unita troops were pouring burst after burst of automatic fire into the water, their apparent target a bloated hippo carcass floating on its back, stubby legs pointing stiffly skywards.

I lost my temper and shouted at them, in English: "What the bloody hell are you idiots up to?" They looked surprised to see me, armed only with a pistol, but one of the men who could speak English, spun a highly unlikely tale about shooting crocodiles which had caught some of their comrades.

The thought crossed my mind that the crocs ought to be commended for their taste, not shot, but I held my tongue.

"What about the hippo?" I asked.

They didn't know where the hippo came from. They had found it there that morning.

I could see that it had been shot, but the Unita men insisted they did not know who the culprits were. Dissatisfied with their explanation, but unable to do any more, I left them to continue shooting at imaginary crocodiles.

The next day, I sent an irate signal to the senior South African liaison officer working with Savimbi. I had pinpointed the source of the hippo slaughter and I was thoroughly disgusted by Unita's hypocrisy and Savimbi's eloquent claims that they were taking particular care of their wildlife, in spite of the Angolan civil war.

I estimated that for eight hippos to end up in the main stream as far south as Kongola, at least four times as many must have been shot. Unita had no boats, so the hippos could only be shot from the banks of lagoons and sidestreams. Wounded animals would be able to make it to the main stream, where some would die in agony. The rest would be trapped in thick reed beds, lagoons and narrow channels. The Cuando River and swamp system form a very efficient net for catching dead or dying animals.

One of my men at a Unita training base north of the cutline saw a Samil 100 truck arriving late one evening, loaded with buffalo carcasses. He counted 14 animals.

The truck crew sought out the camp commandant and asked him to supply them with labour to offload the truck. He told them to get lost, as his men had just received their weekly supply of fresh beef and mutton, courtesy of their South African allies.

The truck driver and co-driver simply moved out of the base, and promptly dumped the carcasses in the bush nearby.

Once a year, the tsetse-fly team arrived at Fort St Michél to spray and eradicate the only organism that stood between the Mafwe cattle and the western Caprivi.

Every year there was a stand-up fight between me and the Department of Veterinary Services about their spraying campaign, but that is another story.

During one of their annual visits, I returned from Katima Mulilo to find a dead hippo on the road at the Kongola bridge. A Unimog from Fort Doppies was standing by to tow it to the tsetse-fly team's camp where the hippo would be cut up and cooked for a big feast. The team consisted of Mafwes from the Singalamwe area where the men were notorious hippo poachers.

I climbed out of my Land Cruiser and began asking some pertinent questions.

According to the white team leader, the hippo had simply floated down the river, as dead as a door nail, and fetched up in the shallows at the bridge. They dragged it from the water, then went to Fort Doppies to enlist some aid in getting it to their camp and to get permission from the Fort Doppies commander (Dewald had already left) to utilise the carcass in any way they saw fit.

"How did it die?" I asked.

"I don't know. There is no sign of any injury on it," the tsetse-fly man replied.

I examined the carcass which was that of a youngish cow and found no indication that it had been shot or fatally injured in a fight. Yet the carcass looked far too healthy for death by disease or any other natural cause.

The Unimog took the strain on the towrope and, as luck would have it, the carcass rolled over onto its back, and I noticed a puncture mark between the animal's forelegs, seemingly penetrating the chest cavity. I remembered the Singalamwe poachers' favourite method of killing hippos.

They planted sharpened stakes in the hippo footpaths after the animals had left the river or lagoons to feed at night. The tips of the stakes pointed away from the water at an angle of about 45 degrees, directly in the hippo paths. Then the poachers would set fire to the reeds over a wide front and make a terrible din by beating drums and tins, firing their rifles, yelling and screaming.

The animals grazing peacefully on the flood plains would, predictably, charge back helter-skelter along their well-worn footpaths, seeking the safety of the river and lagoons. Some of them invariably plunged their massive bodies into the stakes, the sharpened points driving deep into their lungs.

The only problem was that the hippo carcass found by the tsetse-fly team could not have been more than 12 hours old and Singalamwe was too far upriver for the hippo to have drifted down to the bridge in such a short period of time.

The hippo must have come from a herd close by, most probably the one that frequented the pool in front of my house. It just so happened that there had been a fire in the reeds, across the river from Buffalo Lodge the previous night and early that morning. I made the logical deduction that the team members, all of them experienced hippo killers, had bagged a cow right under my nose.

"Can I have the skin?" asked the tsetse-fly man.

"What for?"

"I want to make some sjamboks," he replied.

Hippo-hide sjamboks are extremely expensive and keenly sought-after.

In those days my temper was attached to a very short fuse, especially when it came to poaching. Realising that the tsetse-fly team leader probably knew exactly how the hippo had died, his remarks about the sjamboks set off a verbal salvo from a mouth that suddenly turned into a multiple rocket launcher.

"You bastard!" I shouted. "You and your men killed this hippo!"

"No, we didn't. Nobody did."

"What the hell is this?" I pointed angrily at the entry wound. "Do you think I am a bloody idiot? Neither you nor any of your men will have an ounce of meat from this hippo!"

The team members had been crowding around the carcass expectantly. As my words began to sink in, I could feel their animosity rising. They stared at me with barely concealed hatred and started to murmur among themselves.

That was all I needed.

"Take your men from your camp right now and bugger off back across the river! I don't want you and your poachers anywhere on this side of the Cuando!"

The tsetse-fly man realised with fear that I was close to uncontrolled rage.

"Yes, Colonel, but what about our spraying?" he asked plaintively.

"You will stay in the eastern Caprivi and come over every morning to spray, staying only on the roads. At night you will return to your camp. You've got one hour to get out."

"Yes, Colonel." They moved off in a huff to their nearby base and started to pack.

I rounded up the Fort Doppies Bushmen to cut up the hippo carcass for their own use after the Unimog had dragged it to their *kimbo* about three kilometres away. They, of course, were elated at the unexpected windfall.

After a while, the tsetse-fly team leader approached me, apologising profusely and asked if he could stay in the old base if his men moved to the eastern Caprivi.

I agreed on condition that he use only one particular footpath to the river to wash and collect water. He or his men were not allowed to approach the river at any other point and especially not near any hippos or drinking sites for animals.

"Yes, Colonel," he meekly agreed.

It turned out to be the end of him. Another tsetse-fly man replaced him the following year and I made sure that the Windhoek headquarters of Veterinary Services was informed about the poaching incident.

I had set up a base opposite Singalamwe near the northern extremity of the St Michél training area. Across a sidestream and some beautiful lagoons, lies a sizeable island beyond which, to the east, flows the main stream of the Cuando River.

The island is about four kilometres across from west to east and on the far side was a magnificent horseshoe lake, populated by about 35 hippos, easily the biggest herd along the whole Cuando. Some four kilometres further, perched on high ground on the east bank of the Cuando flood plain, lay the village of Singalamwe, home to a nest of expert hippo poachers.

They used to come across with *makorros*, along a labyrinth of numerous sidestreams and lagoons to take potshots at the hippos. By the time we got to the scene of shooting, across the four-kilometres-wide island, they would already be well on their way back to Singalamwe.

During one of my rubber-duck patrols, I found their footprints and the *makorros'* beaching marks. This enabled me to pinpoint on a map the point at which the *makorros* landed. It was about 50 metres from the nearest horseshoe lake which was, and probably still is, cut off from the main stream by a dense stand of reeds and papyrus.

I went back to the training base called Cassinga, and Piet Brink and I plotted several fire tasks for an 81mm mortar on an ordnance map. We got out a mortar, plus a number of high explosive bombs and did some silent registration on the prospective targets. There were three of them: the *makorro* landing site, a spot closer to the hippo herd and one in a small sidestream along their getaway route.

Then we sat back and waited.

Several days later, we heard a shot from a heavy-calibre rifle in the direction of the hippo herd.

Piet rushed to the mortar pit, laid the mortar on the target near the hippo herd and dropped a bomb down the barrel.

The bomb climbed rapidly at a steep angle into the blue sky over the island. We waited for long seconds and then we saw a cloud of smoke and dust shooting up above the distant trees, followed by a satisfying "crump!"

Piet waited a minute or so before sending the second bomb on its way to the *makorro* landing site.

Another cloud of smoke and dust, another "crump!"

Target number three followed swiftly after that.

No more shots were heard that day, or for at least a week afterwards.

But then we heard another shot. The poachers must have thought that they had just been unfortunate enough to stumble into one of our mortar exercises, so three more mortar bombs went hurtling towards their hunting ground.

This time they did not return for several weeks, and when they did, it was at night. Of course they had no way of knowing that we were shooting predicted fire on map-plotted targets and assumed the cloak of darkness would hide their movements from our observation.

It came as no surprise when I heard a shot ring out from the direction of the hippos late one night. I jumped out of bed and shouted for Piet. The shot had woken him too and he was already on his way to the mortar pit.

Soon the first bomb was on its way. On the eastern horizon a brilliant flash appeared, followed by the "crump!" of the exploding bomb. The other two bombs were also launched into the night sky after suitable intervals, to give the poachers time to run to their *makorros* and attempt their escape along the side channel.

This put a full stop to any further hippo poaching in the vicinity of Cassinga by the Singalamwe gang for the remainder of my time at Fort St Michél.

The poachers must have puzzled long and hard over how we could be so quick off the mark with our mortar without actually sighting them. They probably ascribed it to white man's magic.

As far as I know, no poacher was actually hit by shrapnel from a mortar bomb and it was never our intention to kill or wound them anyway. But we certainly scared the hell out of them.

It was my deep misfortune to find several elephant carcasses up and down the river, most of them shot and subsequently dying of their wounds in or near the water.

It seems that badly wounded elephants will always head for water if they can. They then stand belly deep in the stream or pool, until they keel over, or die close to the water's edge, probably after trying to slake their thirst or kill the gnawing pain with the cool water washing over their wounds.

We also found a number of carcasses well away from the river, especially in the vicinity of Malombe pan on the Angolan cutline, and near a place called Delta Base. These animals either fell where they were shot, or couldn't make it to the water. Delta Base, filled with so-called Unita refugees, was situated inside the western Caprivi and therefore in the game park.

I constantly had problems with these people when it came to poaching because they were considered to be immune and therefore above the law. Some of these refugees were armed with AK-47 rifles, which they said were for self-protection. My complaints to the various authorities produced no results, not even when I found elephant carcasses near their base with the tusks removed. The tusks probably went to Savimbi's headquarters at Jamba for later export along a smuggling pipeline to the Far East.

Unfortunately, the area between Delta and Cassinga was also the last habitat in perhaps the whole of Africa of the only remaining black rhinos of the Chobiense subspecies. The bush was especially dense there, and therefore ideal for the animals to hide in. The protection of these rare animals became my number one headache.

The herd, as far as we could tell, consisted of three adult bulls, a cow, a young heifer and a small bull calf. The cow and calf were always together, sometimes accompanied by a bull. The heifer disappeared after a while, but more about her fate later.

When one of my men reported that he had found two elephants shot on the way to Malombe pan, I got hold of the Fort

Doppies Bushmen and asked them to follow the spoor of the poachers. While tracking, they found a third elephant carcass.

The spoor led to a road construction camp, but a search of the camp produced no sign of the ivory or the rifle that was used.

The Bushmen had picked up two .375 H&H shell casings, and were therefore looking for a .375 heavy-calibre rifle.

The next day, while driving along the Golden Highway towards the site of the original Fort Doppies, I was stopped by the road construction foreman. By that time we had the western Caprivi well cordoned off so as to catch anybody trying to sneak the tusks out of the game park.

The foreman and a gang of his men were working on a leak in a waterpipe alongside the road and he informed me that he had stumbled across some tusks lying, most conveniently, right under a bush at the precise place where the pipe had sprung a leak.

I looked at the tusks, small as they were, and noticed that they had been hacked out of elephant carcasses the previous day. There were five. The blood, although dry, was still a dark red, merging into a brownish black.

They had not yet started to smell, so I informed the foreman that the tusks came from the three elephants shot the previous day, probably by some of his men.

I then asked him how he managed to find them. "One of the men just stumbled over them when he went into the bush to relieve himself," he replied.

"Where is tusk number six?" I asked.

"I don't know," he answered sourly.

"At least one of your guys shot those elephants or removed the tusks," I insisted.

He swore high and low that this was not the case. I asked his labourers about the tusks, but they refused to answer any questions.

I then searched around and found the sixth tusk neatly tucked under a bush some distance away. I could not figure out why this one had been hidden separately from the others and I said so. It seemed to me that someone had succumbed to second thoughts about handing over all the tusks and was hoping to sneak one of them out after the hue and cry had died down.

By this time, of course, these men were subject to regular searches for ivory at roadblocks set up on the route between their road construction camp and Katima Mulilo.

But, apart from the spoor that had led to their camp, I had no concrete proof of their involvement in the shooting of the elephants and was placing my hopes on finding the rifle that was used.

I confiscated the six tusks and left the construction crew sullenly repairing the leak in the pipe while I reflected on the suspicious circumstances surrounding the recovery of the ivory.

A few days later I went to Katima to hand over the tusks to the conservation officer. One of the conservators informed me that the foreman of the road crew had telephoned with a special message for me. The next time I interfered with his work while he was carrying out maintenance tasks in the game park, he would shoot me.

As already mentioned, it took little to arouse my temper in those days and, for reasons that only a psychologist could explain, physical threats – especially to shoot me – were guaranteed to light my fuse.

I jumped into my Land Cruiser and drove the 180 kilometres back to the western Caprivi at a furious pace, grimly intent on confronting the foreman, even if this meant a western-style "shootout".

He was a tall, lanky fellow with unkempt, greasy, blond hair and pale blue eyes. He always wore the shortest of khaki shorts and a pair of "vellies" (tanned hide shoes) without socks. He was obviously a man with a pretty rough background.

I went to every one of his road gangs, but none of them could enlighten me about the foreman's whereabouts.

For an entire week I went looking for him every day, still seething with anger. No one knew where he was or when he would return to his job.

Then one day while I was working in my garden at Buffalo Lodge he suddenly appeared.

"I believe you wanted to see me," he said coldly.

My temper had subsided somewhat and I had to dig deep into the ashes to summon up a fresh blaze of red-hot anger.

"Yes, I've been looking for you all week. I got a message that you want to shoot me."

"Well, yes," he replied. "I don't like being questioned by you as if I am a thief right in front of my men."

"Listen here, mister," I replied, my temper flaring quite nicely by then, "I don't care what you like or do not like, but I take bloody strong exception to being threatened by somebody like you."

His temper was also rising. "I certainly will shoot you if you come barging into my workplace again as if I am a bloody criminal!"

My wife came rushing out to calm us down, but I would have none of it.

"I don't mind you taking shots at me," I shouted. "In fact I would welcome it. There is nothing I like better than a two-sided fight. I have killed a lot more people than you have shot elephants!" It was perhaps fortunate that neither of us was armed at the time.

For the first time he seemed to realise that I meant what I said and, without another word, he turned around, got into his vehicle and drove off.

I never saw him again in the western Caprivi. He stayed in Katima for a while, then shook the dust of the border area off his feet forever.

To this day, I believe that he had one of the men in his gang shoot the three elephants and for a long time, I strongly suspected that the foreman was deeply involved in a well-established ivory-smuggling operation throughout northern Namibia.

When he realised that the tusks could not be smuggled out of the Caprivi, he decided to "dump" them, perhaps hoping I would let him, the finder, take them through to Katima legally. He could then get past the roadblock on the Kongola bridge and, after that, it would be my word against his if he failed to hand in the tusks as arranged at the conservation office.

At the time, there was a collection point for ivory in Katima, one of many run by a particular organisation which was, in fact, behind the smuggling of a large amount of illegal ivory and rhino horn throughout central and southern Africa.

There remains no doubt in my mind that the foreman wanted to get the six tusks to this collection point, but when I confiscated the loot, his entire plan collapsed. No wonder he was so incensed by my interference that he threatened to shoot me. Unfortunately, before we could lay our hands on the .375 rifle, he left the Caprivi.

When Dewald left Fort Doppies, Don Kondermann, a staunch German who was left in charge, kept his finger on the wildlife pulse and poaching to an absolute minimum.

On his departure, the post of commanding officer went to a paunchy former Royal Marine, who claimed to have served in the special boats section.

This man, jocular but with a giant-sized ego, turned out to be an utter disaster in the field of conservation. His right-hand man was Staff Sergeant Dap Maritz, a man of the highest integrity and exceedingly keen to follow in the footsteps of Dewald de Beer.

So the fat marine promptly confined him to the Fort Doppies base area and the Bushman platoon members were put to work as labourers rather than carrying out their primary task, which was patrolling the area to guard against infiltration by both poachers and Swapo.

Poaching began to rise by leaps and bounds. I tried various approaches to get the marine to have his Bushmen patrol the river line, but he obstinately kept them at manual work inside the base.

Some of the students on training courses caught poachers deep inside the Fort Doppies training area, so deep that the suspicion arose that poachers were permanently based in the western Caprivi.

One Recce instructor, out on his own, unexpectedly ran into

two poachers on horseback. They were armed with AK-47s and immediately raised their weapons to their shoulders, ready to fire. The instructor carried only a 9mm pistol but, nothing daunted, he took the initiative by dashing behind a tree from where he opened fire on them. The poachers got such a fright that they galloped off at breakneck speed through the trees, towards the west.

I immediately deployed Bushmen in the area. They followed the spoor of the horses as far as a Bushman *kimbo*, occupied by auxiliary constables, and missed the poachers by minutes. They disappeared into the depths of Botswana by stepping across the cutline within metres of the village.

On another occasion, we found three sables that had been trapped by poachers from a Mafwe *kimbo* called Lazauli. After Maplanke's crowd, the Lazauli Mafwes were the worst criminals on the Cuando River.

From information that reached me, it appeared that skins, ivory and horns were collected by a shopkeeper at Choi, a *kimbo* near Kongola Fort. Game rangers from Katima raided the shop and found some elephant tusks. The shopkeeper was duly tried and fined a ridiculously low sum which he was happy to pay with the small change from his back pocket.

Later he was caught again, this time with Maplanke's son and I'm happy to say that he was sentenced to a well-deserved ten years in jail plus a hefty fine. But that was only after the depravity and extent of poaching finally penetrated the thick skulls of the Windhoek bureaucrats and after magistrates from the circuit court had been hauled over the coals for their inappropriate leniency in the past.

The game in the Fort Doppies area decreased at an alarming rate. During Dewald's tenure there were about 50 waterbuck, reduced in less than one year to a lone bull. The sable herds were cut by half, while roans virtually disappeared. Giraffes were slaughtered until only three were left. Long stretches of the river were completely denuded of hippos. The large island, right under the nose of the marine major, had once been home to 85 lechwes. Over a six-month period, the number dropped to 33. The moribund major actually sat on his verandah and watched Maplanka's poachers killing lechwes. This man, a product of London's East end, proved beyond doubt that he had neither affinity for, nor understanding of, the African savannah.

I fumed, I stormed, I pleaded, but the obdurate Cockney marine would not budge. Oh, he made promises by the hundred but had no intention of keeping any. For him, the post of commander was a soft billet with plenty of cheap booze, more than enough to eat, a huge allowance in danger pay and a continuous holiday thrown in as a bonus.

As the situation deteriorated, I decided to take a helicopter ride to get some idea of how many elephants were left in the Fort Doppies area. I counted none, but located 20 elephant carcasses within ten kilometres of the river. All the tusks had been removed.

A week or so later, one of the training groups came directly to me at Fort St Michél, bypassing their commander at Fort Doppies, to inform me that Dewald had collared three poachers near the Botswana cutline after returning to Fort Doppies for a short visit two weeks before. I contacted Nature Conservation at Katima and Dewald de Beer and I looked around for any further kills.

In the space of a single square kilometre, we found the remains of three sables, three roans, one elephant, one impala and one kudu. The meat had already been cut into strips and was hanging on poles to dry, the tusks despatched across the river to Lazauli. The poachers were operating from a permanent base, deep inside the park, visited at intervals by trains of porters who would carry the spoils to Lazauli.

The Bushmen searched around the poachers' base camp in ever-increasing circles while the trussed-up culprits watched us warily. The rifle they used was, inevitably, a military G3 issued to a Caprivi soldier whose home was the Lazauli *kimbo*.

I sat in my Unimog, bitterly cursing the major and watching the Bushmen. Suddenly they halted their search, turned around and looked in my direction with concern written clearly on their faces. They started to jabber and argue excitedly among themselves while pointing at me every now and then.

For a while I took no notice, but then I realised they had spotted something important, but were not sure what to do about their find. The Bushmen were well acquainted with my explosive temper.

I got out of the Unimog and walked towards the little group. The jabbering stopped and they backed away into the bush as if I was infected with some deadly plague.

As I came nearer, I spotted the bulk of a large, dead animal lying among thick shrubs. I went closer and, to my utter devastation, found myself staring at one of the black rhinos. It was the heifer and, of course, her horns had been removed.

In those days I was not only notorious for my temper, but also for the strings of curses I could spit out like long bursts from a Vickers machine gun.

I simply exploded. The Bushmen ran into the bush and I stormed to the three poachers. Fortunately for me and for them, Dewald came hurrying along to determine the cause of the commotion. My anger swung from the poachers, crouching miserably beside the heap of smelly meat, to the fat major comfortably ensconced in his base like a medieval robber baron.

I jumped into my Unimog with Dewald and drove back furiously to Fort Doppies.

In a rage I stormed into the major's office and launched into a vicious tirade. His usual bombastic attitude was demolished before he could say a word.

I vowed that I would have him run out of the Caprivi and sent back to South Africa in disgrace as soon as possible.

That same night, I compiled a strong letter to the general commanding Special Forces and gave it to a Special Forces friend to deliver by hand when he got back to Pretoria.

A board of inquiry descended on Fort Doppies like an avenging angel. Within days the major was sent packing from the Caprivi and out of Special Forces. A real Special Forces operator was appointed as base commander to sort out the mess left behind by the marine.

Once more, poachers began to feel the wrath of those who cared, running into patrols, being tracked down even inside Botswana, having their *makorros* sunk, their *kimbo* raided and generally experiencing a very hard time from game rangers and the Fort Doppies personnel.

The game within the training area could breathe again and start to recover, at least for a while.

But, as far as I know, there is only one rhino cow left, in the whole world, of the Chobiense subspecies.

Note: Nkasa and Lupala islands have been declared game reserves, hopefully in time to save the remnants of game species still found there.

TWELVE
Taking on the Authorities

When the Department of Nature Conservation in Windhoek appointed me as a conservator, I made it my business to reconcile military activities in the western Caprivi with protection of the flora and fauna in the region. Points of conflict between myself and various organisations within the SADF arose almost immediately.

It was my contention that since the western Caprivi was a declared nature reserve, military activity had to be conducted with minimum disturbance to the wildlife.

However, some military brass were of the opinion that conservation should take a back seat, since we were fighting a war.

I pointed out that a war could be fought and troops trained for combat with minimum disruption of the indigenous flora and fauna. There was never any fighting in the western Caprivi, only large numbers of troops based there for training purposes.

All the training establishments centred on 32 Battalion, Fort St Michél, Fort Doppies, Omega and camps run by Military Intelligence. There were very few areas of conflict with the first three, but endless problems with the others. Inevitably, I made a number of lifelong enemies among the officers at Omega, home of the Bushman Battalion, and particularly the officers from Military Intelligence.

However, on the positive side, I could count among my friends many in the conservation-minded 32 Battalion and the pioneer conservators of Fort Doppies. I ran Fort St Michél myself and between these three units, proved over and over that one could carry out intensive training, including field-firing exercises, without unduly disturbing the game.

Needless to say, the ever-present plunderer's sword hovered over the Caprivi, manifesting itself in large-scale ivory poaching and intense hunting pressure on the few remaining rhinos. Obviously, no black Mafwe poacher had direct access to the Hong Kong ivory market. There had to be an organisation conveying ivory and rhino horn along to the location from where the products could be exported illegally to overseas markets.

Soon after becoming an official conservator, I became aware of a tremendous increase in donkeys and horses at the various Bushman *kimbos*.

These *kimbos* radiated outwards from Omega, established mainly by family members of Barakweña soldiers serving in the Bushman Battalion. The soldiers injected a fair amount of cash into the Bushman community and introduced them to rations which could be bought from a huge self-service store at Omega.

This made the Bushmen less dependent on game than they had been when they were still hunter-gatherers and should have been beneficial to the game but, unfortunately, the reverse was true.

There was no longer a need for Bushmen to manage the herds of wild animals as a constant food source. The game could now be shot indiscriminately for sport, for orgiastic feasts and particularly to make money from products such as skins and tusks.

The Stone Age hunter-gatherers eagerly embraced the evils of Western-style business but had no idea how to handle the money it generated. They bought everything in sight, from the most useless to the barely necessary. They all wanted to drive cars or pick-up trucks and, at the very least, acquired bicycles as an interim measure. All owned expensive radios.

Poaching began to flourish because white members of the Bushman Battalion and other units found a ready market for tusks, leopard skins, lion skins, horns and even otter skins.

It was almost a passion among a great many South Africans who served on the border to return to the Republic with a well-matched pair of elephant tusks. The second most desirable item was a leopard skin.

Some Bushmen in the *kimbos* became entrepreneurs in the game product trade. Others emerged as expert butchers. They could turn a carcass into choice strips of biltong in no time at all and their customers were often South West African policemen who patrolled the cutlines regularly.

The butchers also supplied venison to other Bushmen, particularly giraffe meat for which most had a special weakness. Another animal that was greatly sought after was the eland which offered the tenderest of steaks with just enough fat to make the meat nice and juicy.

Unfortunately, a market was also created for all sorts of rackets. The second-hand car trade was probably the most lucrative, followed by a black market in alcohol. There were also well-established brothels in which young Bushman girls were ruthlessly exploited, mostly by blacks passing through the Caprivi.

The second-hand vehicles were rarely licensed and would never have passed a roadworthy test. The Bushman drivers, or owners, had never heard of drivers' licences and the accident rate was consequently high.

Towards the end of my stay in the Caprivi, another evil took its place among the existing criminal practices: gun-running.

Rifles disappeared, mostly from the Bushman Battalion, and were sold to the indigenous population. The weapons included AK-47s such as those wielded by the mounted poachers who had been confronted by a Recce instructor.

Ammunition was plentiful and easily stolen from military or police installations.

The manager of the store at Omega began selling expensive hunting rifles to the Bushmen, complete with properly signed firearm licences that had been forged in Windhoek. He was eventually caught and brought to justice, but I'm willing to put my head on a block that not many of the rifles were retrieved because it would have been politically inexpedient.

The veritable army of racketeers included in its ranks horse dealers, chief among them one of the commanders of the Bushman Battalion. He sold horses to the Bushmen for up to R600 for a broken-down old nag. I don't know where he acquired them, but they were mostly animals that had been retired from their labours, so he probably bought them for a song in the south of Namibia or Ovamboland.

It deterred him not at all that the possession of a horse or any other pack animal in a game reserve was expressly forbidden by law. In his capacity, as a senior army officer, he quite clearly considered himself to be above the law and became quite aggressive when I confronted him about his contemptuous disregard for nature conservation regulations and the efforts made by the game rangers to protect the Caprivi game park.

He and some of his compatriots also smuggled cattle and sheep into the Caprivi, again in contravention of the nature conservation laws, but the mighty men of Omega, charged with the safety and security of the Caprivi, clearly considered themselves entitled to certain "perks".

The donkey and goat trade was mostly conducted among Bushmen or by black Botswanas who sold the animals to Bushmen at or near the cutline.

There was also a flourishing trade in wood. While establishing an infrastructure to serve the many military bases, desirable hardwood trees had to be hacked down. The logs were often cut up at a particular sawmill and the wood exported to South Africa. The wood included mukwa (or kiaat), pod mahogany, African ebony and false mopani which, by law, was supposed to be disposed of by the Department of Nature Conservation.

My first clash with the authorities occurred after I discovered a black man, who claimed to be a policeman, living deep in the bush in a magnificent *kimbo* with his family and satellite Bushman huts spread all around him. The occupants of the huts were at the beck and call of the rogue policeman: he was their owner and they were his slaves.

The western Caprivi had been designated for settlement exclusively by Bushmen as protection against their exploitation, and no other indigenous people were allowed to establish *kimbos* there. What really angered me, however, was that I found two other black policemen indulging their sexual appetites with a young and rather pretty Bushman girl. The owner of the *kimbo* was acting as a pimp for Bushman prostitutes.

This camp became a well-known halfway house for black travellers through the Caprivi, a place where they could break their long journey and indulge their baser appetites at leisure.

I also found a .303 hunting rifle and a pot filled to the brim with buffalo stew. The two policemen were tucking into this stew regardless of the fact that it was illegal to be in possession of game meat inside a reserve and blatantly oblivious to the fact that they were supposed to be law enforcement officers.

The policemen and family members were loaded into one of my Unimogs and dumped at Kongola bridge. I threatened them with the direst of consequences if they should ever come back to the Caprivi.

I then took the owner of the rifle and the owner of the buffalo meat to Katima to have them charged for contravening the nature conservation regulations.

The police refused to do so.

This resulted in an angry exchange between me and the SWA Police station commander who argued that the Caprivi was not a nature reserve. I produced the relevant documentation in terms of which the territory was proclaimed a nature reserve in 1967 and the station commander reluctantly agreed to investigate the charges.

Meanwhile, one of my men, Marius Heymann, returned to the den of iniquity to burn it down and ensure that the Bushmen had returned to their original *kimbo* at Ndashwa pan, under the rather ineffective control of Tokoloshe.

Marius got out of his Unimog a short distance from the *kimbo* and proceeded on foot towards the huts, almost stumbling over a tripwire designed to activate an automatic ambush consisting of claymore mines arranged to devastate anything that moved into the killing ground in a hail of shrapnel. The claymores were South African military mines and must therefore have been laid by either SWA police or the South African army.

No one in the army had the slightest notion that this den of evil existed deep inside the Caprivi bush, so it had to have been policemen who set up the ambush for me or my men.

Marius burned the whole *kimbo* down, the Bushmen having already left, deactivated the claymores and reported back to me.

I went to Katima to have another word with the police captain, but I said nothing about the claymores. He informed me that the Rundu magistrate had "signed off the docket" as not worthy of prosecution. I insisted that I wanted to see the docket and the captain had it brought to me with barely concealed impatience. There was no magistrate's signature to be found anywhere in the docket.

The police captain looked uncomfortable for a while and then said a particular sergeant would deal with the complaint.

The days went by. When I enquired about progress in the case, the sergeant was extremely rude and virtually told me to bugger off. This got my blood boiling and a shouting match ensued.

The sergeant toddled off like a spoiled brat to complain to his captain that I, a senior officer, had insulted him. This, of course, was quite true, and he wanted a redress of wrongs.

The captain and I then had a shouting match and the whole experience was most unpleasant. The case was never brought to trial despite my adamant insistence. I even went to the secretary general of the Caprivi to force the hand of the SWA police, but to no avail.

However, the incident did lead to the police giving me and the western Caprivi a wide berth in future, especially after a second incident which will be related later.

The proliferation of donkeys and horses had become a gigantic headache. I once again confronted the commander of Omega and asked him to have the unlawfully imported pack animals removed. He promised to attend to the problem, but nothing happened, and even more horses streamed into the reserve.

It was discouraging to see a larger number of horses and donkeys each time I drove along the Golden Highway. They were everywhere, at Omega, in every *kimbo* and often grazing unattended.

What really annoyed me was that lions that killed horses, donkeys, cows or sheep were diligently tracked down and shot by Bushmen from Omega at the instigation of their commander.

I went back to the commander in a final attempt to get his cooperation, only to be fobbed off with "we are working on the problem". I wrote reports about the pack animals to both army headquarters for Sector 20 in Rundu and Nature Conservation headquarters in Windhoek. There was no response from either. It seemed that Nature Conservation was too weak-kneed to upset the army.

When the confrontation between the Recce instructor and the mounted armed poachers occurred, I had no option but to push the whole pack-animal question to a conclusion, once and for all.

We followed the spoor of the horsemen as far as a *kimbo* on the Botswana cutline, from where it continued across the border into Botswana. I attached some paratroopers to the Bushman patrol from Fort Doppies and ordered them to keep the vicinity of the *kimbo* under surveillance and capture the horsemen should they return to the Caprivi. At the *kimbo* they found four or five donkeys and a horse which belonged to a particular Bushman, known to make his living from poaching elephants and rhinos. This Bushman had a *kimbo* some 20 kilometres to the south, in Botswana. He also had some stolen AK-47 and R1 rifles obtained from contacts at Omega and it was an established fact that he led mounted poachers into the Caprivi on a regular basis.

Omega was singularly disinterested in the stolen weapons when I informed them that we could trace the thief to a particular *kimbo* in Botswana. I was therefore obliged to disregard the theft of firearms except where this led to or formed part of poaching offences.

As luck would have it, the chief of the *kimbo* was caught red-handed while poaching a duiker, but two paratroopers who apprehended him were physically attacked by the rest of the Bushman clan and the chief was set free. The paratroopers managed to retain the Rl rifle he had been hunting with.

I traced the rifle back to the SWA police at Rundu. A white sergeant with the nickname of Bek (mouth) had left it with the chief to do some biltong hunting for him, collecting the meat on a regular basis. The rifle also offered a ready means for the Bushman auxiliary constables to augment their regularly provided rations.

I informed the police that one of their rifles had been seized in a poaching incident. To this day, they have not retrieved the weapon. Naturally, I bent the barrel the moment we got our hands on the rifle, our usual drill with all weapons confiscated from poachers.

I rushed off to the Bushman *kimbo* in the Unimog and cornered the chief and the clansmen who had set him free. All of them were auxiliary constables and members of the SWA police. I took them back to St Michél where we interrogated them separately, each one locked up in his own pitch-dark and virtually airtight freight container.

They had no idea what to expect and since they were strictly segregated they could offer no encouragement to one another.

It soon transpired that the Bushmen were using horses extensively for lucrative hunting expeditions aimed particularly at giraffes. The mounted poachers would isolate a giraffe victim from a herd and chase it in the direction of their *kimbo*, until the animal was too tired to resist. They then dismounted and killed the animal with assegais (spears). The meat was cut up and transported on donkeys to their *kimbos*, where it was sold to the local inhabitants or visiting Bushmen from other *kimbos*.

I deployed more patrols to confirm this information and a slaughtering site was soon discovered just outside Tokoloshe's kraal.

The wily little Bushman chief soon admitted under interrogation that his people, too, used this method of killing giraffes. He could hardly do otherwise than make a clean breast of things because he had vivid memories of a sjambok hiding administered by Dewald de Beer after he had killed a giraffe near Malombe pan.

When I got back to St Michél I mustered two patrols to go out and shoot as many horses and donkeys as they could find.

We also released the Bushman constables and returned them to their kraal.

Soon every donkey and horse east of Bwabwata had been shot. After a week I requisitioned a helicopter from the air force and we shot more of the animals, including a number of donkeys at an auxiliary police *kimbo* on the cutline.

Then the reaction started. I was at Fort St Michél when the military police turned up with a Bushman corporal to investigate my deliberate "liquidation" of the corporal's horse – estimated value R600.

As usual, I blew my top. I informed the military police lieutenant that he had better investigate who the hell was responsible for selling horses and donkeys illegally in the Caprivi game park and that he should at least get hold of a copy of the nature conservation regulations before starting to investigate a possible crime. The Bushman corporal insisted that he wanted his R600 back. I told him bluntly that I was inclined to have him charged for transgressing the law on pack animals and that I would make sure he was locked up for a long time.

Incidentally, the same regulations also empower a conservator to kill pack animals and dogs summarily and on sight if they are found in a game reserve. When the corporal saw that he was getting nowhere with me, he began bewailing the fact that his commandant had duped him by selling him the horse while neglecting to inform him that it was illegal to keep horses in the reserve.

The corporal's outburst pinpointed the chief culprit. I immediately sent a signal to Sector 20, explaining that the commander of Omega was involved in illegal horse trading. The corporal supplied information that the commandant had developed a thriving business and that prices ranged from R200 to R600 for a horse.

I also notified Sector 20 that I had information that the same commandant was in possession of illegal ivory, probably obtained from Bushman poachers. We were still investigating the precise origin of the tusks, but we already had a particular poacher in mind.

I requested that the commander be disciplined and removed from the Caprivi as soon as possible.

There was no response from Sector 20, but I was summoned by army headquarters in Windhoek to attend an urgent meeting in Omega.

I took the precaution of having the chief conservator of Katima, Alistair MacDonald, and the local biologist, Manie Grobler, accompany me to the meeting. I had requested that the Omega commander also should attend the meeting, but the commandant suddenly found that urgent and important business required his presence elsewhere. His second-in-command was designated to attend.

The meeting began on an acrimonious note. A brigadier whom I knew well launched into an attack, accusing me of upsetting the Bushmen during a particularly sensitive political phase by irresponsibly slaughtering their horses and donkeys. The animals were, after all, their property for which they had paid large amounts of money.

The best way to regain ground lost during an enemy attack is to launch a more violent counterattack. I could see that my conservator friends were somewhat overawed by the brigadier's rank and status as well as the seriousness of his accusations. Since I knew him well as a soldier, I had a fairly good idea of his weak spots and knew that the best way to deal with the brigadier's blustering attack was by means of a counterattack that was so devastating that it would force him to abandon his moral high ground in favour of a face-saving rearguard action.

I cited the relevant regulations in support of my contention that the army was breaking the law and that the offending commander could face criminal charges for selling horses to the Bushmen. This would not augur well for the army in the media. People throughout South West Africa and South Africa would start asking questions, and conservation societies in particular would raise an uproar and demand that the whole question of the army's occupation of the western Caprivi be thoroughly investigated.

The attack made way for reasonable discussion when the

brigadier saw that I was so incensed by the horse situation that my determination to carry out my threats would not be shaken.

In fairness, I should mention that of all the officers at headquarters in Windhoek, this brigadier supported our conservation efforts to the hilt. The problem lay at the higher echelon and he was only carrying out orders given to him by his general.

Our meeting ended in a decision that the army would appoint an officer to deal with the problem of getting the horses, donkeys and other livestock out of the Caprivi as soon as possible. The proliferation of *kimbos* would also be addressed. The indiscriminate hunting by Bushmen was making extremely hurtful inroads into the game herds and Omega undertook to control the poachers. Because of the artificial situation created by the so-called upliftment of the Bushmen, it had become necessary to set aside specific areas in the game park where they could keep a limited number of cattle and goats.

The commander of Omega was transferred shortly afterwards. Whether this was the result of his involvement with horse trading and the illegal possession of ivory is difficult to say. The whole business was handled unobtrusively, almost secretly, in fact. He left Omega without the fanfare usually due to a departing commander.

We left the meeting with high hopes. A deadline had been set for the pack animals to be removed from the Caprivi and Alistair MacDonald would monitor the situation by requesting progress reports.

I had left the army and the nature conservation service by the time the due date arrived, but Alistair's continuous enquiries revealed that the number of horses and donkeys was once again on the increase. Cattle were also building up into quite sizeable herds.

Through patrolling the southern cutline, it was found that a cattle-smuggling route existed between the Botswana settlements on the east bank of the Okavango River and Omega. The smuggling was conducted on such a large scale that the Caprivi virtually became the scene of Texas-style cattle drives.

Alistair took his complaints to his Windhoek headquarters, but as usual, the mealy-mouthed senior officials preferred to turn a blind eye to the problem.

The officer placed in charge of the livestock problem had meanwhile decided that it was best to leave the situation as it was inside the Caprivi game park, while halting any further imports of cattle, goats and pack animals. His argument was that the livestock would eventually die off.

Evidently, he had never learned the facts of life, namely that big horses and donkeys make lots of little horses and donkeys.

So, as was customary in all conservation matters, the entire plan foundered on the rocks of procrastination, indecision, bureaucratic deviousness, moral cowardice and official antipathy towards the savannah environment.

While acting as a conservator I believed, with misguided enthusiasm, that the hierarchy of both the army and conservation could be swayed towards a proper regard for the Caprivi as a game park, if only I could produce a well thought-out development plan. What was needed was a blueprint to channel development in one direction, instead of constantly trying to extinguish bushfires.

I tackled the problem using proven military techniques for making an in-depth analysis, or "military appreciation".

This meant that I had to interview Bushmen, soldiers and conservators, travel all around the game park, study the wildlife (in particular their habitat requirements, survival problems and migration patterns) and the major flora species, taking into account military activity and training, looking at the poaching problem in depth, determining the effects of fire on the environment and studying the impact of seasons and climate on the veld and migration.

I eventually produced a document containing several suggestions which could be considered controversial by conservators schooled in the old philosophy that nature reserves and game parks should not form the basis of lucrative hunting.

I wanted certain training establishments run by Military Intelligence shifted outside the Caprivi into areas more suited to their requirements.

272

Shooting ranges had to be reduced in number and shared by several units and were to be established in areas not frequented by the major game species. There was far too much unnecessary duplication in field training facilities.

Access roads had to be reconciled with game movement and their feeding areas. Use of roads along the edges of flood plains and perennial water pans had to be discontinued to avoid disturbing animals as they moved to and from their drinking sites.

I pinpointed several areas inside the reserve which could be set aside as sanctuaries. It is perhaps incongruous to think of sanctuaries inside a game reserve, but the high incidence of vehicle movements, frequent training exercises and other military activities made this necessary. Only nature conservators were to have access to these sanctuaries.

I also suggested specific points where boreholes were to be sunk to provide water during the dry season in areas away from the rivers. This would increase the carrying capacity of the Caprivi which at that time was largely determined by the food available on the two relatively narrow river fronts. I hoped that, in time, game would disperse into areas away from the rivers where plenty of sustenance was available throughout the year, but from which they were forced by lack of water in winter. I also hoped that the game across the cutline in northern Botswana could be enticed to move to the vicinity of permanent water, perhaps with the additional help of salt licks.

Control of these water points could then be used to manipulate the veld and thus improve its overall condition. By closing down water holes in areas that were becoming overutilised and opening up other water holes, game could be forced to move away, giving the veld time to recover.

There was one particular area of mopani veld which cried out to be effectively used. There were no permanent water holes there, so that for a large part of the year only the smaller antelope species were found in reasonable numbers. The usual rainy season population moved into nearby Botswana during the dry season and became legitimate prey for the clients of concession hunters. This situation applied particularly to sables, zebras, wildebeest, eland and a fair number of elephants.

In the final section of my paper I addressed the problem of future development of the Caprivi. Conservators have adopted the principle of making the establishment of nature reserves and conservation of animals and plant life economically attractive to the country concerned and its citizens. This generally translates to tourism along the lines of the Kruger National Park or ecotourism.

My overriding suggestions were based on the concept of ecotourism. To my mind, the Caprivi game park had to be run for the sole financial benefit of the Barakwena tribe, rather than for the national coffers. I did not foresee the total disbandment of the Bushman Battalion, but I did anticipate the scaling down of military operations with the accompanying discharge of a large number of soldiers. This meant that most of the Bushmen would be forced to seek a livelihood outside the army.

It was part of my proposed solution that they should run the Caprivi game park for their own benefit, at the same time making it quite clear that overall conservation would be a major factor in their continued physical and cultural survival.

I suggested that game numbers had to be built up with the help of permanent water holes away from the rivers, the use of fire in veld management, relocation of elements of some species, such as impalas, to suitable habitat inland and other measures to be applied until game culling became feasible. The Bushmen could then be allocated a quota in certain prescribed hunting areas, rotated from time to time in accordance with game numbers and veld conditions, where they could hunt, preferably with bows and arrows. Any other excess game culled by using more modern methods such as helicopters and hunting rifles was to be disposed of for the benefit of the Bushmen and their game park. Profits could be ploughed back into the park to improve its overall viability and to cover running costs.

Trophy hunting had to be considered as perhaps the major source of income but, again, profits had to revert back to the park and the Bushman communities.

A few exclusive tourist camps could be established, particularly at scenic spots such as the Popa Falls on the Okavango River.

All employment, excluding that of trained nature conservators, had to be reserved for Bushmen. They had to be employed as game guards, guides, trackers, labourers, road maintenance personnel and in various other categories. In time, the better educated Bushmen, such as Shuffle Foot, could become conservators themselves, ultimately aiming for the post of park warden.

In addition, they could be trained to turn game products into souvenirs. Skins could become karosses, rugs, shoes and boots, belts, handbags and other items prized by the European market. Horns and heads could be mounted, elephant bones (definitely not tusks!) could be carved into attractive curios. The scope for small industry was tremendous and virtually inexhaustible. There was plenty of potential for crocodile farming and fish farming on a large scale along both rivers as well.

However, this plan meant that the Bushmen would have to be moved into areas where they could have space enough to spread out sufficiently, while simultaneously being restricted to locations where their presence would have a limited impact on the game population of the surrounding park.

An agricultural survey in 1966 had shown that only one area in the whole of the western Caprivi, confined to the flood plain around Bagani bridge, was suitable for agriculture. The army started an agricultural development there which became quite a successful venture. Plenty of water was available from the Okavango River and the soil was fertile enough to plant crops. Bagani was therefore an obvious choice for relocating some of the Bushmen and was, indeed, already the home of a fairly large section of the Barakwena tribe.

Another suitable location was to be found around Bwabwata, formerly home to the tribe whose chief was Tokoloshe. They had been forcibly removed by Military Intelligence for security reasons, because MI elements wanted to utilise the bush airstrip and its immediate vicinity for their own nefarious purposes. I proposed that the Military Intelligence facility be relocated to a more suitable area and that the Bwabwata clan be returned to their former home. The area could be improved agriculturally to make it suitable for stock farming. There were no tsetse flies there and the underground water was plentiful and close to the surface. Wells dug in the past always struck water at a depth of three to four metres.

My report encompassed many other points, such as trails, including canoe trails, fishing camps on the rivers and traffic control.

I sent off my blueprint with great expectations to both the Department of Conservation and to the army sector headquarters in Rundu and waited anxiously for what I thought would be a favourable reaction from both quarters.

Army sector headquarters in Rundu began implementing some of the suggested measures before a policy had even been formulated which encouraged me considerably and raised my hopes enormously.

Nature Conservation in Windhoek, on the other hand, gave not the slightest indication that they had taken note of my magnificent treatise on the Caprivi problem. However, subsequent developments seemed to indicate that they had indeed given it considerable thought.

I was unexpectedly summoned to Katima to see the director of conservation management, who lost no time in offering me the job of warden in the Caprivi game park after my retirement from the army. He wanted an immediate answer and I accepted with alacrity, reaching the inevitable conclusion that my proposals had made a favourable impression on these august gentlemen, some of them first-rate conservators.

I had a rather different reaction from Military Intelligence. They threatened me with a court martial unless I withdrew the document in toto. According to them, I had breached security by writing about their secret installations in a document that was sent to a department outside the ambit of the Defence Force. All copies of my blueprint had to be collected and destroyed.

One signal after another was sent to me personally, asking about progress regarding the collection and destruction of the documents. I remained noncommittal, said I was looking into the situation, that some documents had already been withdrawn and destroyed and whatever else came to mind to utilise the full spectrum of bureaucratic delaying tactics in order to dilute and finally dissipate the onslaught. The same tactics had often been used against me by Military Intelligence, so I was only getting my own back.

I destroyed all spare copies of the offending paper but withdrew none from Nature Conservation channels. The accusation was, in any case, one of the most specious I had ever come across. Everyone in the border area, including conservators, Bushmen, indigenous black people, civil servants, people of high moral calibre and hardened criminals, casual lorry drivers, road workers, national servicemen (who had no security clearance), citizen-force troops and career soldiers, knew exactly where Military Intelligence had their "secret" installations in the western Caprivi. The locations were certainly not secret to Swapo or to any other enemy forces. I was perplexed by their heated reaction. A Military Intelligence general was emphatic that none of the top structure in conservation circles could be trusted with state secrets and the locations of sensitive installations, yet he saw no contradiction in entertaining some very shady characters in those same installations.

I decided to ignore the general and treat his threats against me with the contempt they so richly deserved.

Little did I know that something far more sinister lay behind this highly indignant reaction. My paper had the potential of hampering their exploitation of the Cuando-Cubango's natural resources on behalf of Unita, and worst, if the recommendations were to be implemented, it would be only a matter of time before I, as park warden, uncovered one of the biggest ivory-smuggling rackets ever to operate in Africa.

Meanwhile, I was making enemies in the Department of Veterinary Services as well. I did not realise at the time that this department and the Department of Nature Conservation were controlled by the same man, a former veterinary surgeon whose sympathies lay with his former colleagues rather than with the conservators.

The crux of the problem was the department's use of Dieldrin for exterminating tsetse fly in the western Caprivi. I, of course, had a great affection for the little fellow since wherever they were present, the human species tended to stay out. Someone once said that the tsetse fly is the best game ranger in Africa, and I agree wholeheartedly.

However, this view was not shared by the veterinary surgeons in Windhoek. They wanted to destroy the fly so that areas formerly inaccessible for cattle farming, could be opened up for this purpose. Stock farming always results in competition between game and cattle for grazing. Game numbers have to be reduced, particularly as regards buffalo and wildebeest, since these two species carry some of the most fatal cattle diseases which are only rarely fatal to their own.

The western Caprivi buffaloes carry foot-and-mouth disease and, some claim, also the dreaded anthrax. Wildebeest, as is generally known, carry "snotsiekte" or malignant catarrhal fever.

Another danger presented by extended stock farming was that my favourite animals, the big cats, would automatically become public enemy number one. They love tucking into juicy beef steaks.

I fought veterinary services with everything at my disposal to prevent the eradication of the tsetse fly from the eastern edge of the western Caprivi, which fell outside the game park, compliments of a certain commissioner general. My big chance came when I discovered that they were using Dieldrex – which contains Dieldrin – to spray the flies' habitat. The use of this extremely dangerous substance had already been prohibited by law in South Africa.

There was a huge controversy in the South African media about the use of Dieldrex in Botswana by vets spraying tsetse-fly infested areas and the operation was stopped as a result of the outcry. When the Namibian Department of Veterinary Services was asked by the media whether they used Dieldrex, they replied rather vaguely, but in the negative.

Yet that same year, I spotted the hated blue drums being off-loaded from trucks at their field camp, in preparation for an attack on the flies in the Fort St Michél training area.

I objected immediately and stated unequivocally that no spraying would take place in my area. My information was that Dieldrin was not easily biodegradable with the result that the poison would build up in the tissue of various organisms, the highest toxic levels being reached in those animals at the top of the food chain. This would invariably cause reproduction problems, particularly in raptors such as the fish eagle.

I had to provide the men to do the actual spraying and it was with considerable alarm that I read on the warning label on the drums that sprayers had to wear protective clothing, including masks, gloves and overalls. The substance could be absorbed into the bloodstream through exposed skin.

The department could not provide my men with protective clothing and this gave me added incentive to stop the spraying.

We were deadlocked. Signals flashed all round southern Africa: "That difficult colonel of yours has put a spoke in our wheel again. We want you to discipline him and order him to toe the line."

A real corker reached me from Military Intelligence, ordering me to cooperate forthwith. I replied that I would do so, provided they were prepared to bear the consequences of chronic ill health and possible death among the sprayers. They backed off quickly when this potentially nasty problem was deposited in their lap.

The next development was a visit from a vet who was a deputy director at the Windhoek headquarters. He explained in great detail that the perceived dangers of Dieldrin were just so much poppycock, the product of fevered imaginings by Greenpeacers who saw a threat to the environment from a multitude of directions and virtually every human-driven development project.

He assured me that the amount of Dieldrin left in the habitat and flushed into the Cuando River system would be infinitely small and could not possibly endanger any species.

I asked him about the warning labels on the drums which stated categorically that they contained top-grade poison.

That, he said, was merely to comply with regulations. The substance was actually quite harmless and there was no need to take any special precautions when handling Dieldrin.

He was talking absolute nonsense. The learned doctor thought he could bamboozle me with his scientific knowledge and his background as a vet. After all, I was only a dumb infantryman whose knowledge of such matters could be expected to be pretty sketchy. I can read, however, and I took the trouble to read the labels, whereas the good doctor evidently never did, although he was in charge of the tsetse-fly eradication campaign in Namibia.

The labels stated quite clearly that Dieldrex contained Dieldrin and, according to the manufacturer, it was imperative that protective clothing, including face masks, should be worn when handling the substance. If this was not done, a build-up of poison would result, which could lead to death after prolonged exposure. The labels further stated that the substance was non-biodegradable and described various symptoms of Dieldrin poisoning and how to deal with it if the symptoms were observed.

This kind of information, I explained to the doctor, did not appear to be the general kind found on all tins with poisonous contents.

He sat there for a while at a loss for words, then abruptly changed tack.

They had another substance – biodegradable over short time periods and not as poisonous as Dieldrex. However, it was still in the experimental stage, but he was willing to try it in Fort St Michél.

Reluctantly, I agreed.

It transpired through discussions with tsetse-fly fieldworkers that the department was stuck with a mountain of very expensive Dieldrex. They had stockpiled the drums and were caught flatfooted when continued use of the poison was outlawed in South Africa. At the time, of course, the department was an extension of the South African civil service and therefore subject to South African policy decisions.

But Windhoek decided to continue using Dieldrex, hoping that the media or environmental pressure groups would not become aware of their underhand way of reducing the unwanted mountain of poison.

Sometime later the same doctor sent me a report on autopsies performed on bream from the Cuando River system. The report indicated that the amount of Dieldrin per gram of tissue was clearly within accepted tolerance levels. In fact, the amounts were almost negligible.

But, once again, the doctor took me for an ignoramus. What he did not state, either deliberately or because he did not understand the food-chain concept, was that a fish eagle eating one Dieldrin-infected bream a day will eventually build up a level of non-degradable poison in its system that will actively threaten the continued existence on this planet of one of the most magnificent birds ever created.

So I ignored the doctor's useless information.

A year later, Manie Grobler informed me that the Department of Veterinary Services intended cooperating with Botswana in exterminating the tsetse fly once and for all along the Cuando River system. They were getting a Dakota that would spray from tree-top height, at night, all along the riverine forests and islands as well as some kilometres inland from the river. The aircraft would take off from Maun every night and be manned by a British flight crew.

Manie objected because he thought the poison would prove fatal to the fish.

"No," said the good doctor, "it kills insects, not fish."

The fact that many fish species would be eating poisoned insects was neither here nor there.

Eventually Manie succeeded in keeping the Dakota away from the Linyanti swamps and Nkasa and Lupala islands.

I sent a strong signal to Windhoek army headquarters explaining the situation and pointing out that it was unacceptable to have a British-manned, foreign aircraft flying at low level over secret military training establishments.

Windhoek, as usual, hummed and hawed for a while until they got my next message reminding them that we did anti-aircraft training at night and that I did not want to be held responsible for the safety of a foreign aircraft.

The spraying of the western Caprivi was halted but it continued in Botswana, just to the south.

Manie's fish died by the thousands as he had predicted, since the aircraft strayed into the Linyanti swamps. The good doctor was unrepentant. The tsetse fly was his enemy number one, and he was one of the main culprits undermining the viability of both Caprivis as nature reserves.

THIRTEEN

Wholesale Slaughter

In the winter of 1986 some of my men and I were despatched to assist Savimbi as military advisors in his forthcoming campaign against Cuito Cuanavale. He and his officers preferred to call us liaison teams as a face-saving ploy, though it was not clear who we were expected to liaise with.

This was the first time I had set foot deep inside the Cuando-Cubango since the late 1970s. We drove in our Casspirs along the old and well-remembered sand track from Mucusso to Coutada de Mucusso and from there eastwards to a place called Likua, further downstream on the Luengue River. This was the major logistics base for the Unita forces.

As we progressed northwards, I became aware that there was no sign at all of any game. Moving eastwards along the Luengue, the contrast between the prolific wildlife of the late 70s and the paucity of 1986 was shocking.

The teeming herds of the past had completely disappeared. Now there was nothing at all, not even a duiker or steenbuck ducking and diving to get away from the labouring Casspirs.

The tall red syringas were as profuse as ever. The sand tracks were much more deeply rutted by the heavy traffic. The few *omurambas* we passed through were still clothed in acacias and combretums. The extensive reed and papyrus swamps were still there.

But over it all hung an atmosphere of utter desolation. There was no life.

There were plenty of signs of human presence: discarded tyres, gearboxes dumped in the tracks right where they had been replaced with new ones, bits of canvas side panels torn off where lorries rubbed against forest giants and, of course, a stream of Unita Samil 100s plying the sandy tracks between Mucusso and Likua, heavily laden with military supplies and equipment, courtesy of South Africa.

Although I kept a sharp lookout, I could not spot the spoor of a single elephant. Where there used to be tens of thousands of lumbering, grey hulks, now there was nothing.

We spent the night at Likua and pushed on northwards towards Mavinga in the morning.

The deciduous tropical vegetation gradually gave way from savannah to evergreen tropical savannah, but the subsurface remained deep sand all the way.

The *omurambas* all contained small perennial streams which became wider and more like rivers further north. Just before Mavinga we crossed one which had the clearest water I had ever seen in any river. It was like looking through glass straight down to the pebble strewn bottom. The scenery was pleasant, green and restful with the little river rushing along to the Cuando in the east. The valley through which it flowed was fairly narrow and steep-sided, the high ground on both sides heavily covered in thick evergreen forest.

But permeating the indisputable loveliness was a depressing silence. I cannot recall hearing the song of a single bird. I saw none darting through the warm air or circling in the blue sky above, riding the currents rising from the valley below.

There was an eerie absence of all four-footed animals. It was as if they had been banished from paradise forever by Unita. The animals would have been totally out of place amid the display of energy required to transport tons of war material northwards and deeper into Angola and they had either been shot into oblivion by Unita hunters, or had to scuttle for safety in a few remote areas far removed from the path of the war machine.

The further north we went from one logistics base to the next, laid out as if they were stepping stones, the stronger the contrasts became. As the tree canopies got higher and the forests got thicker, the silence in them became deeper and more oppressive, like the deathly silence of the grave.

Some considerable distance to the north we started to skirt vast swamps which, at a first cursory glance, appeared to be grassy plains. Closer examination revealed oozy, black turf underneath the grass surface along the rims of the swamps and, deeper in, a messy, black porridge of mud and water that could swallow a vehicle in seconds.

Once or twice, vehicles did inadvertently stray into the soft black turf only to get stuck up to their mudguards in the ooze. It took long hours of struggling to extricate the heavy Casspirs, using a whole train of the vehicles linked to one another by stout towbars.

I had been as far north as Mavinga before during the late 70s, but the area beyond this wrecked little town was completely new ground for me.

For the first time, I understood why the Cuando flooded in the late winter and early spring rather than during the summer months, as the Kavango and Zambezi rivers did.

The vast swampy areas have to first fill up during the rainy season before releasing their floods into the rivers towards the end of summer. The swamps also maintain a constant and copious flow of water in the Cuando system throughout the year.

The rivers to the north of Mavinga are all fringed with extensive, swampy flood plains. The Lomba River, constantly in the news during 1987 and 1988, is a narrow, fast-flowing river flanked by plains which are black, porridgy bogs covered over with a layer of grass. It is a formidable obstacle. There are only one or two places where the surface is firm enough to admit access to vehicles and allow a crossing to be made.

As we skirted the northern edge of one of these flood plains I spotted, with some amazement, a sitatunga feeding on the fringe of a large patch of reeds.

Accompanying us were Unita "bodyguards", travelling in their own vehicle, further back.

Imagine my disgust on being presented at our next stop with the skinned carcass of the sitatunga I had spotted that afternoon. Our Unita escort had shot the animal and obviously thought they were doing us a big favour by giving us fresh meat.

To make matters worse, they had shot the animal through the stomach, so that the contents had spilled all over the meat. At the best of times, sitatunga meat is unappetising and tastes like rotting swamp water because the animal spends its life in oozing mud, but this was totally inedible.

What I did see on our journey, with some satisfaction, were several pairs of wattled cranes.

But in all those swamps I saw not a single hippo or crocodile. No doubt there were crocodiles, because a Recce operator was bitten by one a year later in the Cuito River not too far from Cuito Cuanavale.

But I did not see one. Hippos, in any event, are not secretive animals like crocodiles, if only because of their frequent snorting and chuckling, yet I saw none and heard none. There were simply no hippos left in the most suitable habitat to be found for them anywhere in Africa.

Where did they go? There is no doubt in my mind that they were shot, brutally exterminated in their thousands within ten to fifteen years.

Our travels took us north as far as Tempue, over the Cuanavale River, then across the Cuito to a place called Cuvelai (not to be confused with the much more substantial town of that name in the Cunene Province), and south again almost as far as Masseca, a small place some 80 kilometres north-west of Cuito Cuanavale. We were approaching Cuito Cuanavale's northern back door.

Apart from the wattled cranes, the sitatunga and two reedbuck, no other wildlife was spotted, nothing at all. The landscape was sterile, as far as the eye could see.

There were no spoor, no burrows of animals such as jackrabbits or ant bears, a complete silence in the branches of the profusion of trees with not even a miserable-looking snake anywhere.

Nothing, nothing at all ... only emptiness.

Formerly, while the Portuguese were in control, these areas were lucrative hunting concessions. Hunters came from Europe and America, perhaps even Japan, to bag the Big Five. They always went home satisfied.

Savimbi, meanwhile, changed his war plans and we meekly retraced our steps back to Tempue, across the Cuito and Cuanavale rivers and down to the south of the junction of these two rivers, to start planning for an attack on Cuito Cuanavale itself.

I was now back in an area which, in 1976, teemed with elephant, buffalo, rhino, giraffe, sable and other species, while lechwes splashed through the water of the Cuito flood plains and islands.

By the time we got to Cuito Cuanavale I knew what to expect. I was proved correct in all respects. All traces of wildlife had disappeared from the face of the earth.

All I saw was an owl that came and sat in a tree to look solemnly at me, a stupid soldier, trying to sleep after four futile days trying to attack and occupy Cuito Cuanavale.

The entire operation was a total failure, not because of bad planning, but because of nonexistent leadership among the senior Unita officers, starting with Savimbi himself. He left the battle in the hands of bumbling brigadiers after his personal contribution sabotaged it to such an extent that no one could salvage it.

Unita troops were running all over the place like frightened rabbits. Only one brigadier pulled his weight and quite respectably too, but unaccountably, his artillery support was simply removed, without explanation, and given to Savimbi's brother-in-law who commanded the other brigade.

The whole operation was a nightmare, not because of heavy fighting, but because of a succession of blunders and acts of downright cowardice by some of Unita's senior officers.

We drove back after this farcical campaign, the same way we had come. I found the spoor of a kudu in one of the more secluded spots we had selected for a stopover, and further south, towards Likua, I actually found the spoor of five elephants that had crossed the track the night before.

When I got back to St Michél – welcomed, incidentally, by several herds of elephants as we turned off the Golden Highway towards the base – I added up the score for the Cuando-Cubango. We had travelled a total of 4000 kilometres, much of it retracing our steps, and we found the spoor of five elephants and one kudu, spotted one sitatunga, two reedbuck and perhaps a dozen pairs of wattled cranes.

There were birds about, of course, but very few of them.

That was the sum total of all the animals left in an area formerly bursting at the seams with virtually all the savannah game species found in Africa.

Savimbi's headquarters was at a place called Jamba, a sort of squatter camp 10 kilometres south of the Biongue *omuramba* and about 15 kilometres south of the Luiana River.

When journalists went to visit Savimbi they were always shown elephant, zebra, giraffe and other species dotting the Biongue *omuramba* and the adjacent bush. Another pocket of game was to be found around the old Portuguese military post at Luiana. Down the Cuando River as far as the cutline with Namibia, one could, with luck, come across pockets of elephants and, of course, the big herd of buffalo that straddled the Angola/Namibia cutline.

Savimbi used these pockets of game as proof that he had a strong and working conservation policy. He also used these areas as a private hunting ground for himself and his friends, especially foreign politicians, generals and economists who could assist him in his war against the MPLA.

The fact that his troops had denuded at least 90 per cent of the vast Cuando-Cubango by indiscriminate and often planned slaughtering of all game species is therefore considered a myth, particularly by journalists sympathetic to his cause.

I don't want to discuss the merits of Unita's war against the MPLA or even their efficiency as guerrilla fighters. I have seen far too much of their performance on the ground to get excited about their soldier-like qualities. What I do object to, and want to discuss, are the moral issues involved when wild animals are slaughtered to support a war effort.

288

Bear in mind that apart from vast numbers and a tremendous variety of African savannah game species, the Cuando-Cubango had nothing else to offer. There were no mines, industries, cities, energy sources or agricultural potential that could be tapped to support Savimbi's long, drawn-out war. The only resource available was the game, particularly the vast herds of elephant and a considerable number of rhinos.

Savimbi considered his fight for his version of democracy to be of greater importance than the continued existence of elephant herds and black rhinos belonging to the scarce Chobiense subspecies.

He started to shoot these two species on an organised basis. The tusks and rhino horn were stockpiled at Jamba, while a means was sought to export the loot to the Far East, particularly Hong Kong.

Savimbi claimed that he had to pay South Africa for its assistance with ivory and diamonds, according to Fred Bridgland in his book *Jonas Savimbi – The Key to Africa*. However, this is a misrepresentation by Savimbi. I know that the support budgeted by Military Intelligence in 1986/87 amounted to R400 million. I also know that with that money the South Africans bought virtually all Savimbi's military hardware fuel and clothing. The money for supporting Unita came out of the South African taxpayer's pocket.

I am all for a just war, but I have great difficulty in reconciling the justness of war against the wholesale rape of the African savannah's last outpost.

Savimbi might have been a better ruler for Angola than Dos Santos, but then again, he might not. From what I have seen of Africa and experienced at first hand through a whole string of wars in at least six different African countries, an improvement in government does not automatically follow change, which in any event is usually achieved by violent means. More often than not, a change in government ushers in deterioration. Sometimes the new broom will sweep clean for a while, only to lapse into mediocrity on a par with most other governments in Africa.

To sacrifice the last stronghold of the African savannah for the precarious freedoms promised by Savimbi, which would go unnoticed by at least 80 per cent of the Angolan population any way is, to my way of thinking, utterly despicable and an offence against God's creation.

Then there was the inherent deviousness that formed an integral part of the whole process of getting the ivory to the Hong Kong markets that tended to corrupt those running the operation. In this particular case, the operation resulted in former well-respected officers in the Defence Force becoming tainted with the rotten smell that permeates the process of smuggling game products.

What really rankled was the calculating way in which those beautiful animals were appraised by the scheming eyes of South African Military Intelligence officers. To them, an elephant was a huge piece of worthless, mobile meat, carrying towards its front end valuable tusks under its ludicrous, hosepipe nose. These were the same men who thought I had a screw loose because I befriended the big cats. Waxing lyrical about a herd of buffalo or sable was considered tantamount to knocking at the door of a lunatic asylum. To show emotion over the unnecessary death of a kudu run down by a speeding truck at night, served only to confirm one's madness.

These were people whose idea of getting close to nature was to have a braai, somewhere in a wild spot along the Cuando, with plenty of booze to accompany the feast. If one could do that every night for a week or so, with a spot of hunting thrown in, preferably from the back of a Land Cruiser, one was really communing with nature.

Someone who strolled through the bush – unarmed – following elephant footpaths and spending hours observing the antics of the various animals while coping patiently with tsetses and the pesky little mopani flies, was not considered a red-blooded South African whose roots were embedded in African soil. He was placed on a par with the fanatical Greenpeacers from Europe and treated with the same derision.

I got my first inkling of what was going on when Manie

Grobler cornered me one day and asked if I had any knowledge of several million rands worth of ivory waiting to be picked up from an airstrip in the Caprivi.

I had no knowledge of such a huge cache. Evidently, Manie had been approached by a private pilot who informed him that he was on his way to the Caprivi to pick up ivory for Military Intelligence.

There are three airstrips in the Caprivi. One is an all-weather tarred runway at Omega, capable of taking virtually any plane. A shortish dirt strip, known as Immelman, served Fort St Michél and Fort Doppies. A third dirt strip served the Military Intelligence installations in the vicinity of Bwabwata.

I came to the conclusion that the ivory was to be flown out of Bwabwata and advised Manie to contact his counterpart in Rundu with a request that he approach a certain colonel who had regular contact with Savimbi. I was of the opinion that the ivory could be a Unita stockpile.

A week or so later, Manie – fuming with anger – informed me that he had received a message from this colonel – via an alcoholic middleman – to lay off enquiring about the ivory or else he would get "sorted out".

Now Manie Grobler, although a biologist, was also a nature conservation officer and therefore a law enforcement officer. Notwithstanding Manie's position, the army colonel clearly considered himself and the organisation for which he worked to be above the law.

As a military man myself and one who was proud of my profession, I was disgusted that a senior officer should drag the name of the SADF through the mud by ignoring the laws of the country he was fighting for. But his action also set alarm bells ringing. Something was obviously not right.

I began making enquiries and putting together the few facts I could glean. The picture that gradually began to emerge was an ugly one and, at first, I found it hard to believe. Not in my worst nightmare could I have imagined that officers in the SADF would get involved in something that would be worthy of the Mafia.

The eccentric editor of a well-known Windhoek newspaper printed several incredible reports about a Portuguese crime boss, based in Rundu, who ran a smuggling ring operating between southern Angola and South Africa. Week after week, more startling disclosures were made.

The editor himself went to Rundu to investigate persistent rumours about the smuggling ring and ended up in a potentially dangerous confrontation.

The Portuguese had erected a high and sturdy security fence around his property, but somehow, the intrepid journalist managed to get inside. Subsequently, photographs were splashed all over the front page of his newspaper showing a mean-looking Portuguese in a cowboy hat, threatening the editor with a rifle.

All this made good copy, as the newsmen say, but none of it was taken seriously. I laughed with the best of them over the editor's fertile imagination.

But when Manie Grobler told me about the ivory hoard, I began to have second thoughts, especially when a series of unexplained events came to my attention.

There were the accidental deaths of a policeman and Rundu nature conservator, the only two "outsiders" who knew about the ivory racket at that time. The death of the conservator coincided with the mysterious disappearance of incriminating tapes from his briefcase before nature conservation officials from Grootfontein could retrieve them from the car wreck. Unfortunately, those were the only copies of the tapes in existence.

Then there was a cache of 70 tusks dug up in the kitchen of a Portuguese employee of the Rundu "godfather". He was working on a road being constructed by his boss between Kongola and Lianshulu when he was arrested and his employer lost no time in getting to the courthouse to pay the paltry R50 fine that was imposed, then promptly packed the fellow off to Swaziland, where he probably became engaged in opening up the Mozambique arm of the ivory-smuggling racket.

Another load of ivory, comprising 270 tusks, was intercepted in Namibia and the two smugglers, both Angolans, were given another ludicrously small fine which was promptly paid. They worked for the same Portuguese man from Rundu.

In all these cases, the accused simply pleaded guilty, thus avoiding having to give evidence and run the risk of cross-examination by the prosecution.

The Portuguese businessman then expanded his enterprises, placing one of his countrymen in charge of a shop he had bought in Katima. Soon the ivory flood to the south increased.

A Portuguese greengrocer would travel from the Republic every week in a pantechnicon crammed with fresh produce, making the return trip with an empty vehicle – or so we thought. Following a tip-off, he was searched at the Ngoma customs post on his way out and 80 tusks were found in false compartments. He was also given a ludicrous fine, something like R1000, which he paid out of his small change.

Thanks to the help of other conservators, reliable information from a policeman friend stationed in Rundu, and the Windhoek editor's reports, which cut close to the bone, a grim picture materialised.

South African Military Intelligence had set up an organisation to ferry equipment into southern Angola for Unita and transport wood back to the Republic, with the idea of making money for Savimbi. This organisation, known as Inter Frama, was under the control of two Portuguese – one in Rundu named Lopez, or Lops, and one in Johannesburg, named Maya. I knew Lopez well and I had met Maya.

I heard about Inter Frama from colleagues who, like me, worked for Military Intelligence. It was supposed to be a "secret" organisation, but in due course, Inter Frama became an open secret, known throughout Namibia.

The organisation's trucks pounded the roads between Angola and Pretoria, attracting the attention of our editor friend. The drivers all had passes exempting them and their vehicles from searches at police or army roadblocks on the grounds of security.

The trees were felled in Angola and sawn into planks or railway sleepers at a sawmill belonging to Inter Frama at Bwabwata in the western Caprivi. I must confess that without the slightest pangs of conscience, I pinched some of the sleepers for use in our house at Buffalo Lodge.

Savimbi had pushed for his stockpile of ivory to be exported via South Africa to the Far East and Military Intelligence had agreed, roping in a certain Chinese to take care of the disposal and export of the ivory once it reached Pretoria.

This Chinese, originally from Hong Kong, had previously been used extensively in sanctions-busting operations and was connected via family ties to Hong Kong ivory dealers.

The pipeline was in position and the illegal ivory began to flow down it in a constant stream.

The Official Secrets Act gave more than adequate protection for the covert operation, but greed is a strange thing. Like cancer, it begins to feed on what is healthy, firm tissue and turn it, in time, into a rotten, smelly mess.

This is precisely what happened. This extremely effective and secret pipeline was operating under the protection of the Official Secrets Act for the illegal export of ivory and rhino horn, so why could it not be used to serve individual greed?

Soon ivory and rhino horn started to come in via a collection point in Katima from Zambia, Zimbabwe and points further north.

The collector was a Portuguese shopkeeper in Katima, running the business for his boss, Mr Lopez. In addition to the ivory, they also channelled mandrax that originated in Lusaka through the store.

I had already accepted the post of park warden for the western Caprivi, but I was still serving in the army, and therefore felt that my first loyalty was to the SADF. I had an impression at the time that the pipeline established by Military Intelligence had unavoidably been corrupted and that the officers in control did not really know what was going on.

So when I was visited by one of the senior intelligence officers in control of support to Unita, I decided to inform him about my suspicions and misgivings, including the mandrax that was being transported along the pipeline from Lusaka to Johannesburg.

I cornered this guy one night on his own in our boma beside the glowing coals of a warm fire. I gave him all the details and asked him to close the pipeline, to disband the whole operation, to get rid of the Portuguese Mafia and take urgent steps, since the elephant herds and few remaining rhinos were being slaughtered.

He regarded me in stony silence, but a few weeks later I received a message via Alistair Macdonald that my appointment as park warden had been withdrawn at the insistence of the SADF.

I had already indicated that I would retire from the army at the end of 1987 and my immediate reaction was to write a personal letter to the Chief of the SADF, asking on what grounds they had objected to my appointment as warden of the Caprivi game park. This letter was only answered after I had left the army, at which time the Chief of the SADF informed me that he had the matter investigated and found that there were no reasons why I should not stay on in the Caprivi as a park warden. He had informed the Nature Conservation authorities accordingly.

But Military Intelligence, who seemed to be behind the whole affair, refused to let matters rest. They flew a brigadier to Windhoek to have a personal interview with the senior official who had offered me the job in the first place.

Meanwhile, I had been reinstated and was looking forward to being able to develop the park in accordance with my blueprint.

So it came as a double blow when Alistair once again turned up at Buffalo Lodge to inform me that the offer had been withdrawn for the second time.

A brigadier in Military Intelligence had succeeded in overturning a decision made by the Chief of the Defence Force himself.

Of course, this unusual interference raised not only my hackles, but my suspicions regarding the involvement of some very senior officers in the smuggling racket. It seemed to me that far from losing control of their own corrupt creation, as I had thought, they had actually decided to enrich themselves along the way.

A certain officer who worked for Military Intelligence informed me that on returning from an operation deep inside Angola one day with his ammunition depleted, he had gone to a store in Rundu to restock. He opened a large box he thought contained ammunition and, to his surprise, found that it was filled with tusks. He then went to another box and found that one also filled with tusks. A third box revealed the same contents, as did one box after another.

The tusks were stored in an official SADF equipment store under control of Military Intelligence. Like a good soldier, the young officer decided to report the matter to his senior commander. This officer listened with some irritation, closed the door to prevent intrusion, and proceeded to lay into the young man in a rather menacing manner, promising all sorts of repercussions, including physical harm, if he should disclose his discovery.

Shortly afterwards, the young officer was posted back to South Africa suffering from "battle fatigue".

He had lost his confidence in Military Intelligence and asked for a transfer back to the army. In due course he was posted back to Rundu, this time with the rank of major. He was then an army intelligence officer, which is quite a different thing. An army intelligence officer obtains tactical information in support of the unit or formation for which he works, while a Military Intelligence officer gathers information, mostly of a strategic nature, over a much wider front.

This officer deployed agents inside the Okavango and the western Caprivi in order to obtain information about infiltrated Swapo agents and, in the process, snippets of other intelligence inevitably also came to light.

He soon picked up a poacher who had been hunting elephants in the western Caprivi with a rifle belonging to a Portuguese officer who acted as a Military Intelligence officer in Rundu and worked closely with the SADF's liaison team with Unita.

The rifle was confiscated and so were twelve tusks found with the man. The army intelligence officer reported the incident to the police and handed over the rifle and the tusks to the authorities.

Then the army officer decided he should tell the Portuguese officer what he had done.

For the second time in his career, he found himself being threatened with extreme physical injury and was informed that he would be dealt with at a level far higher than Rundu unless he desisted.

Not long afterwards, the police bungled the arrest of an Angolan who smuggled diamonds for the Rundu Mafia. The smuggler had to be released, but not before he had divulged the name of his contact man, an Ovambo, who brought the diamonds to him from one of the De Beers mines.

Within days the contact man was stopped at a roadblock by Angolans dressed in police uniform, and he, his wife, his daughter and a hitchhiker were brutally murdered.

The real police soon caught the imposters and interrogation implicated the smuggler who had been released, a military intelligence officer and a policeman in the murders.

The police went to the intelligence officer's house to question him but their bird had flown. The police then went to Military Intelligence and were told the officer in question had gone on leave and had failed to return to his duties. He was posted as AWOL (absent without leave) and they did not know where to find him.

About six months later a friend of mine in Durban told me that he had read in an African publication, I think it was called the *East African Gazette*, that a certain colonel, the man who had been posted as AWOL, was running an office for Military Intelligence in Lisbon where he acted as liaison between MI and Renamo, the Mozambican resistance movement.

To me it was as clear as daylight that he had been spirited out of reach of the police to protect the smuggling operation from being compromised.

Towards the end of my army career I managed to infiltrate one of my sergeants into the smuggling ring. He was friendly with one of the Portuguese shopkeeper's sons in Katima. The sergeant promised his friend that he would get him some ivory from Angola if he could be assured of an adequate return for his efforts. He pretended to have an uncontrollable desire to own a BMW, but made it clear that acquiring one was beyond his means.

The friend referred him to his brother, who handled all ivory transactions. He told the sergeant that he, himself, handled only diamonds!

The two sons did their national service, by arrangement, in Katima Mulilo, and it is known that on at least one occasion, they smuggled a load of ivory from Katima to Rundu in a military truck. Whoever manipulated their posting to Katima for their national service is anyone's guess, but I have my suspicions.

I eventually had the opportunity to compare notes with the detective inspector assigned to crack the smuggling syndicate, and his version supported mine entirely, except that he could add much more to it, especially as regards the involvement of highly placed persons.

Sometime after I had left the Caprivi I saw a report in the press about a haul of nearly 1000 tusks confiscated by the SWA police near Otjiwarongo. This occurred shortly after Military Intelligence had responded to smuggling allegations in the media by claiming that they had been involved on a one-time-only basis, through Inter Frama, in moving ivory for Savimbi, but that Inter Frama had since been disbanded.

The truth is, according to the detective inspector responsible for the huge haul, that exactly the same Inter Frama people were involved. They had merely changed the name of the company. He also confirmed that the same military officers involved during the late 1970s were still at it in a big way in the late 1980s.

Since then, information has come to hand indicating that the web was extended into Mozambique and that the same people were yet again involved, but, because of the extent of the operation, the organisation was significantly larger. Renamo became the beneficiary, presumably because Savimbi no longer needed to trade in ivory, as his war moved north into the diamond-rich areas of Angola after Namibia's independence.

It is my feeling that the smuggling will only end when the last elephant has dropped, unless conservationists and counter-smugglers can get their act together.

Until then, all elephants, no matter where they are, remain endangered, even the few left in Savimbi's stomping ground, the Cuando-Cubango.

FOURTEEN

Sound the "Last Post!"

I once nourished a dream of being involved in saving the last of the African savannah. All conservators must have dreams on which to live, because their salaries certainly can't fulfil that necessary function.

My dream went something like this. Concerted international efforts restored the Cuando-Cubango, the western and eastern Caprivi, northern Botswana, south-western Zambia and northern Zimbabwe to their former grandeur as a highly productive savannah environment and I was there to see it.

I saw the elephants in their hundreds of thousands ranging widely over the lush terrain and clearing the bush like bulldozers, so that the grasses would grow for the benefit of the vast herds of grazers such as buffalo, blue wildebeest, zebra, sable and roan antelope and all the other species.

I saw the browsers, including a recovering rhino population, nibbling at the leaves of trees and shrubs, growing fat while making their natural contribution to sound veld management.

I saw the dredging hippos working at their channels to keep the water flowing, at the same time fertilising the pools and lagoons for the benefit of fat bream, water birds and plants.

And I saw the big cats selectively catching the weak and the unproductive, their predatory lifestyle genetically enhancing the overall performance of this vast variety of species.

The plains and swamps would be covered with thousands of species and millions of animals, all of them interlocked in a complicated pattern of feeding at different levels, as ordained by their creator in a way no human farmer can equal, no matter how scientifically he manages his well-bred cattle, sheep and goats.

In short, I saw at least a partial solution to Africa's chronic protein deficiency and its uphill struggle to feed its starving millions in perpetuity.

But to achieve this dream, man would have to allow the land to return to its natural state without interference. His sole function would be to monitor progress and study the deepest mysteries of a creation that he does not understand and therefore cannot respect.

There are still some game populations in parks such as the western Caprivi, the Chobe, Moremi and Wankie that could spread outwards to populate the vacuum created by man especially in the Cuando-Cubango.

Unfortunately, my dream will forever remain just that – a fantasy that no one wants to buy, not even the reputable wildlife conservation organisations, nationally or internationally.

Like all conservators, they have been defeated by progress. The excess elephants that have sought asylum in the Chobe reserve from uncontrolled shooting and poaching must now be culled to save the flora of the park.

The Orapa diamond mines need huge amounts of water and the Okavango swamps present a most convenient source. Cattle farmers want to expand into the Okavango swamps so an anti-buffalo fence must be built to keep out foot-and-mouth disease and game must be shot or driven out of large parts of paradise. A veterinary inspired foot-and-mouth fence just south of the swamps has already taken a toll of tens of thousands of blue wildebeest.

In short, the Okavango swamps must suffer severe damage, if not total destruction, for the sake of progress and the economy of the country.

Meanwhile, the western Caprivi has been split in two to accommodate the uplifted Bushmen, now turned poachers, in one part, and the surviving game, their prey, in the other.

Elephants are still being slaughtered in their hundreds and thousands. The Wankie game reserve, the Zambezi Valley and the area south of the Kariba Dam have become battle grounds. An ivory- and rhino-horn smuggling ring based in Harare numbers senior politicians, civil servants, conservationists and military personnel among its beneficiaries.

Thousands of Savimbi's troops still squat in the Cuando-Cubango. Forests have been wrecked by thousands of rutted tracks and the wholesale exploitation of timber. Mines were planted everywhere, but, by a cruel twist of fate, these now threaten only human beings, the vast majority of animals having long since been shot out by Savimbi's troops.

Poachers spread over a broad front hunt down and shoot the few remaining elephants and other game species skulking in remote corners to escape violent death.

And somewhere in the Caprivian bush, three rhino bulls – sole survivors of the Chobiense subspecies – wander around disconsolately. The cow and calf have long since been removed, for their own protection, to elsewhere in Namibia, a move that spells the end of *Diceros bicornis chobiensis*.

In northern Botswana, eradication of the tsetse fly has opened up the savannah to invasion by thousands of head of cattle. Botswana's extraordinary wealth in cattle is concentrated in the hands of only a few, some of them cabinet ministers, but still they want more, and to get it, they are prepared to sacrifice the wild beauty of the Okavango swamps and the woodlands of northern Botswana.

It is becoming a dying landscape of empty plains, lifeless swamps and majestic but meaningless rivers.

I can visualise the tragic end, heralded by the lonely call of the last fish eagle sounding its version of the "Last Post" over the remains of the last outpost of the African bush.

The day before I left the Caprivi for good, I went for a final jog. It was my last chance to savour the bush, the riverine forest, the lagoon, the edge of the flood plain and the well-trodden elephant footpath past Rufus and Dayan's feeding site.

I ran past the troop of baboons, screeching insults at me because I had eliminated two of their members the previous evening. They were no doubt waiting to move into Buffalo Lodge the moment Ros and I drove off in our Suzuki and trailer.

Some kudu cows bounced across the elephant footpath in front of me. In the clear sky above, a bateleur eagle was quartering its domain in circles. In the swamps off to the right, a fish eagle proclaimed its ownership in clarion calls.

I ran over fresh elephant spoor and passed warm elephant dung. The animals were probably somewhere up ahead browsing off camelthorns and sickle bush. The heat of the day had not yet set in, so they would be filling their ever-growling stomachs.

I turned around and started back towards the house. The baboons had disappeared, but a troop of feeding monkeys were moving peacefully through the branches of the swamp figs at the lagoon's edge.

I detoured to the place where I had shot the baboons. I wanted to check on the spoor around the carcasses, particularly the movements of our resident hyena.

But there was no sign of the carcasses. Something had dragged them off into the bush.

Filled with curiosity, I began to follow the drag marks. As usual I was unarmed, an indication perhaps that I was beginning to take the bush a little too much for granted.

The drag marks went through some camelsfoot shrubs into a stand of tall grass. I was still trying to identify the indistinct pad marks of whatever it was that had laid claim to the baboons when an angry snarl was hurled at me from the depths of the grass.

I would recognise that snarl anywhere in the world. It was Taunu.

Gingerly, I moved to the edge of the grass. It would be stupid to burst in on a feeding leopard, even if it was Taunu.

I called him by his name and he answered in his usual fashion, with a cross between a miaow and a whine.

I squatted on my haunches and started to tell him how sorry I was to be leaving the Caprivi, and especially him.

He assured me that he felt the same and that he was unhappy about me leaving him there to face whatever the future held for him all on his own.

I told him to keep out of the way of all men, because they would shoot him on sight if they saw his beautiful, spotted coat.

He said that he would.

I wished him the best of luck for the future and many small cubs with his lady love to the south.

He just miaowed.

I moved off to the lodge, empty of all our possessions, and to my Suzuki waiting to take Ros and me back to the Republic and civilisation ... for good.

Editor's Note

Subsequent to allegations made, the Kumleben Commission of Inquiry was appointed to investigate and report on the alleged smuggling and illegal trade in ivory and rhinoceros horn in South Africa.

One of the allegations investigated was that "the SADF was covertly involved in the receipt, transportation, sale and export of *inter alia* ivory and rhino horn. By doing so, it aided and abetted the slaughter and destruction of elephant herds and rhino in neighbouring countries, particularly Angola and Mozambique. Such operations were conducted with this knowledge of, and sanctioned by, highly placed personnel of the SADF, state officials and Ministers of State."

Col Jan Breytenbach gave evidence before the Commission about the vast destruction of wildlife – including elephant and rhinoceros – that he observed from 1975 to 1987.

In January 1996, the Commission published its report and found:

"(i) During the period from mid-1978 to about 1986 the SADF (Military Intelligence Division) officially, though covertly, participated in the illicit possession and transportation of ivory and rhino horn from Angola and Namibia to the RSA. Initially the SADF was directly involved and at a later stage collaborated with its 'front' company, Frama Inter-trading (Pty) Ltd, in continuing such illicit handling of ivory and rhino horn.

(iii) There are no grounds for believing that after 1986 the SADF, or its successor the SANDF, has been engaged in smuggling ivory or rhino horn."